THE APOCRYPHAL ACTS OF ANDREW

STUDIES ON THE APOCRYPHAL ACTS OF THE APOSTLES

Edited by T. Adamik, J. Bolyki, J.N. Bremmer (*editor-in-chief*), A. Hilhorst, G. P. Luttikhuizen and J. Roldanus.

In recent years the Apocryphal Acts of the Apostles have increasingly drawn the attention of scholars interested in early Christianity and/or the history of the ancient novel. New editions of the most important Acts have appeared or are being prepared. We are therefore pleased to announce a new series, *Studies on the Apocryphal Acts of the Apostles* (edited by Jan N. Bremmer), which will contain studies of individual aspects of the main Acts: Those of John, Paul, Peter, Andrew, and Thomas. Initially, six volumes are scheduled.

1. *The Apocryphal Acts of John*, J.N. Bremmer (ed.), Kampen 1996
2. *The Apocryphal Acts of Paul en Thecla*, J.N. Bremmer (ed.), Kampen 1996
3. *The Apocryphal Acts of Peter: Magic, Miracles and Gnosticism*, J.N. Bremmer (ed.), Leuven 1998
4. *The Acts of John: a Two-stage Initiation into Johannine Gnosticism*, P.J. Lalleman, Leuven 1998
5. *The Apocryphal Acts of Andrew*, J.N. Bremmer (ed.), Leuven 2000
6. *The Apocryphal Acts of Thomas*, J.N. Bremmer (ed.), Leuven 2000

The Apocryphal Acts of Andrew

JAN N. BREMMER (ED.)

PEETERS

© 2000, Uitgeverij Peeters, Bondgenotenlaan 153, 3000 Leuven
ISBN 90-429-823-8
D. 2000/0602/28

All rights reserved. No part of this book may be reproduced or transmitted in any form or by any means, electronic or mechanical, including photocopying, recording, or by any information storage and retrieval system, without permission in writing from the publisher.

Contents

Preface		vii
Notes on contributors		ix
List of abbreviations		xiii
I	A. Hilhorst and P.J. Lalleman, *The Acts of Andrew and Matthias: Is it part of the original Acts of Andrew?*	1
II	J.N. Bremmer, *Man, Magic, and Martyrdom in the Acts of Andrew*	15
III	T. Adamik, *Eroticism in the* Liber de miraculis beati Andrea apostoli *of Gregory of Tours*	35
IV	M. Pesthy, *Aegeates, the Devil in Person*	47
V	I. Czachesz, *'Whatever Goes into the Mouth…'*	56
VI	J. Bolyki, *Triangles and What is Beyond Them. Literary, historical, and theological systems of coordinates in the Acts of Andrew*	70
VII	F. Bovon, *The Words of Life in the Acts of Andrew*	81
VIII	G. Luttikhuizen, *The Religious Message of Andrew's Speeches*	96
IX	J. Bollók, *Poimandres and the Acts of Andrew*	104

CONTENTS

X   C.T. Schroeder, *Embracing the Erotic in the Passion of Andrew. The Apocryphal Acts of Andrew, the Greek novel, and Platonic philosophy*   110

XI   A. Jakab, *Les Actes d'André et le christianisme alexandrin*   127

XII   P.J. Lalleman, *The Acts of Andrew and the Acts of John*   140

XIII   V. Calzolari, *La version arménienne du Martyre d'André*   149

XIV   J.N. Bremmer and P.J. Lalleman, *Bibliography of the Acts of Andrew*   186

Index of names, subjects and passages   190

Preface

After the fall of the Berlin Wall the Rijksuniversiteit Groningen decided to intensify contacts with universities in Eastern Europe. In 1991 the then Head of the Department of Church History, Professor Hans Roldanus, took this opportunity to forge links with the Károli Gáspár University of Budapest. In the search for a common research project, which would also prove to be attractive to classicists of the Loránt-Eötvös University of Budapest, it was decided to focus on the Apocryphal Acts of the Apostles. This particular choice hardly needs to be defended. The world of early Christianity is currently receiving an ever increasing attention from New Testament and patristic scholars as well as from ancient historians. Various Apocryphal Acts have recently been re-edited or are in process of being re-edited, but the contents of these Acts are still very much under-researched.

It is the object of the Dutch-Hungarian cooperation to study the major Apocryphal Acts in a series of yearly conferences, of which the proceedings are published in the series, *Studies in the Apocryphal Acts of the Apostles*. The editors in principle envisage the publication of six volumes, but they are open to further suggestions.

Following the first three volumes of the new series on the *Acts of John* (1995), the *Acts of Paul and Thecla* (1996) and the *Acts of Peter* (1998), this new volume is devoted to the *Acts of Andrew*. After a study of the relationship between the *Acts of Andrew* and the *Acts of Andrew and Matthias*, the major part of the book studies various persons, aspects and passages of the *Acts*: Aegeates, Alexandrian Christianity, eroticism, gnosticism and Neo-Platonism, magic, man, Poimandres, scatology and several triangles. The penultimate chapter analyses the relationship between the *Acts of Andrew* and the *Acts of John* and the book concludes with a close study of the important Armenian translation. As has become customary, the volume is rounded off by a bibliography and an index.

The conference which formed the basis of this book took place at the Károli Gáspár University of Budapest in the autumn of 1997. I am most grateful to my Budapest colleagues, in particular István Czachesz, for their generous reception and to the Faculty of Theology and Science of Religion of the Rijksuniversiteit Groningen for its financial support. Susan Ketner and Lautaro Roig Lanzillotta most helpfully assisted with the editing of the proceedings. Without the generous help of these colleagues and institutions it would have been impossible to prepare this volume once again in such an efficient manner in these hectic times.

Jan N. Bremmer   Groningen, July 1999

Notes on Contributors

Tamás Adamik b. 1937, is Professor of Latin at the Loránt-Eötvös University of Budapest. He is the author of the following studies in Hungarian: *A Commentary on Catullus* (1971), *Martial and His Poetry* (1979), *Aristotle's Rhetoric* (1982), *Jerome's Selected Works* (1991), *A History of Roman Literature* I-IV (1993-96). He is also the editor of new Hungarian translations of the *Apocryphal Acts of the Apostles* (1996) and the *Apocryphal Gospels* (1996).

János Bollók b. 1944, is Associate Professor of Latin at the Loránt-Eötvös University of Budapest. He is the author of the following studies in Hungarian: *Firmicus Maternus: Astrology. The Error of Pagan Religions* (1984), co-author of *A Commentary on Vergil's Aeneid I-VI* (1988) and *Philo of Alexandria: The Life of Moses* (1995).

János Bolyki b. 1931, is Professor Emeritus of New Testament Studies at the Károli Gáspár University of Budapest. He is, in Hungarian, the author of *The Questions of the Sciences in the History of Theology in the 20th Century* (1970), *Faith and Science* (1989), *Principles and Methods of New Testament Interpretation* (1990) and *The Table Fellowships of Jesus* (1992), and co-author of *Codex D in the Book of Acts* (1995).

François Bovon b. 1938, is Frothingham Professor of the History of Religion at the Harvard Divinity School. He is the author of *De Vocatione Gentium. Histoire de l'interprétation d'Act. 10,1-11,18 dans les six premiers siècles* (1967), *Les derniers jours de Jésus* (1974), *Place de la Liberté* (1986), *Luc le Théologien (Vingt-cinq ans de recherches* (1983²) = *Luke the Theologian: thirty-three years of* *research (1950-1983)* (1987); *Lukas in neuer Sicht* (1985), *L'oeuvre de Luc* (1987), *Das Evangelium nach Lukas*, 2 vls (1989-96), *Nouvel Âge et foi chrétienne* (1992), *Écritures et Révélations* (1993), *L'Évangile et l'Apôtre* (1993) and *New Testament Traditions and Apocryphal Narratives* (1995), co-author of *Genèse de l'Écriture chrétienne* (1991), editor of *Analyse structurale et exégèse biblique* (1971), *Exegesis. Problèmes de méthode et exercices de lecture* (1975) = *Exegesis: problems of method and exercises in reading* (1978); *Les Actes apocryphes des apôtres* (1981), co-editor of *Écrits apocryphes chrétiens* I (1997) and *The Apocryphal Acts of the Apostles* (1999).

Jan N. Bremmer b. 1944, is Professor of History and Science of Religion at the Rijksuniversiteit Groningen. He is the author of *The Early Greek Concept of the Soul* (1983) and *Greek Religion* (1999²), co-author of *Roman Myth and Mythography* (1987), editor of *Interpretations of Greek Mythology* (1987), *From Sappho to de Sade: Moments in the History of Sexuality* (1989), *The Apocryphal Acts of John* (1995), *The Apocryphal Acts of Paul and Thecla* (1996), *The Apocryphal Acts of Peter* (1998), and co-editor of *A Cultural History of Gesture* (1991), *Between Poverty and the Pyre. Moments in the history of widowhood* (1995) and *A Cultural History of Humour* (1997).

Valentina Calzolari b. 1964, is co-Director of the Centre de recherches arménologiques of the University of Geneva, where she teaches Armenian Language and literature (ancient and modern). She is co-editor of *Apocryphes arméniens. Transmission, traductions, création et iconographie* (1999) and prepares *Apocrypha Armeniaca* I for the *Corpus Christianorum Series Apocryphorum*. She has also published several articles on the Armenian *AAA* and on Armenian language and literature.

István Czachesz b. 1968, currently prepares a dissertation on the canonical Acts of the Apostles at the Rijksuniversiteit Groningen. He is, in Hungarian, the author of *Gaia's Two Faces* (1996) and co-author of *Codex D in the Book of Acts* (1995).

A. Hilhorst b. 1938, is Associate Professor of Early Christian Literature and New Testament Studies at the Rijksuniversiteit Groningen. He is the author of *Sémitismes et latinismes dans le Pasteur d'Hermas*

(1976) and co-author of *Apocalypse of Paul: a new critical edition of three long Latin versions* (1997), editor of *De heiligenverering in de eerste eeuwen van het Christendom* (1988), and co-editor of *Fructus Centesimus. Mélanges G.J.M. Bartelink* (1989), *The Scriptures and the Scrolls. Studies A.S. van der Woude* (1992), *Early Christian Poetry* (1993) and *Evangelie en beschaving. Studies Hans Roldanus* (1995).

Pieter J. Lalleman b. 1960, is a free-lance theologian and the author of *The Acts of John: A Two-Stage Initiation into Johannine Gnosticism* (1998).

Gerard Luttikhuizen b. 1940, is Professor of Early Christian Literature and New Testament Studies at the Rijksuniversiteit Groningen. He is the author of *The Revelation of Elchasai* (1985) and *Gnostische Geschriften* I (1986), editor of *Paradise Interpreted* (1999) and co-editor of *Interpretations of the Flood* (1998).

Monika Pesthy b. 1954, teaches Classical Greek and Patristics at the Loránt-Eötvös University of Budapest. She is the author of the following studies in Hungarian: *Origen: Commentary on the Songs of Songs* (1993); *Origen, Interpreter of the Bible* (1996).

Caroline T. Schroeder b. 1971, is a Ph.D. candidate in Religion at Duke University (Durham, North Carolina). She is preparing a dissertation on the writings of the fourth- and fifth-century Coptic monk Shenute of Atripe.

List of abbreviations

AA	*Acts of Andrew*
AAA	*Apocryphal Acts of the Apostles*
AJ	*Acts of John*
ANRW	*Aufstieg und Niedergang der römischen Welt*
APt	*Acts of Peter*
ATh	*Acts of Thomas*
Bremmer, Acts of John	Jan N. Bremmer (ed), *The Apocryphal Acts of John* (Kampen, 1995)
Bremmer, Acts of Paul	Jan N. Bremmer (ed), *The Apocryphal Acts of Paul and Thecla* (Kampen, 1996)
Bremmer, Acts of Peter	Jan N. Bremmer (ed), *The Apocryphal Acts of Peter* (Leuven, 1998)
CIL	*Corpus Inscriptionum Latinarum*
JAC	*Jahrbuch für Antike und Christentum*
JTS	*Journal of Theological Studies*
NTA	W. Schneemelcher, *New Testament Apocrypha*, tr. and ed. R. McL. Wilson, 2 vols (Cambridge, 1992^2)
PG	*Patrologia Graeca*
PL	*Patrologia Latina*
RAC	*Reallexikon für Antike und Christentum*
RE	*Realencyclopädie der classischen Altertumswissenschaft*
SBL	*Society of Biblical Literature*
SEG	*Supplementum Epigraphicum Graecum*
TRE	*Theologische Realenzyklopädie*
TWNT	*Theologisches Wörterbuch zum Neuen Testament*
VigChris	*Vigiliae Christianae*

ZNW   *Zeitschrift für die neutestamentliche Wissenschaft*
ZPE   *Zeitschrift für Papyrologie und Epigraphik*

The Greek, Latin and Coptic versions of the *Acts of Andrew* are referred to by *AA*, *AAlat* and *AAco*, respectively. All translations, if not otherwise indicated, are from *NTA* II (by J.-M. Prieur).

I. The Acts of Andrew and Matthias: Is it part of the original Acts of Andrew?

A. HILHORST AND PIETER J. LALLEMAN

While studying the *Acts of Andrew* (*AA*), we are fortunate in having, in addition to the careful but old text of Max Bonnet, two valuable modern editions: those of Jean-Marc Prieur and of Dennis Ronald MacDonald. Both of these contain the new text material, published for the first time by Detorakis, and both are provided with a translation[1]. So we seem to be equipped with everything we need. Yet there is a problem. Apart from the text comprising the events from the arrival of the Apostle in Patras to his death on the cross (this is the *AA* proper), there are a number of other writings dealing with Andrew's activities. What is their relationship to the *AA*? Most of them are clearly from a later period, and some of them belong to a different literary genre, so we may safely leave them aside when studying the finer points of the *AA*.

One text, however, cannot be skipped so easily, and that is the *Acts of Andrew and Matthias* (*AAM*). The sixth-century bishop, St Gregory of Tours, presented it, together with the *AA*, as one complex in his abridged rendering of the Andrew story. Was he right in doing so? MacDonald is quite sure he was; Prieur, on the other hand, dismisses the *AAM* as serious evidence of the original *AA*[2].

---

[1] J.-M. Prieur, *Acta Andreae*, 2 vols (Turnhout, 1989); D.R. MacDonald, *The Acts of Andrew and the Acts of Andrew and Matthias in the City of the Cannibals* (Atlanta, 1990); Θ. Δετοράκης, 'Τὸ ἀνέκδοτο μαρτύριο τοῦ ἀποστόλου 'Ανδρέα', *Acts of the Second International Congress of Peloponnesian Studies, Patrae, 25-31 May 1980* I = *Peloponnesiaca. Journal of the Society of Peloponnesian Studies*, Suppl. 8 (Athens, 1981-82) 325-52.
[2] Cf. the discussion in D.R. MacDonald, 'The *Acts of Andrew and Matthias* and the *Acts of Andrew*', *Semeia* 38 (1986) 9-26, with responses by J.-M. Prieur (27-33) and D.R. MacDonald (35-9), and also Prieur, *Acta Andreae*, 32-5 and MacDonald, *The Acts of Andrew*, 6-47.

In this chapter we shall discuss the question once more by comparing both texts in order to know whether they are the remains of one common text, the original *AA*. Taking the contents of the *AA* for granted, we will begin with summarizing the less familiar *AAM*[3].

The story of the AAM

In the opening scene the apostles cast lots to divide the regions where each will preach. The lot falls on Matthias to go to the city of the cannibals. He goes there, is seized by the people of that city and is imprisoned to await his being consumed by them. He prays to the Lord Jesus Christ for rescue. Jesus answers him that he will send Andrew, who will lead him and those with him out of the prison (1-3). Jesus appears to Andrew in a city of Achaia where he is teaching and tells him to go and liberate Matthias; a boat will be ready on the shore. Andrew obeys. Together with his disciples, he finds the boat and boards it, invited by the captain, who is none other than Jesus, a fact of which Andrew is unaware because Jesus is hiding his divinity (4-6).

During the voyage, the captain interrogates Andrew about his Lord Jesus. Andrew tells him a number of facts we know from the gospels (7-10). On his prayer, his disciples, who are seasick, fall asleep. Andrew continues the conversation. Asked by the captain why the Jews refused to believe in the Lord Jesus, he describes at length a miracle Jesus performed before the Jewish chief priests in the temple of the gentiles. He tells how Jesus addressed one of the sphinxes in the temple and made it declare that Jesus is God. The chief priests rejected this as magic. Thereupon the sphinx walked before them, went to the field of Mambre and called the patriarchs

---

[3] The Greek text has been edited by M. Bonnet in *Acta Apostolorum Apocrypha* II.1 (Leipzig, 1898 = Darmstadt, 1959), xix-xxiv and 65-116 and by MacDonald (n. 1) 63-169. MacDonald overlooked the sixth- or seventh-century papyrus fragment from *cc.* 30-3 published by J.B. Bauer, 'Ein Papyrusfragment der Acta Andreae et Matthiae: Pap. Graec. Vindob. 26227', *Jahrbuch der Österreichischen Byzantinischen Gesellschaft* 16 (1967) 35-8. Modern translations are provided by M. Erbetta, *Gli Apocrifi del Nuovo Testamento*, II, *Atti e Leggende* (1966) 493-505 and by MacDonald facing his Greek text.

out of their tomb, who refuted the chief priests. Jesus ordered the sphinx to go up to its place, which it immediately did. Nevertheless, the chief priests did not believe in him (11-5).

When land is near, Andrew too falls asleep and is brought by angels to the gate of the city of the cannibals, together with his disciples; Jesus and the angels ascend into heaven (16). Andrew and his disciples awake. It turns out that during their sleep the souls of the disciples experienced a visit to heaven, where they saw the Lord Jesus sitting on a throne of glory and all the angels surrounding him, along with Abraham, Isaac, Jacob, David, and the twelve apostles with their angels (17). On Andrew's prayer, Jesus comes to him appearing like a beautiful child, orders him to rescue Matthias and his co-prisoners and reveals to him the afflictions he will suffer at the hands of the inhabitants of the city (18). Andrew goes to the prison without anyone seeing him; he prays silently and the seven guards standing at the door of the prison fall dead. The door opens automatically. Andrew enters and leads Matthias and his co-prisoners out. The end of this episode runs as follows:

> He made Matthias go with his disciples out of the city toward the east. Andrew commanded a cloud, and the cloud lifted Matthias and Andrew's disciples and placed them on the mountain where Peter was teaching, and they stayed with them.

Exit Matthias, never to return in the *AAM* (19-21).

In the meantime, in the city of the cannibals, the executioners, who are to fetch people for their food according to their daily custom, find the doors of the prison open, the seven guards lying dead and the prisoners flown. The rulers of the city decide to eat the seven dead guards instead, but on Andrew's prayer the executioners are unable to prepare them for their meal (22). The rulers give the order to gather the old people of the city and to choose seven of them as substitutes, but again on Andrew's prayer this is thwarted (23). Then the devil incites the citizens to search for Andrew. They are unable to find him, for he is invisible, but Jesus tells him to reveal himself (24). The citizens seize him, tie a rope around his neck and drag him through the streets of the city (25). He weeps and prays, and back in prison is mocked by the devil and his demons (26-7). The next morning he is dragged again through the city and again he weeps and prays for relief, reminding Jesus of his own words on the cross 'My Father, why have you forsaken me?' (28; Matthew 27.46 par). Then

Jesus strengthens Andrew in the prison. Andrew sees a statue, which he commands to spew forth water to flood the city. The flood causes the death of men, women, children and cattle. This brings about a general change of mind among the citizens. They cry 'O God of this stranger, remove this water from us.' Andrew makes the statue stop the flood (29-30). After some more temporary punishments, Andrew restores to life the people and animals killed by the flood, establishes a church and baptizes the citizens. They ask him to stay with them a few days, because they are neophytes. Andrew, however, is determined to leave them and to go to his own disciples (31-2). Thereupon the Lord Jesus, having become like a beautiful child, appears to Andrew and rebukes him for his lack of compassion. Andrew turns back to the city, saying 'I bless you, my Lord Jesus Christ who wants to save every soul, that you did not permit me to leave this city in my rage', and spends seven days teaching and confirming them in the Lord Jesus Christ. Only then does he depart, sent off by the whole population of the city (32-3).

Elements in common

In order to do justice to the text, we have summarized it according to the extent it has in the chief textual witnesses. Part of it, however, namely *cc.* 11-15, which is absent from a number of secondary witnesses, is regarded as a late interpolation by MacDonald for a historical reason: 'Insofar as these chapters tell of a sphinx forecasting the transformation of temples into churches, they probably were not composed prior to the fifth century and thus could not have appeared in *The Acts of Andrew*'[4]. Therefore it seems to be superfluous to adduce proof of the late date of this section, a date which nobody disputes. Accordingly, from now on, when talking about the *AAM*, we intend its 33 chapters minus 11-15. How does this text relate to the *AA*? To answer this question, we shall discuss the points they have in common and then the discrepancies.

In discussing the common features, it is of little use to state general facts, such as the central role of the great and mighty apostle

---

[4] MacDonald, *Acts of Andrew*, 92, also 46-7. This does not prevent him from using these chapters as evidence for the original *AA* in his *Christianizing Homer* (a book to be discussed below) 29, 43-6, 60-1, 68, 304-5, 321.

Andrew. Any story about this character is bound to show this characteristic. But there is a more specific point. In both texts, Jesus appears to his followers in different shapes: in *AA* 32 he appears to Maximilla as a beautiful young boy, and in *AA* 46 likewise to Maximilla in the shape of Andrew; in *AAM* 5-16 he appears to Andrew as a human captain and in *AAM* 18 as a beautiful child. This metamorphosis, however, occurs in all *AAA*[5].

MacDonald mentions some additional common themes and motifs[6]. The *AAM*, he says, is fascinated with the sea and the same fascination is in Gregory's epitome. However, nothing of the sort is in the Greek *AA*. Both texts, MacDonald continues, are obsessed with the devil and his minions. From the summary above it is clear that the devil and his demons are important in the second half of the *AAM*. In the *AA* they also come up[7], but the struggle is here much more an inner one. Moreover, this theme can hardly be regarded as a specific one; it is omnipresent in early Christian literature. Both texts touch on magic, but whereas in *AAM* 22 a concrete act is meant, namely the death of the prison guards[8], the *AA* characterizes Aegeates' advances to Maximilla as filthy wizardry (37); this is the sole example MacDonald can adduce from the *AA* regarding this theme. Both texts mention heavenly mysteries, the *AAM* in *c.* 32 and the *AA* in *cc.* 47 and 50, but their contents are totally different. Furthermore MacDonald mentions speculations concerning Adam in *AAM* 20 and *AA* 37-9. However, the *AAM* does not speculate at all: it simply refers to Adam's fall, while the *AA*, on the other hand, presents Andrew and Maximilla as counterparts of Adam and Eve. In conclusion, we can do no better than quote MacDonald himself: 'To be sure, many of these similarities appear elsewhere in early Christian literature and therefore by themselves cannot demonstrate the literary cohesion of the AAM and the AA'[9].

---

[5] See P.J. Lalleman, 'Polymorphy of Christ', in Bremmer, *Acts of John*, 97-118 at 108-9.
[6] MacDonald (n. 2), 17-9.
[7] Chs. 2, 4, 5, 11, 16, 21, 29, 40, 42, 45, 49, 58, 62, 63.
[8] The same is true of the sphinx speaking in *cc.* 14-5.
[9] MacDonald (n. 2), 19; cf. Prieur (n. 2) 31.

Differences

What, however, about the disagreements? In a discussion published in the journal *Semeia* of 1986, MacDonald is silent about them and Prieur devotes only a short paragraph to them. In our opinion, the following features deserve mentioning.

1. Whereas in the *AA* the apostle is, so to speak, of a superior race, shows no weakness and makes no mistakes[10], in the *AAM* he is, admittedly, a hero but at the same time has his imperfections. When Jesus tells him to go and rescue Matthias, he asks to be relieved of that task, because he cannot go there quickly and does not even know the route. Jesus has to call him to order by saying 'Obey the one who made you, the one who can speak but a word and that city and all its inhabitants would be brought here.' (4). The tortures he undergoes make him weep, although he has been informed beforehand that he will have to suffer them (27 and 28). And the Lord blames him for the fact that he is harsh towards the citizens even after their conversion (33).

2. Although there are some miracles in the *AA*, in the *AAM* they are both more numerous and more fantastic. Suffice it to mention the removing of Matthias and his followers on a cloud (21) and the punishment of the citizenry by producing a flood spewed by a statue (29-30)[11]. As Prieur has it: The taste of the *AAM* 'for the prodigious (anthropophagites, cataclysm, being borne on the clouds) is less marked in the *AA* which relate sober miracles meant less to astonish than to cause faith to be born and confirmed. These then are almost always exorcisms, resurrections, and healings as in the New Testament'[12].

3. Whereas the propaganda of continence is a prominent feature of the *AA*, in the *AAM* it is non-existent. Indeed, no woman is mentioned in it.

4. In the *AA*, the points of contact with Scripture are unimportant[13]. There are only two allusions to the Old Testament, Andrew

---

[10] Cf. A. Hilhorst, 'The Apocryphal Acts as martyrdom texts: the case of the Acts of Andrew', in Bremmer, *Acts of John*, 1-14 at 6.
[11] From the section 11-5 we may add the sphinx evoking the patriarchs from their tomb (15).
[12] Prieur (n. 2), 31. In the same vein Prieur, *Acta Andreae*, 304.
[13] See Prieur, *Acta Andreae*, 12, 397, 404-5.

comparing Maximilla with Eve and himself with Adam (*AA* 37 and 39) and the expression 'works of Cain' used for marriage (*AA* 40). Also the New Testament is represented only in some allusions; for instance, Andrew asks whether the inner man in Maximilla has anywhere to lay his head (*AA* 42), which mirrors Jesus' words about himself in Matt. 8.20 par, and in a vision Jesus calls the devil Aegeates' father (40), like he calls him the father of the Jews in John 8.44. There are no quotations nor are there references to biblical events. In the *AAM* the picture is quite different[14]. To begin with Old Testament features, Andrew's disciples behold Abraham, Isaac, Jacob and David while they are being transported into heaven during their sleep before the gate of the city of the cannibals (17). In prison, when Andrew rebukes Satan, he refers to Adam's fall (Gen. 3), the transgression of the angels with the daughters of men (Gen. 6.1-4) and the flood which Noah survived (Gen. 6-8, and an allusion to Gen. 9.11: *AAM* 20). When addressing the statue in the prison, Andrew mentions such features as the moulding of man from the earth (Gen. 2.7) and the tablets of stone which Moses received (Ex. 31.18: *AAM* 29).

The New Testament is represented better still. In the prison, Matthias prays, 'Lord Jesus Christ, for whom we have forsaken everything to follow you', which is a quotation from Matthew 19.27 par (2). Andrew tells Jesus, whom he takes for a human captain, a lot about the Lord Jesus Christ. Thus in *c*. 6 he states:

> He chose us twelve and gave us this command: 'When you go to preach take on the road no money, no bread, no bag, no sandals, no staff, and no change of tunic.'

This is a direct quotation from Matthew 10.7-10 par. In *c*. 8 Andrew describes Jesus' calming of the storm (Matthew 8.23-7 par), in *c*. 10 his curing the blind, the lame, the deaf and the leper (Matthew 11.5 par), as well as his changing water into wine (John 2.1-10). Also the miracle of the loaves (Matthew 14.14-21 par) is told there. When Jesus reveals to Andrew that he will have to suffer many tortures, he reminds Andrew that his opponents beat him, spat in his face, and said, 'He casts out demons through Beelzebul', a quotation from

---

[14] Even omitting *cc*. 11-5, in which many biblical elements occur. The Latin versions of *AAM* contain still more biblical references than the Greek, see F. Blatt, *Die lateinischen Bearbeitungen der Acta Andreae et Matthiae apud Anthropophagos* (Gießen, 1930) 32, and his index s.v. Biblisches Sprachgut.

Matthew 12.24 par (18). In his turn, Andrew comforts Matthias with Jesus' words 'Behold, I send you as sheep in the midst of wolves' (Matthew 10.16 par: 19). When about to be arrested, Andrew says, 'Look, I am Andrew whom you seek' (25), which sounds like an echo of John 18.4-8. In the prison, the devil says to Andrew, 'We will kill you as Herod killed your teacher Jesus', an incorrect reminiscence of Luke 23.8-12 (26). *C.* 28 yields no less than three references. Andrew prays for relief of his tortures, reminding Jesus both of his own words on the cross: 'My Father, why have you forsaken me?' (Matthew 27.46 par) and, on the other hand, Jesus' promise, 'If you walk with me, you will not lose one hair from your head' (cf. Luke 21.18; Acts 27.34). Jesus replies by quoting himself: 'Heaven and earth will pass away, but my words will never pass away' (Matthew 24.35 par). From books of the New Testament apart from the Gospels, we may add possible reminiscences of the singing of Psalms in prison of Acts 16.25 in *cc.* 3 and 19[15], of the holy kiss of Rom. 16.16 in *c.* 19[16], and of the statement that God wants everyone to be saved of 1 Tim. 2.4 in *c.* 33. There are also many biblical phrases such as 'Peace be with you' (*cc.* 3 and 4).

5. In the *AA*, there is but one apostle, Andrew; the other ones are completely ignored. In the *AAM* the situation is different. Andrew turns out to be the hero of the story, but initially we hear only about Matthias, a situation comparable with the canonical Acts, where Paul enters the scene after many events in which Peter was the main character. And as we mentioned when summarizing the story, there is even a third apostle mentioned in the *AAM*, namely Peter, even if the author obviously does not feel like explaining what has brought Peter to teach on a mountain (21)[17]. As a collective, 'all the apostles' are mentioned in *c.* 1, 'the twelve' in *c.* 6 and 'the twelve apostles' in *c.* 17.

6. Turning to theology, we find that in the *AA* Jesus is God and that there is no God but Jesus. God the Father as distinct from God

---

[15] This is a common feature in martyrdom texts, e.g. *Acts of Justin* 6; *Martyrdom of Pionius* 11.5, 18.12. Also, Joseph praises God in prison (*Testament of Joseph* 8.5).

[16] This was familiar from liturgy, cf. F.L. Cross and E.A. Livingstone (eds), *The Oxford Dictionary of the Christian Church* (Oxford, 1997³) s.v. 'Kiss of Peace'.

[17] Is it in imitation of Jesus' Sermon on the Mount, cf. Matthew 5.1 and 8.1?

the Son is never mentioned[18]. In the *AAM* too, Jesus' divinity is stressed; he is mentioned as the creator of the world in *cc.* 4, 8 and 10 and of man in *c.* 4. The Father, however, is not absent; thus, Andrew reminds Jesus of his own words on the cross: 'My Father, why have you forsaken me?' (Matthew 27.46 par) in *c.* 28. Furthermore, there is an absence in the *AAM* of philosophical and gnosticising tendencies. To say it pointedly: the *AA* is a treatise in philosophical religion whereas the *AAM* is just a juicy story.

7. In the *AA*, we do not hear about angels[19]. In the *AAM*, however, they play an important role in the narrative. When Jesus orders Andrew to go and rescue his fellow apostle, Andrew suggests sending an angel instead (4). Jesus, acting as a captain of the boat which will transport Andrew, has two angels as his crew (5). These angels lift Andrew and his disciples and transport them to the city of the cannibals, after which they ascend to heaven with Jesus (16). Andrew's disciples, when being exalted into heaven during their sleep, behold Jesus there with all the angels surrounding him and in particular the twelve angels standing behind the apostles and being of the same appearance as the apostles (17). When about to punish the citizens, Andrew asks Jesus to send his archangel Michael (30).

8. In the *AA*, the Jews are never mentioned, either in a friendly or in a hostile sense[20]. In the *AAM*, on the other hand, Andrew depicts them as stubborn opponents of Jesus, and not even the most spectacular miracles are able to convert them from their hardness of heart[21]. True, in prison, Jesus strengthens Andrew by saying to him in Hebrew 'Our Andrew, heaven and earth will pass away, but my words will never pass away', but this use of Hebrew, comparable with Jesus speaking Hebrew to Saul on his way to Damascus (Acts 26.14), cannot be interpreted as compensating for the anti-Jewish bias of the text. Actually, we have here the idea of the true Israel from which the faithless Jews are excluded.

9. The literary and stylistic properties of both texts are completely at variance. Prieur points to the fact that the language in the two texts is quite different: 'The language in the AAM is simple and uses a limited vocabulary. The language in the AA, on the contrary, is much richer

---

[18] Prieur, in *NTA* II, 113 (German original: II, 105).
[19] Prieur, *Acta Andreae*, 370 n. 1.
[20] Prieur, *Acta Andreae*, 397.
[21] This is still more worked out in *cc.* 11-5.

and more literary'[22]. Both texts have much direct speech, but whereas in the *AAM* it consists of dialogues in short statements, quick prayers or story-telling, in the *AA* there are a number of long effusions and initiatory speeches. The plot of the story is much more sophisticated in the *AA* than in the *AAM*. Thus in the latter text the character Matthias can be dropped without detriment to the story, and indeed Andrew sends him away on a cloud just as a host might dispense with a boring visitor by calling a taxi. On the other hand, the *AAM* shows some literary subtlety by having Jesus in disguise speaking with Andrew about Jesus.

10. The *AAM* includes elements that point to a moment of origin which lies much later than that of the *AA*. Partly, these are of an intertextual nature. Flamion has shown that the *AAM* has a whole series of traits in common with other late *AAA* like the *Acts of Peter and Andrew*, and the B-version of the *Acts of Thomas*[23]. A. de Santos Otero argues that the *Life of Shenute* by Besa (5th century) contains the motif that Jesus acts as a captain with two angels as sailors, also found in *AAM* 5; he concludes that this motif was current in Egypt in the fourth century[24]. MacDonald tells a different tale, contending that the *ATh* depends on the *AAM*[25]. If that were correct, the *terminus ante quem* for the *AAM* would be no later than the early third century. However, the evidence in favour of this hypothesis is very slight. MacDonald mainly bases it on the beginning of the *ATh* (Act 1) which allegedly has parallels in the beginning of the *AAM*. In his reasoning he lumps together the scene in which Matthias is sent (*AAM* 1) and the scene in which Andrew is commanded to come to his rescue (*AAM* 4). Both scenes contain elements that also occur in *ATh* 1, but whereas in the *AAM* it is Matthias who draws a lot and departs from Jerusalem and Andrew who protests against his task, in the *ATh* both acts are told of Thomas. In our opinion, rather than assuming that the

---

[22] Prieur (n. 2), 31. For a similar conclusion, cf. now D.H. Warren, 'The Greek Language of the Apocryphal Acts of the Apostles: A Study in Style', in F. Bovon *et al.* (eds), *The Apocryphal Acts of the Apostles* (Cambridge MA, 1999) 101-24; E. Zachariades-Holmberg, 'Philological Aspects of the Apocryphal Acts of the Apostles, *ibidem*, 124-42.
[23] J. Flamion, *Les Actes Apocryphes de l'Apôtre André: Les Actes d'André et de Mathias, de Pierre et d'André et les textes apparentés* (Louvain, Paris and Brussels, 1911) 272-300.
[24] A. de Santos Otero, in *NTA* II, 444-5 (German original: II, 400).
[25] MacDonald, *Acts of Andrew*, 31-8.

ATh is secondary, we should say that the *AAM* follows the general pattern or convention for the beginning of both earlier and later *AAA*, a pattern which was partly influenced by the canonical Acts[26]. The similarities which MacDonald discovers between the rest of the *AAM* and the *ATh* are of so general a nature that they carry no force.

11. Different times of origin. The *AAM* shows several grammatical features that are characteristic of early Byzantine Greek, although some of them may sporadically occur earlier:

periphrasis of the pluperfect with the aorist participle, e.g.
ἦσαν ... συναχθέντες (*c.* 1 [65.3-4])[27],
ἦν ... κρύψας (*c.* 5 [70.9-10]),
ἦν τελευτήσας (*c.* 22 [114.7]);

subjunctives in main clauses used as optatives, e.g.
διαμένῃ (*c.* 3 [67.19]),
παράσχῃ (*c.* 6 [72.9]),
γενώμεθα (*c.* 7 [74.7]);

participle forms like
παραδώσαντες (*c.* 8 [74.17-18])[28].

In the sphere of Church history, late elements include the occurrence in the *AAM* of church buildings (30 and 32) and the suggestion of the demons at the end of *c.* 26 that temples are lying deserted because of the advance of Christianity[29].

---

[26] Cf. J.-D. Kaestli, 'Les scènes d'attribution des champs de mission et de départ de l'apôtre dans les Actes apocryphes', in F. Bovon *et al.*, *Les Actes apocryphes des Apôtres: Christianisme et monde païen* (Geneva, 1981) 249-64.

[27] The figures between square brackets refer to page and line of the edition by M. Bonnet (n. 3).

[28] Other grammatical features, although attested earlier, are also unthinkable in the *AA*. Some examples must suffice here: subjunctives in main clauses used as future indicatives, e.g. πορευθῇς and μείνητε (*c.* 31 [113.2,4]), ἐπανέλθω (*c.* 32 [115.4]); ἵνα and μή with the indicative, e.g. ἵνα ἐξάξει (*c.* 4 [69.2-3]), μή ... ὑπάρχουσιν (*c.* 7 [73.1]), μή ... ἰάσεται ... καὶ παραδώσει (*c.* 27 [105.17-18]); participle forms like γεναμένης (*c*3. 0 [110.9]); imperfects ending in -αν, e.g. προσέδεναν (*c.* 3 [68.9]), ἔλεγαν (*c.* 25 [101.15]), προέπεμπαν (*c.* 33 [116.13]). Cf. also Zachariades-Holmberg (n. 22), 140.

[29] This is the very argument which made MacDonald assume that *cc.* 11-5 are late, cf. n. 4.

All this is indicative of a date in the fourth century A.D. for the *AAM* at the earliest, much later than the *AA*, dated 'probably... no later than 200' by MacDonald and to the second half of the second century by Prieur[30].

A Christian Homer?

So much for the agreements and disagreements between the *AA* and the *AAM*. It would not be too bold, we trust, to state that they strongly plead against the argument that both texts originally belonged together. However, before drawing our conclusion from them, we should discuss still another contribution by MacDonald. Indeed, he has given us not only papers on the Andrew texts and a bilingual edition, but also his book *Christianizing Homer*[31]. In it, he argues that the original *AA*, in which he includes the textual material of *AAM*, Gregory, the Utrecht papyrus and the *AA*, is to a large extent inspired by or even modelled after Homer and Plato. This thesis has, of course, a consequence for our question: if it can be shown that the *AAM* is a piece of such a jigsaw puzzle of a Homeric/Platonic pattern, it is difficult to deny its belonging to the original *AA*.

In our opinion, however, the thesis is far from being proven. Confining ourselves to the *AAM*, we want to make the following remarks. First, unlike the biblical elements dealt with above, which are direct references or quotations, the Homeric and Platonic features are only parallels, and most of them far-fetched ones. MacDonald seems to adduce one exception to this. The name Myrmidonia, he argues, points 'directly to its classical antecedent: Myrmidonia designates the city of Homer's Myrmidonians'[32]. But although he builds so much on this datum, no Greek witness to the text of *AAM* offers this name, and MacDonald has to borrow from Gregory's epitome in order to replace τῶν ἀνθρωποφάγων of the Greek MSS. with Μυρ-

---

[30] MacDonald, *Acts of Andrew*, 59; Prieur, *Acta Andreae*, 414; see also Bremmer, this volume, Ch. II.
[31] D.R. MacDonald, *Christianizing Homer:* The Odyssey, *Plato, and* The Acts of Andrew (New York and Oxford, 1994).
[32] MacDonald, *Christianizing Homer*, 7, 35 (the manuscript variants of the name).

μιδονία (*AAM* 1, 4, 5, 16, 18; cf. 17, 33) or τῶν Μυρμιδόνων (*AAM* 5)[33]. At best some of the parallels can make an intertextual relationship credible, but none of them suffices to prove that the author of the original *AA* has sought to produce a 'baptized Odysseus' or a 'baptized Socrates'. Unfortunately, it is impossible to show this in the compass of an article; it would take a volume at least as large as MacDonald's. Second, MacDonald creates the impression that the *AAM*, as the first part of the Andrew story, runs parallel to the *Iliad*, whereas the rest of the *AA* would form a parallel to the *Odyssey*. But, judging from Gregory's epitome, the *AAM* can only have been one among many episodes: it takes only the first of its 38 chapters. It is unlikely that this single episode would parallel half the Homeric epos, and the rest of the text the other part of it. Moreover, a closer look at MacDonald's discussion of the thesis reveals that the *AAM* has markedly more parallels with the *Odyssey* than with the *Iliad*[34]. Third, whereas the *AA* is replete with allusions to Socrates and his role as a midwife, these are not to be found in the *AAM*. In short, as far as the *AAM* is concerned, MacDonald's thesis is unconvincing[35].

Conclusion

Thus, there is no obstacle to come to the only possible conclusion: that the *AAM* was not part of the original *AA*. Gregory's combination of it with the *AA* is no proof to the contrary. There are many exam-

---

[33] From MacDonald, 291 we learn that the unpublished MS. *Paris graecus 1313* does have this name Myrmidonia; actually, the name reads Σμυρμήνη (ib. 35), but this is, according to him (p. 78), 'a variant spelling to the word "Myrmidonia"'.

[34] MacDonald, *Christianizing Homer*, 35-76.

[35] Although he does not say so, MacDonald is not the first to discover parallels between Homer and the *AAM*. R. Söder, *Die apokryphen Apostelgeschichten und die romanhafte Literatur der Antike* (Stuttgart, 1932 = Darmstadt, 1969) 43, 79, 103 and 203, already did (cf. also 168: the miraculous sea voyage in *AAM* 4 parallels on Apollonius Rhodius 2.537ff. and 598ff). Still earlier, E. von Dobschütz, 'Der Roman in der altchristlichen Literatur', *Deutsche Rundschau* 111 (1902) 100 wrote: 'In manchen dieser Sagenzüge erkennt man noch deutlich den alten Mythus. Wer dächte bei jener wunderbaren Fahrt des Andreas nicht des Phäakenschiffes, das einst Odysseus schlafend an das Ziel seiner Wanderung brachte...?'

ples of omnibuses of texts relating to a common subject: the *First Book of Enoch*, for example, or, a more close analogy, the *Alexander Romance*, which contains sophisticated parts alongside much more primitive ones[36].

---

[36] We are grateful for help received from Professor W.J. Aerts.

II. Man, Magic, and Martyrdom in the Acts of Andrew

JAN N. BREMMER

Of the Apocryphal Acts of the Apostles (*AAA*), less has been preserved of the *Acts of Andrew* (*AA*) than of any of the other *Acts*, although the recent edition by Prieur has made considerable progress in comparison with earlier editions[1]. Fortunately, its general plan still remains visible in the reworking by Gregory of Tours of the lost Latin translation (*AAlat*), but this skeleton version has surely robbed us of many details which might have enabled us to determine with more certainty where and when the author lived and worked. Confronted with these handicaps, what can we nevertheless say about the author?

According to Prieur, the *AA* could just as easily have been composed in 'Greece as in Asia Minor, Syria or Egypt'[2]. The last region is not a very strong possibility, since the name of one of the protagonists of *AA*, Maximilla (to whom we will return below), is not attested for Egypt[3]. Prieur has also overlooked the fact that our author uses the expression 'first of the city': in the Pontic town of Amasea Andrew resurrected an Egyptian slave of *Demetrii... primi civitatis Amaseorum* (*AAlat* 3). This expression, variants of which also occur in the *AJ* and *AP*[4], was probably inspired by local custom, since a Pontic inscription mentions a grandson of an '*andros proteuontos en tei metropolei Amaseiai*'[5]. As the author of the *AA* knew the *APt*, which may well have

---

[1] J.-M. Prieur, *Acta Andreae*, 2 vols (Turnhout, 1989).
[2] Prieur, *Acta Andreae*, 414-64 and *NTA* II, 115.
[3] As a computer search in the papyri and inscriptions has shown.
[4] See my 'The Novel and the Apocryphal Acts: Place, Time and Readership', in H. Hofmann and M. Zimmerman (eds), *Groningen Colloquia on the Novel* IX (Groningen, 1998) 157-80 at 165-70.
[5] IGR III.115, republished by B. Le Guen Pollet, *Epigraphica Anatolica* 13 (1989) 65-6 and T.B. Mitford, *ZPE* 87 (1991) 181-243, no. 12.

been written in Bithynia, but also the *AJ*[6], we may at least wonder whether the *AA* was not written in Pontus: a Pontic origin would explain the awkward scope of the *AA*, which somewhat uneasily combines a stay in Pontus and Bithynia with a death in Achaia. In any case, its vocabulary of elite and civic virtues (below) makes it unlikely to have been written anywhere other than in Asia Minor.

Such an origin is also supported by the mention of the wife of the proconsul Lesbios and her steward (*AAlat* 23). Although a real Roman proconsul could have taken his wife with him to his province, he would have hardly taken along her steward[7]. On the other hand, stewards (*oikonomos* or *pragmateutes*) of wealthy Greek women are epigraphically attested, especially in areas with large estates, such as Central Anatolia and Bithynia, and they must have been a sufficiently common and distinctive feature for the author of the *Historia Apollonii Tyrii* (31 RA, RB) to introduce one into his novel[8]. In this respect too our text points to Asia Minor.

What else can we say about the author? Most likely, he was a cultivated man. He was not only well versed in Platonic philosophy[9], but also mentions a woman Calliope (the name of one of the Muses: *AAlat* 25), a slave Alcmanes (a probable reference to the famous Spartan poet Alcman: 4, *AAlat* 34), a Sinopean citizen Gratinus (probably Cratinus, the name of the famous poet of Old Comedy: *AAlat* 5), a Megarian citizen Antiphanes (the name of a famous poet of Middle Comedy: 15; *AAlat* 29), and the proconsul Lesbios, whose name in this literary company evokes the island of Lesbos, famous for its poets Alcaeus and Sappho (*AAlat* 22)[10]. One may be sceptical

---

[6] *AA* and *APt*: Prieur, in *NTA* II, 115. Date and place of *APt*: Bremmer, *Acts of Peter*, 14-20. *AJ*: Lalleman, this volume, Ch. XII.

[7] For stewards see J. Carlsen, *Vilici and Roman Estate Managers until AD 284* (Rome, 1995); Wives: M.T. Raepsaet-Charlier, 'Épouses et familles de magistrats dans les provinces romaines aux deux premiers siècles de l'empire', *Historia* 31 (1982) 56-70.

[8] *Oikonomos*: *SEG* 43.441 (*BCH* 1993, 384-94); *I. Iznik* 196, 1062, 1201, 1208; *RECAM* ii.324; L. Robert, *BCH* 103 (1979) 429 n. 13; S. Mitchell, *Anatolia* I (Oxford, 1993) 160; R. van Bremen, *The Limits of Participation* (Amsterdam, 1996) 267-9.

[9] See Schroeder, this volume, Ch. X.

[10] Prieur misses all these literary references, except Alcmanes. A literary interpretation of the name Cratinus is supported by its virtual absence in second-century Asia Minor.

about these identifications, but our author was certainly sensitive to names. It can hardly be chance that the wife of the proconsul Lesbios was called 'the most beautiful', Callista (*AAlat* 23), and the wife of the proconsul Aegeates 'the most important', Maximilla, even though the latter name was not very common in the Greek world.

There are also other indications that our author did not belong to the lowest strata of his city. Any reader of the *AA* will be struck by the stress on 'gentleness' in our text. Antiphanes invokes Andrew's help with the words: 'if there is any gentleness (*bonitas*) in you' (*AAlat* 29), just as all the men of Thessalonica loved a young man, Exuos (Exuor, Exoos, Exuus), for 'his gentleness and mildness' (*bonitatem et mansuetudinem*: *AAlat* 12) after his resurrection. And when Stratocles is introduced into the story, he is said to have 'fulfilled his proper duty to his friends, bearing himself kindly (*prosênôs*) to all and greeting all in gracious (*epieikôs*) and seemly (*metrios*) fashion' (1).

These words were key terms of Greek civic life and regularly recur in the honorific decrees so abundantly displayed in the Greek cities of Hellenistic and Roman times. The most frequent of the three Greek terms in the characterisation of Stratocles was *epieikês*, 'reasonable', which in the course of time came to mean 'fair'[11], whereas *metrios* meant 'moderate', and *prosênês* 'gentle'; the latter quality even came to be reflected in names[12]. Sometimes the terms occur in combinations, as in the case of the above mentioned Exuos, who was praised for what in Greek may have been called his *praotês kai epieikeia*, a combination rather popular in Aphrodisias[13]. In all these cases the stress on moderation and mildness is an indication of the growing judicial cruelty of the period which needed to be counterbalanced by praising the moderation and gentleness of the *grands*

---

[11] L. Robert, *Hellenica* IV (1948) 15-8, 133 and XIII (1965) 223-4; J. de Romilly, *La douceur dans la pensée grecque* (Paris, 1979) 269-70; L. Robert, *Le martyre de Pionios* (Washington, 1994) 63-4; *SEG* 43.850.

[12] *Prosênês*: Robert, *Hellenica* IV, 133; De Romilly, *Douceur*, 271; *SEG* 35.1330. Names: H. Solin, *Die griechischen Personennamen in Rom* (Berlin and New York, 1982) II.775 and *Die stadtrömischen Sklavennamen* (Stuttgart, 1996) II.426. *Metrios*: C. Spicq, *Notes de lexicographie néotestamentaire* II (Freiburg and Göttingen, 1978) 563-5; *TAM* II.3.739; *SEG* 35.1363.

[13] De Romilly, *La douceur*, 269.

seigneurs[14]. But whereas at first these terms denoted important civic virtues, they subsequently came to be used to denote more personal qualities, as in our examples[15]. The use of these terms, then, shows that our author was a man well acquainted with the ethical vocabulary of his time and thus, probably, a representative of the higher classes.

The author's theological views have been well studied by Prieur, who has concluded that they have much in common with Gnosticism. His contempt for the flesh also displays itself in his propagation of a very simple diet, encratism and the renunciation of sexuality[16]. This last element is demonstrated by various scenes, one of which deserves a closer look. In Philippi, Andrew prevented a wedding between two pairs of cousins (*AAlat* 11). The moment itself is narrated with a feeling for drama, since the marriage is nearly consummated and the parents are already wearing the wedding garlands, as befitted such a festive event. At that very moment, the apostle arrived and spoilt the party. Prieur has persuasively suggested that Gregory has tinkered with the story, but the question is of course in what way he did so[17].

A marriage in the urban elite between the children of brothers, so-called parallel cousins, was not uncommon at the time of the *AA*. In fact, Achilles Tatius' contemporary novel *Leukippe and Kleitophon* is a striking example, since the homonymous protagonists of the novel are the children of two brothers. Achilles Tatius probably came from southern Anatolia, the same region where we have situated the *AJ* and *AP*[18], and it is exactly in Lycia that endogamy in the elite is repeatedly attested[19]. Another interesting example can be

---

[14] See also C. Spicq, *Notes de lexicographie néo-testamentaire. Supplément* (Freiburg and Göttingen, 1982) 570-82. For the growing cruelty see R. MacMullen, 'Judicial Savagery in the Roman Empire', in his *Changes in the Roman Empire* (Princeton, 1990) 204-17, 357-64 (notes).
[15] Robert, *Le martyre de Pionios*, 63.
[16] Prieur, *Acta Andreae*, 319-30.
[17] Prieur, *Acta Andreae*, 42f.
[18] Bremmer, 'The Novel', 165-8.
[19] S. Pembroke, 'Last of the Matriarchs: a study in the inscriptions of Lycia', *J. Ec. Soc. Hist. Orient* 8 (1965, 217-47) 231 n. 2; A. Balland, *Inscriptions du Létôon* (Paris, 1981) 152ff; M. Wörrle, *Stadt und Fest*, 70; M. Adak, *Epigraphica Anatolica* 26 (1996) 136.

found in Apuleius (*Met.* 4.26), whose Greek model, the *Metamorphoseis* ascribed to 'Lucius of Patrai', was probably also composed in Southern Anatolia[20]. Here a girl relates that on the very day of her wedding bandits had taken her away from her intended husband and *consobrinus*, 'cousin', whom *omnis civitas* had elected as *filium publicum*, that is, as 'son of the city', a honorary title especially popular, once again, in Southern Anatolia in the second century[21]. Her husband-to-be was also three years older than herself, an interesting indication of the age difference at marriage in the region[22].

On the other hand, Prieur is quite right in stating that incest between cousins was not objectionable in those days. In fact, the prohibition of a marriage between cousins appears first in the Councils of Epaon (AD 517: *canon* 30) and Auxerre (*canon* 31), that is, in the time of Gregory himself. Unfortunately, the date of the latter Council is debated. If it indeed took place some time after AD 585, as the latest discussion hesitantly suggests, that would be an additional argument for dating the *Liber de miraculis* to Gregory's last years, since 'incest' between cousins does not seem to have been a burning issue in the earlier part of the sixth century[23]. In any case, in the original *AA* the episode will have been directed against marriage rather than against incest.

So when did the intellectual from Asia Minor write the *AA*? On the basis of the absence of institutional details and of their Christology, Prieur has suggested that the *AA* were composed 'probably about 150 rather than about 200'. However, in the first English edition of *NTA*, M. Hornschuh pointed to *AA*'s close contacts with Tat-

---

[20] Bremmer, 'The Novel', 168.
[21] Bandits: for the most recent bibliography see B. McGing, 'Bandits, Real and Imagined, in Greco-Roman Egypt', *Bull. Am. Soc. Papyr.* 35 (1998) 159-83. 'Son of the city': Van Bremen, *Limits of Participation*, 167-9.
[22] Add the example to the material in Bremmer, *Acts of Peter*, 2.
[23] P. Mikat, *Die Inzestgesetzgebung der merowingisch-fränkischen Konzilien (511-626/7)* (Paderborn 1994) 119f (Epaon), 131f (Auxerre); add to his bibliography M. de Jong, 'To the Limits of Kinship: anti-incest legislation in the early medieval west (500-900)', in Bremmer (ed), *From Sappho to De Sade. Moments in the History of Sexuality* (London, 1989) 36-59. Late date of *Liber*: J. Flamion, *Les Actes Apocryphes de l'Apôtre André* (Louvain, 1911) 54f.

ian's theology and therefore suggested a date closer to, but not after, 190, particularly considering the *AA*'s close relationship with the *APt*, a relationship also accepted by Prieur[24].

Such a date of origin for the *AA*, close to 200, is supported by the development already observed from civic virtues towards personal characteristics as reflected in the *AA*. There is also another indication which has been insufficiently taken into account by Prieur and Hornschuh. When Stratocles is introduced, the author tells us that Caesar had excused him from the army so that he could dedicate himself to philosophy (1). Evidently, it was impossible to represent the emperor as being opposed to military service, but the author's intentions become clearer in the Coptic fragment, where we hear of a young man who, like the centurion mentioned by Tertullian in his *De corona* (1), had thrown off his uniform and dropped his sword (*AAco* 9)[25] – a passage perhaps to be connected, as Prieur suggests, with the soldiers who threaten the apostle in Thrace (*AAlat* 9)[26]. Now the question of the acceptability of military service hardly occurs in the Christian literature of the first and second centuries, but suddenly becomes prominent around the beginning of the third century, when, presumably, the Christian faith had started to make inroads into the Roman army[27]. In other words, the theme of the rejection of military service also points to a date for the *AA* towards the end of the second century or the beginning of the third.

After these observations on the author, place and period of the *AA*, it is time to look at some of its more prominent aspects. In line with my earlier investigations of the *AJ*, *AP* and *APt* I will look at (1) man, (2) magic and exorcism, and (3) martyrdom as reflected in the *AA*.

[24] M. Hornschuh, in W. Schneemelcher (ed), *New Testament Apocrypha* II (London, 1965) 395-7. Prieur: see note 6.

[25] I quote the Coptic fragment from the edition in Prieur, *Acta Andreae*, 655-71. For the Coptic translation note now also T.S. Richter, 'P. Ien. inv. 649: Ein Splitter vom koptischen Text der Acta Andreae', *Arch. f. Papyrusforschung* 44 (1998) 275-84.

[26] Prieur, *Acta Andreae*, 588, who on p. 327 notes the author's rejection of military service, but does not draw any chronological conclusions from his observation.

[27] A very full bibliography on this theme: F. Ruggiero, *Tertulliano, De Corona* (Milan, 1992) XLIV-XLVIII; add J. Roldanus, 'De vroege kerk en de militaire dienst', *Kerk en Theologie* 33 (1982) 182-202; P.W. van der Horst, *De onbekende God* (Utrecht, 1988) 210-28.

1. *Man*

How are males and females represented in the *AA*? Let us start with the depiction of the brothers Stratocles and Aegeates, both noble Romans. When Stratocles saw his beloved servant Alcmanes in the grip of a demon, he wanted to commit suicide because of his great grief (2). Moreover, he is depicted as groaning, sighing and incessantly weeping (8, 43) – hardly the accepted behaviour of the Roman upper class.

Aegeates does not fare much better. To start with, his status is evidently compromised by his own admission that he was of a lower status than his wife (36; *AAlat* 24). Relationships in which a Christian woman was socially superior to her pagan partner did indeed occur. They were even condoned by Pope Callistus, but it is not clear whether our passage presupposes such practices[28]. Aegeates' lower status was also reflected in his behaviour. He was a drunkard (18), a glutton (46) and, like his brother, he threatened to commit suicide when his wife was very seriously ill (*AAlat* 30). In addition, he was slow-witted, since for eight months a female slave, Eukleia, could pretend to be his wife in bed, despite the fact that he is pictured as being a husband in love – a mistake admittedly made easier by the Roman upper-class custom of making love in the dark[29]. Aegeates also did not always move in the right way. When once he was acting as a judge, he suddenly remembered the apostle, rose from the bench and ran 'like a madman' to the praetorium (35), whereas a real Roman (or Greek) gentleman of course was never seen running in public; even Maximilla, although in haste, moved 'not rashly or without set purpose' (46)[30].

Even worse, when Aegeates was at the point of discovering Andrew and the brethren in Maximilla's chamber, he was struck with a stomach-ache and had to sit a long time on a kind of toilet (13) – not a very dignified sight for a Roman governor! In this passage the

---

[28] Hipp. *Ref.* 9.12.24-5; Tert. *Ad uxorem*, 2.8.
[29] Ov. *AA* 2.619f, *Am* 1 5.7f; Mart. 11.2.4, 11.104.5, 12.43.10; Tac. *Ann.* 15.37.
[30] For walking among the Greeks and Romans see Bremmer, 'Walking, standing and sitting in ancient Greek culture' and F. Graf, 'Gestures and conventions: the gestures of Roman actors and orators', in J. Bremmer and H. Roodenburg (eds), *A Cultural History of Gesture* (Cambridge, 1991) 15-35 at 18-20 and 36-58 at 55, respectively.

author has visible pleasure in depicting the highest Roman official in a less than respectable situation: an interesting testimony to the possibilities which Greeks had of expressing their true opinion about their rulers[31].

Moreover, Aegeates was very cruel. After his detection of Eukleia's cheating he had her fellow slaves, who had informed him about her deceit, crucified. As for Eukleia herself, her tongue, hands and feet were cut off and 'after remaining some days without nourishment she became food for the dogs' (22). Crucifixion was a customary Roman penalty for slaves, although not uncommon in the Greek world, whereas the other measures seem to have been typically Greek in origin[32].

Similar cruelty was also displayed by the anonymous proconsul in, perhaps, Amaseia, who ordered a young man, Sostratus, with whom his mother had fallen hopelessly in love, to be executed using the *culleus* of the parricide (*AAlat* 4)[33]. This typically Roman penalty may seem out of place in this Greek environment, but in the Greek mentality incest and parricide were closely related[34], and the passage may thus reflect the original. In both these cases the behaviour of the Roman pagan proconsuls is in sharp contrast with the gentleness and affability of the converted Stratocles.

In one case, even a Christian prostitute could be more imposing than a pagan male. The wife of the proconsul Lesbios, whom we will

---

[31] The example is not mentioned by H. Fuchs, *Der geistige Widerstand gegen Rom in der antiken Welt* (Berlin, 1938); J. Palm, *Rom, Römertum und Imperium in der griechischen Literatur der Kaiserzeit* (Lund, 1959).

[32] Greek crucifixions: M. Hengel, *Crucifixion* (London, 1977) 69-83; J. and L. Robert, *Fouilles d'Amyzon en Carie* (Paris, 1983) 259-63; É. Puech, 'Notes sur 11Q19 LXIV 6-13 et 4Q524 14, 2-4. À propos de la crucifixion dans le *Rouleau de Temple* et dans le judaïsme ancien', *Revue de Qumran* 18 (1997) 109-24. Tongue: 2 Macc.7.4; Plut. *M*.849B; 4 Macc. 10.19, 12.13; Origen, *Mart*.23. Hands and feet: Pol. 5.54.10, 8.21.3; 2 Macc. 7.4; Diod.Sic. 34.8; 4 Macc. 10.20; Aug. *De gestis cum Emerito* 9 (*PL* 43.704: a bishop's tongue and hands cut off).

[33] For a fascinating study of the penalty with rich bibliography, see F. Egmond and P. Mason, *The Mammoth and the Mouse* (Baltimore and London, 1997) 133-56 ('The longue durée of ritual punishment').

[34] Parricide and incest: Bremmer (ed), *Interpretations of Greek Mythology* (London, 1988²) 49-51; add A. Moreau, 'La liaison entre parricide, inceste et cannibalisme. Compléments', *Cahiers du GITA* 1 (1985) 49-56.

meet again as a real sinner, condemned her husband's former concubine, Trophime, to a brothel, a not uncommon penalty[35]. Here she was protected by an *euangelium* hidden in her bosom. Apparently, this method of protection proved very helpful, since it made impotent all those who wanted to 'touch' her (*contingerent*) and helped to kill a youth who wanted to 'sexually humiliate' her (*inluderet*: AAlat 23)[36]. This power of the gospel also becomes apparent in the case of an old man of 74, evidently still *compos mentulae*, who had converted after a life of debauchery and carried an *euangelium* with him[37]. Yet life-long habits are not easily shed. He again succumbed to his lust and approached a prostitute, but this time she did not let him get near her – evidently, she had felt the presence of the gospel (28).

According to Prieur, these episodes must have been introduced by Gregory or a later translator (revisor?) of the text, since contemporary testimonies for 'magical' use of a gospel are non-existent. Now it is true that Christian miniature codices are usually later than the time of the *AA*[38], but, as Prieur also recognises, such a use of the gospel as talisman might have been derived from contemporaneous Jewish practice, which used small codices of the Torah for magical protection[39]. Moreover, Jerome already reproaches *superstitiosae mulierculae* for carrying small gospels on their persons like the Pharisees with their phylacteries, and small gospels have been found in graves from the fourth or fifth century onwards – surely as amulets[40].

---

[35] Bremmer, *Acts of John*, 51; add now F. Rizzo Nervo, 'La vergine e il lupanare', in *La narrativa cristiana antica* (Rome, 1995) 91-9.
[36] In late Latin, *contingere* is a well attested euphemism for sexual intercourse, cf. J.N. Adams, *The Latin Sexual Vocabulary* (London, 1982) 184; for *inludo* see Adams, *ibidem*, 200.
[37] For the sexual connotation of *exercere* in AAlat 28, cf. Adams, *Latin Sexual Vocabulary*, 158 n. 1.
[38] E. Turner, *The Typology of the Early Codex* (Philadelphia, 1977) 22, 30; add *Historia Lausiaca* 8; *P.Kell.* 91, 92, 94 and *P.Kell.Copt.* 1.
[39] Prieur, *Acta Andreae*, 622 n.6; L. Blau, 'Das neue Evangelienfragment von Oxyrhynchos buch- und zaubergeschichtlich betrachtet nebst sonstigen Bemerkungen', ZNW 9 (1908) 204-15; S. Lieberman, *Greek in Jewish Palestine* (New York, 1942) 110ff.
[40] J. Vezin, 'Les livres utilisés comme amulettes et comme reliques', in P. Ganz (ed), *Das Buch als magisches und als Repräsentationsobjekt* (Wiesbaden, 1992) 100-15 at 103-5.

It is, then, not impossible that these episodes were already part of the original *AA*.

When we now survey our evidence, we cannot fail to observe a clear contrast between men and women, and there can be little doubt as to which category comes off better. On the whole, except for the apostle, males are depicted as rather feeble and having difficulty controlling themselves, just as they are in the *AJ*. As was the case with the *AJ* and *AP*, we thus once again feel that educated, wealthy women were an important part of *AA*'s intended readership[41].

2. *Magic and exorcism*

Any reader of the *AA* will be struck by the multitude of references to magic, demons and exorcism. We cannot discuss in detail all the relevant passages, but we can certainly pose questions such as: who is the magician? Where are the demons and what do they look like? How do they affect the possessed? How does the apostle approach them and how do they react? How does the victim of demonic possession respond to his exorcism? In what kind of context does exorcism take place? And what is the reaction of the public? Investigation into ancient exorcism has rarely transcended the stage of collecting the facts, but we must always take into account that exorcism is a ritual scenario which takes place between the exorcist, the person possessed, the demon(s) and the public. Any analysis which neglects one of these aspects presents us with an only inadequate view of this ancient ritual[42].

Let us start with the magician. In the Coptic fragment a young magician says before 'attacking' a Christian girl: 'If I have spent five and twenty years under the instruction of my master until I was trained in his skill, this is the beginning of my craft' (*AAco* 10). The

---

[41] For female readership see now my observations in Bremmer, 'The Novel', 171-8.

[42] For exorcism see K. Thraede, 'Exorzismus', *RAC* 7 (Stuttgart, 1969) 44-117 (learned but insufficient on the *AAA*); P. Brown, *Society and the Holy in Late Antiquity* (London, 1982) 123-6; R. Lane Fox, *Pagans and Christians* (Harmondsworth, 1986) 327-30; R. Kotansky, 'Greek Exorcistic Amulets', in M. Meyer and P. Mirecki (eds), *Ancient Magic and Ritual Power* (Leiden, 1995) 243-77. For modern Greece, Ch. Stewart, *Demons and the Devil* (Princeton, 1991) 211-21.

passage is an interesting, albeit neglected, testimony for the ancient belief that magic could only be learnt after many years of instruction, preferably in Egypt[43]. So Celsus reproached Jesus for having learned magic in Egypt[44]; according to later legend, Bishop Cyprian had been ten years with the Memphitic priests training to become a magician (*Conf.* 12)[45], and Lucian's lover of lies had spent twenty-three years in subterranean chambers in Memphis where Isis had trained him to become a magician (*Philopseudeis* 34-6). Clearly, after an even longer period of instruction our magician should have been a formidable opponent of the apostle!

The same teacher-pupil relationship perhaps underlies the episode of Exuos, an upper-class youth, who had left his parents in order to follow Andrew. When they tried to smoke out the apostle with the help of a military cohort, their son extinguished the fire with a dish of water. The parents realised that their plan had failed and exclaimed: 'Look, our son has become a magician!' Not wholly surprisingly, they had identified Andrew as a master magician (*AAlat* 11).

The young magician did not speak himself, but, according to the apostle, it was the demon Semmath who had entered him (*AAco* 10). According to Prieur (*ad loc.*), Semmath may well have been the devil and must have been introduced by the Coptic translator, but he rightly does not follow Quispel's suggestion that Semmath is the demon Sammael of the Latin translation of the *Acts of Andrew and Matthias* (24)[46]. Unfortunately, both Quispel and Prieur overlooked a close relative of this demon, the undoubtedly related demon Sammoth from one of the Leiden magical papyri (*PGM* XII. 79).

---

[43] For Egypt as the country of magic *par excellence* see F. Graf, 'How to Cope with a Difficult Life. A View of Ancient Magic' and D. Frankfurter, 'Ritual Expertise in Roman Egypt and the Problem of the Category "Magician",' in H. Kippenberg and P. Schäfer (eds), *Envisioning Magic* (Leiden, 1997) 93-114 at 94-5 and 115-35 at 119-21, respectively.

[44] Origen, *Contra Celsum* 1.28, 38, 46; *bSanh* 107b; B. Kollmann, *Jesus und die Christen als Wundertäter* (Göttingen, 1996) 179-81; E. Bammel, *Judaica et Paulina* (Tübingen, 1997) 3-14 ('Jesus der Zauberer').

[45] For the text see *Acta Sanctorum*, Sept. vol. VII, 204 ff; H.M. Jackson, 'A contribution toward an edition of the *Confession* of Cyprian of Antioch, the *secreta Cypriani*', *Le Muséon* 101 (1988) 33-40.

[46] G. Quispel, 'An Unknown Fragment of the Acts of Andrew', *VigChris* 10 (1956) 129-48 at 137 n.4.

Magicians were traditionally believed to be accompanied by a demon who helped them perform their magic, the so-called *parhedros*[47]. According to Irenaeus, the heretic Marcus had such a 'demonic assistant (*daimona parhedron*), through whom he himself seems to prophesy and through whom he rouses to prophecy those women whom he thinks worthy of participating in the grace' (*Adv. Haer.* 1.13.3). As the assistant was indispensable, he is sometimes even mentioned right at the beginning of a ritual, such as in a Berlin magical papyrus: 'A [demon comes] as an assistant who will reveal everything to you clearly and will be your [companion and] will eat and sleep with you'[48].

Often, though, demons do not belong to a specific magician but seem to be independent beings who sometimes lurk in specific places. It is rather striking for us moderns to find them regularly in the baths[49], a belief abundantly illustrated by the *AA*. When Andrew comes near Sinope, he heals the son of Cratinus, who had been 'struck' (see below) by a demon when frequenting the women's bath (*AAlat* 5). Subsequently, in Patras he resurrected the wife of Lesbios, Callista, who, whilst taking a bath together with her steward (see the introduction), had been 'struck' by a demon (*AAlat* 23). Finally, in Corinth he exorcised both an old man and a youth whom he had met in the baths (*AAlat* 27). Gregory's narration supplies no more information about the last case, but in the earlier ones we can easily recognise the underlying pagan and Christian objection to mixed bathing[50].

---

[47] C. Zintzen, *Kleine Pauly* 4 (1972) 510f; Th. Hopfner, *Griechisch-ägyptischer Offenbarungszauber* I, 1921¹ (Amsterdam, 1974²) §1ff; C. Colpe, *RAC* 10 (Stuttgart, 1974) 621ff; L. Ciraolo, 'Supernatural Assistants in Greek Magical Papyri', in Meyer and Mirecki, *Ancient Magic*, 279-95; F. Graf, *Magic in the Ancient World* (Cambridge MA, 1997) 107-16.

[48] *PGM* I.1-3. All translations from magical papyri are from H.D. Betz (ed), *The Greek Magical Papyri in Translation* I (Chicago, 1992²).

[49] C. Bonner, 'Demons of the Bath', in *Studies Presented to F.Ll. Griffith* (London, 1932) 203-8; Hopfner, *Offenbarungszauber* I §195; K. Dunbabin, '*Baiarum grata voluptas*: pleasures and dangers of the baths', *Papers of the British School at Rome* 57 (1989) 6-46.

[50] For mixed bathing see Mart. 7.35, 11.75; Juv. 6.422f; Clem.Alex. *Paed.* 3.5.32; A. Hilhorst, 'Erotic Elements in the *Shepherd* of Hermas', in Hofmann and Zimmerman, *Groningen Colloquia* IX, 193-204 at 196.

The demons manifested themselves in rather different ways. The demon who had struck the proconsul's wife and her steward is simply called a *daemon teterrimus*, but those who assaulted the proconsul Lesbios were 'Aethiopians', pitch-black men, a favourite manifestation of ancient demons (*AAlat* 22)[51]. They could even show up as animals. In Nicaea seven demons lived in tombs along the road (*AAlat* 5, 7), another place fit for demons, just as their number, seven, is typical of groups of demons in the New Testament[52]. When the apostle arrived in the city, the Nicaeans approached him with olive branches, not, as Prieur suggests (*ad loc.*), in imitation of Jesus' entry into Jerusalem, but in the Greek mode of supplication[53]. The apostle gave in to their entreaties and ordered the demons to show themselves. At that very moment they appeared as dogs, one more indication of the ambivalent standing of the dog among Jews and Greeks[54].

How did the demons affect their victims? As the above mentioned examples show, some victims felt 'struck', 'beaten' or 'whipped' by the demons. We do not find this belief in a 'blow' by a demon in the New Testament, but just as the wife of the proconsul and her steward were *percussi* by a demon (*AAlat* 23), so Stratocles' servant Alcmanes was *ab inpulsu daemonis percussus* (2; *AAlat* 34). Indeed, the explanation of illness or possession as the result of a stroke is very widespread and regularly occurs in the magical papyri, where, for example, in a recipe for a love spell the advice is to 'glue it to the dry vaulted vapour room of a bath, and you will marvel. But watch yourself so that you are not struck'. A variant of the 'stroke' was a 'lash', a belief perhaps reflected in the

---

[51] Bremmer, *Acts of Peter*, 8; and J. Clarke, 'Hypersexual Black Men in Augustan Baths: Ideal Somatypes and Apotropaic Magic', in N.B. Kampen (ed), *Sexuality in Ancient Art. Near East, Egypt, Greece, and Italy* (Cambridge, 1996) 184-98.

[52] Tombs: Mt 8.28; Mk 5.2,3,5; Lk 8.27; *Test. Sol.* 17.2; H. Strack and P. Billerbeck, *Kommentar zum Neuen Testament aus Talmud und Midrasch* IV.1 (Munich, 1928) 515f. Seven: Ez. 9.1f; Mt 12.45; Mk 16.9; Lk 8.2, 11.26; *Test. Sol.* 8.1. Canine demons: H.-J. Loth, 'Hund', *RAC* 16 (Stuttgart, 1994) 773-828 at 822f; add *Test. Sol.* 10.1-4.

[53] Bremmer, 'Scapegoat Rituals in Ancient Greece', *HSCPh* 87 (1983) 299-320 at 318f; add for a contemporary parallel Apuleius, *Met.* 3.8.

[54] Loth, 'Hund'.

proconsul Lesbios' feeling of being 'whipped' by 'Ethiopians' (*AAlat* 22)[55].

From the Middle Ages until virtually our own times, possessed people also display socially unacceptable behaviour and extreme signs of motor disorder, often with contortions and dislocations. It is no different in the *AA*. The old man in the bath (above) trembled (*AAlat* 27). Some servants of Antiphanes were 'grinding their teeth...and insanely laughing' (*AAlat* 29)[56]. Other people even lost all control over their limbs. The son of Cratinus went mad and fell on the ground in front of the apostle (5). In the Coptic fragment the soldier fell on the ground and started to foam at the mouth (*AAco* 9), just like Stratocles' servant Alcmanes, who was moreover 'utterly convulsed' and sitting on a dungheap (2-3; *AAlat* 34), not a very dignified position. One may at least pose the question of how far these possessions, or their descriptions, were dependent on the New Testament where, for example, in Mark the boy with the dumb spirit 'convulsed the boy, and he fell on the ground and rolled about, foaming at the mouth' (9.20)[57].

It could be even worse. The Nicaean canine demons killed the son of aged parents (*AAlat* 7), just as a demon killed the proconsul's wife and her steward (*AAlat* 23), and strangled the son of a Thessalonian (*AAlat* 14). In the latter case one may well wonder whether the narrative here does not exaggerate the feeling of suffocation which is attested for some possessed people. Exaggeration certainly plays a role in the earlier scenes and this raises a problem to which we will return immediately, viz. to what extent these scenes were stock descriptions rather than representations of reality.

How did the apostle react to the demonic powers? Whereas he had taken the initiative in addressing the Nicaean canine demons, it was usually the other way round. For example, in Philippi a youth cried out: 'What is there between you and me, Andrew? Have you

---

[55] *PGM* XXXVI.76; see also *PGM* VII.282; Ptol. *Tetrabl.* 3.14; S. Eitrem, *Notes on the Demonology in the New Testament* (Oslo, 1966²) 36f; A. Stramaglia, *Res inauditae, incredulae. Storie di fantasmi nel mondo greco-latino* (Bari, 1999) 330; for the widespread background of this belief see L. Honko, *Krankheitsprojektile* (Helsinki, 1959).

[56] Teeth: Jerome, *Vita Hilarionis* 12.10. Laughter: Bremmer, *Acts of Peter*, 11; Philostratus, *Life of Apollonius* 4.20; Aretaeus 3.6.

[57] Note also the description in Lucian, *Philopseudeis* 16.

come to chase us from our proper place?' (*AAlat* 17). Virtually the same approach takes place in a Corinthian bath, when a youth addresses Andrew with: 'What is there between you and me? Have you come here to unsettle us from our place?' (*AAlat* 27). These initiatives are clearly influenced by the New Testament, where the possessed Gadarenes address Jesus first with the words: 'What have we to do with you, son of God?' (Mt. 8.29, cf. Mk. 1.24, 5.7, Lk 8.28), and they are thus not likely to be authentic[58], but in Megara all the demons cried out in unison (*unius vocis impetu*): 'Why do you chase us here, holy Andrew?' (*AAlat* 29), which makes a more convincing impression. The demonic initiative is probably to be explained by the public arena in which the confrontation takes place. Before the community can accept that the possessed persons are healed, it has to be convinced that the demons have actually left. So the demons have to make themselves manifest before they can be properly expelled.

Not all demons were highly cooperative, though, and in the magical papyri a magician therefore says: 'I conjure you, every daimonic spirit, to tell whatever sort you may be, because I conjure you by the seal which Solomon placed on the tongue of Jeremiah, and he told'[59]. For those who persisted in keeping silent, the papyri supply an effective recipe: 'If you say the Name to a demoniac while putting sulphur and asphalt to his nose, the demon will speak at once and go away'[60].

Normal people might have been frightened by the sudden outbursts of the demons, but an apostle is of course not that easily impressed. In the case of the possessed house of Antiphanes, Andrew can react as if there is nothing strange about the situation (*nimis* [read: *nihil*] *de his admirans*: *AAlat* 29). Similarly, after having been invoked by Maximilla in order to heal Alcmanes who was 'foaming at the mouth', he entered 'smiling' (3). The reader is left in no doubt that our hero will confront the 'villain' and convincingly despatch him. But how does he do it?

---

[58] For the Old Testament background of the formula (1 Kings 17.18) see O. Bächli, '"Was habe ich mit Dir zu schaffen?". Eine formelhafte Frage im A.T. und N.T.', *Theol. Zs.* 33 (1977) 69-80; P. Guillemette, 'Mc 1,24 est-il une formule de défense magique?', *SCEs* 30 (1978) 81-96.
[59] *PGM* IV.3037-41; see also Lucian, *Philopseudeis*, 16; Theophilos, *Autolyc.* 2.8; *ATh* 74; *Test. Sol.* 5.2ff, 13.2.
[60] *PGM* XIII.242-4; note also Josephus, *Ant.* 8.47.

At first it may seem surprising how unimpressive the actual exorcism sometimes is. In the case of Alcmanes, the apostle simply invokes God in a prayer in the characteristic participial style once so well analysed by Eduard Norden: 'O God, who does not hearken to the magicians... grant now that my request be speedily fulfilled before all these in the slave of Stratocles, putting to flight the demon whom his kinsmen could not drive out' (5; *AAlat* 34)[61]. In the Coptic fragment, he addresses the soldier with: 'It is now fully time for you to come out from this young man, that he may gird himself for the heavenly palace' (*AAco 14*). In other cases the apostle seems to be less quiet. To the son of Cratinus he speaks *increpans*: 'Go away from the servant of God, you enemy of the human race' (*AAlat* 5), and the same verb is used when he expels the demons from the old man and the youth in the swimming pool (*AAlat* 27). This approach was probably more like real practice, since both Jesus and Apollonius of Tyana, too, were sometimes agitated while exorcising demons and rebuked them[62]. The order '*discede*' will also have been part of traditional Jewish exorcism, since the command *exelthe* is a recurrent term in New Testament exorcism stories and occurs in the magical papyri[63], but is absent from pagan exorcisms[64].

Faced with the supernatural power of the apostle, what could a demon do? In the Coptic fragment the demon quietly leaves the young soldier on the order of Andrew and assures him that 'I have never destroyed a limb of his' (*AAco* 14). In the case of Alcmanes, the demon uses the term 'fleeing': 'I flee, servant and man of God, I flee not only from this slave, but also from this whole city' (5) – the

---

[61] For the participle style see E. Norden, *Agnostos Theos* (Stuttgart, 1912) 166-8.

[62] Eitrem, *Some Notes*, 51f, who compares Mk 1.43, 2.12 and Philostratus, *Life of Apollonius* 4.20; add Mk 9.25; Lucian, *Philopseudeis*, 16, 31; Philostratus 3.38; H.C. Kee, 'The Terminology of Mark's Exorcism Stories', *New Test. Stud.* 14 (1967-8) 232-46 at 240ff; Thraede, 'Exorzismus', 51, 66 (many more examples).

[63] Mk 1.25, 5.8, 9.25; Acts 16.18; compare also *APt* 11; *ATh* 73,74 and 77; Cyprian, *Ep.* 69.15; *PGM* IV.1227, 1242-4, 3007ff and V.158; Thraede, 'Exorcismus', 52; D. Jordan and R. Kotansky, 'A Salomonic Exorcism (Inv. T 3)', in M. Gronewald *et al.*, *Kölner Papyri* 8 (Opladen, 1997) 53-69 at 55f.

[64] As is observed by Kollmann, *Jesus und die Christen*, 202.

terminology of actual exorcistic formulae[65]. That was not enough for Andrew, but by ordering the demon to stay away from wherever the Christians were he showed the extent of his power[66].

Not all demons were so placid, however. The demon of Cratinus' son left *multo clamitans* (*AAlat* 5) and a soldier even died when the demon left him (*AAlat* 18). The last example looks like a narrative exaggeration of a traditional theme in exorcism: the demon's dramatisation of his departure by an act of physical violence. The theme is already present in Mark, where evil spirits leave amid loud shouting (1.26, 9.20) or even destroy a herd of swine (5.13), but it must have been part and parcel of the contemporary exorcist's trade[67].

Naturally, not only had the demon to demonstrate his departure, but the exorcised persons too had to show that they had been healed. So Alcmanes rose from the floor and sat down with Andrew 'sound in mind and tranquil and talking normally' (5). Once again these aspects have to be seen against the public character of the ritual. It is only when everybody has noticed the expulsion of the demon and the recovery of the possessed that he can function again in the community.

The last actor in this scenario to be considered is the public. During resurrections crowds are always prominently present and acclaim the apostle with traditional formulae such as: '*Magnus est Deus Christus, quem praedicat servus eius Andreas*' (*AAlat* 7)[68], '*Non est similis tibi, Domine*' (*AAlat* 24) or '*Non est similis deo Andreae*' (*AAlat* 13), the latter exclamation typically being uttered in the theatre[69]. But what about exorcisms? The great Gibbon, who called exorcism 'the awful ceremony', thought that the ritual was performed

[65] Kotansky, 'Greek Exorcistic Amulets', 258f.
[66] For *Geisterbannung* in general see O. Weinreich, 'Gebet und Wunder. Zwei Abhandlungen zur Religions- und Literaturgeschichte', in *Genethliakon. Wilhelm Schmid zum 70. Geburtstag am 24. Febr. 1929* (Stuttgart, 1929) 169-464, repr. in Weinreich, *Religionsgeschichtliche Studien* (Stuttgart, 1968) 1-298.
[67] For more examples see C. Bonner, 'The Technique of Exorcism', *HThR* 26 (1943) 39-49 and his supplement in *HThR* 27 (1944) 334-6; L. Delatte, *Un office byzantin d'exorcisme* (Brussels, 1957) p. 30.1, 54.17, 56.16, 84.11, 90.10, 91.6, 92.2 and 21.
[68] For the acclamation 'Great is...' see H.S. Versnel, *Ter unus* (Leiden, 1990) 194-6; note also *AA Mart. pr.* 6
[69] For the theatre as the place of performance in Late Antiquity see Bremmer, *Acts of John*, 47.

in front of many spectators and so led to the 'conviction of infidels'[70]. And indeed, it is true that in the time of the European religious wars, exorcism had often been the arena in which Catholics and Protestants had tried to establish the superiority of their faith[71]. In the *AA*, however, and other early Christian literature we notice nothing of this crowd activity. On the contrary, Christian and pagan authors alike stress that the Christians exorcised in a manner as simple as possible. Apparently, they wanted at all costs to avoid the dangerous accusation of being magicians, and thus they practised without the usual hocus pocus of traditional magicians[72]. That is also why magicians are shown up in the *AA* in a bad light (*AAco*) and are proved to be ineffective (4), and why accusations of magic are immediately refuted (*AAlat* 18; *Mart. pr.* 3-4). As far as we can see from the surviving parts of the *AJ* and *AP*, the theme of magic played virtually no role in these works. Can it be that the increasing measures taken by the Roman government against magic are also reflected in the prominence of the theme in the *APt* and *AA*, *AAA* which are to be dated later than the earlier two[73]? There is a problem here which cannot immediately be solved.

3. *Martyrdom*

Let us conclude our study with a few observations on the event of martyrdom as represented by the *AA*. We have two scenes which

---

[70] E. Gibbon, *The History of the Decline and Fall of the Roman Empire* II, ed. Bury (London, 1896) 28f.

[71] C. Ernst, *Teufelsaustreibung: die Praxis der katholischen Kirche im 16. und 17. Jahrhundert* (Berne and Toronto, 1972); D.P. Walker, *Unclean Spirits* (London, 1981); S. Greenblatt, 'Loudon and London', *Critical Inquiry* 12 (1985-6) 326-46; idem, *Shakespearian Negotiations* (Oxford, 1988) 94-128; H. de Waardt, *Toverij en samenleving. Holland 1500-1800* (The Hague, 1991) 171-4.

[72] H. Remus, *Pagan-Christian Conflict over Miracle in the Second Century* (Cambridge MA, 1983) 52-72.

[73] For these measures see M.Th. Fögen, *Die Enteignung der Wahrsager. Studien zum kaiserlichen Wissensmonopol in der Spätantike* (Frankfurt, 1993); H. Kippenberg, 'Magic in Roman Civil Discourse: Why Rituals could be Illegal', in Kippenberg and Schäfer, *Envisioning Magic*, 137-63; V. Neri, *I marginali nell' Occidente tardo antico* (Bari, 1998) 258-86.

show us something of the suffering of the early Christians. In the first case, the proconsul Varianus condemns Andrew to the beasts[74]. As was customary, the proconsul let the beasts and the apostle enter the arena early in the morning[75]. First, they let loose a wild boar at Andrew, but apparently the animal was not interested in the apostle. This must have happened relatively often in the arena and could of course easily be interpreted as an act of God[76]. Next came a bull, the use of which animal is well known from Blandina's martyrdom in the *Letter of Lyons*. It killed the *venatores*, the professional fighters against beasts, who had goaded it on; the same fate is suffered by the attendant who had tied Saturus to a boar in the *Passio Perpetuae* (19)[77]. Finally, there came a most ferocious leopard, who spurned the apostle completely but instead jumped up to the special seat of the proconsul and killed his son. The scene is surely legendary, but it must have been illustrative of the ferocity of the leopard: in the *Passio Perpetuae* Saturus hoped to be killed by one bite of a leopard. This whole passage of the *AA* is only sketchy, but it shows something of what the Christians had to suffer for their faith.

The second instance is the death of Andrew. After a long conversation between Stratocles and Andrew, the apostle told him: 'Tomorrow Aegeates will hand me over to be crucified' (45). The term used, *anaskolopidzo*, can mean 'to impale' and 'to crucify'[78]. Given the cruel treatment of the slave Eukleia, for a moment the reader is left in doubt in which way Andrew is to be killed. However, his doubts are soon resolved, since the proconsul opted for crucifixion (46).

As was the case earlier, the preparations for the execution started at dawn. In the customary Roman way, the apostle was whipped first[79], but Aegeates gave orders 'to leave his sinews uncut' (51), a

---

[74] Unlike Prieur (*ad loc.*), I prefer the name Varianus, which also occurs in *AAco* 9 and which is widely attested, cf. *P.Oxy.* 3.486.1, 9.1201.16, 12.1475.10, 14.1642.4 and 1727.1; *P.Kron.* 3.1; *P.Diog.* 6.3 (Egypt); *SEG* 37.544.2, 4 (Macedonia); *I.Prusias* 7.2.22; *TAM* III. 118.3, 180.3, 596.2 en 697.1 (Termessos); C. Marek, *Stadt, Ära und Territorium in Pontus-Bithynia und Nord-Galatia* (Tübingen, 1993) 136 nr. 3 (Pompeiopolis).
[75] Add this case to Bremmer, *Acts of Paul*, 53.
[76] Prieur (*ad loc.*) compares *AP* 28, 33-5; Eus. *HE*.5.1.41-2.
[77] L. Robert, *Opera minora selecta* V (Amsterdam, 1989) 809f.
[78] P. Franchi' de Cavalieri, *Scritti agiografici* II (Rome, 1962) 160.
[79] Hengel, *Crucifixion*, 21.

detail for which I have been unable as yet to find a parallel. Unlike normal Roman practice[80], Andrew did not need to carry his own cross, as Jesus had to do, but a cross had been prepared for him at the edge of the sea. The place is intriguing but may be a reminiscence of the Greek practice to dispose of polluted beings at the beach, a typically ambivalent place between land and sea[81].

To prolong his suffering, the proconsul had given orders that instead of using nails he should be tied to the cross by his hands and feet. Once again, we feel the contrast between the gentleness of Stratocles and the cruelty of his brother. As was the case with Thecla, the population now became restless and protested to Aegeates[82], who had apparently remained in the city to continue with his court cases. He immediately left his *bêma*, his seat, which is repeatedly mentioned in the *AAA*[83]. However, he arrived to speak with the apostle, who died after glorifying God and after being glorified by the author. The wretched proconsul committed suicide shortly afterwards.

The difference in values manifested by the pagan proconsul and his Christian brother, as well as those displayed in the deaths of the proconsul and the apostle, already suggest the turning of the tables, but more than a century was to pass before Christianity won a definitive victory[84].

---

[80] S. Lieberman, *Texts and Studies* (New York, 1974) 92f.
[81] R. Parker, *Miasma* (Oxford, 1983) 226f.
[82] For such protests see Bremmer, *Acts of Paul*, 51; add *AA* 60 and *AAlat* 18.
[83] Bremmer, *Acts of Paul*, 46; add *AA* 36, *AAlat* 4; E. Dinkler, *Signum crucis* (Tübingen, 1967) 118-33 (archaeological evidence); Lieberman, *Texts and Studies*, 69, 83 (occurrence in Jewish sources).
[84] For comments, information and correction of my English I am most grateful to Kathy Coleman, David Frankfurter, Stephen Harrison, Ton Hilhorst, Peter van Minnen and Jacques van der Vliet.

III. Eroticism in the *Liber de miraculis beati Andreae apostoli* of Gregory of Tours

TAMÁS ADAMIK

Georgius Florentius Gregorius became bishop of Tours in 573 and died in 594[1]. He composed several hagiographic works: *In gloria martyrum, Liber de virtutibus S. Iuliani, Libri IIII de virtutibus S. Martini, Liber vitae patrum, Liber in gloria confessorum* and *Liber de miraculis beati Andreae apostoli*. In the preface to this latter work he writes as follows: *Nam repperi librum de virtutibus sancti Andreae apostoli, qui propter nimiam verbositatem a nonnullis apocrifus dicebatur; de quo placuit, ut, retractis enucleatisque tantum virtutibus, praetermissis his quae fastidium generabant, uno tantum parvo volumine admiranda miracula clauderentur* (5-10), 'For I discovered a book of miracles of the holy apostle Andrew, which some regarded as apocryphal because of its excessive verbosity. I reduced and removed it to the virtues only, having omitted whatever would breed disgust, in order that only a small book should contain the wonderful miracles'.

According to Dennis R. MacDonald, 'This *Liber de virtutibus sancti Andreae apostoli* almost certainly was *The Acts of Andrew*; by the late fourth century ecclesiastical authors were loath to refer to apocryphal Acts as *Praxeis/Acta*, reserving the title instead for Luke's canonical Acts. Gregory read no Greek, so he must have found the *Acts* in Latin translation'[2]. I agree with MacDonald and other scholars that the book discovered by Gregory was the *AA*[3]. In

---

[1] Unless indicated otherwise all citations are from *AAlat*. I have gratefully used the translation by D.R. MacDonald, *The Acts of Andrew and Matthias in the City of the Cannibals* (Atlanta, 1990).
[2] MacDonald, *The Acts of Andrew and Matthias*, 1.
[3] A. Hilhorst, 'The Apocryphal Acts as martyrdom texts: the case of the Acts of Andrew', in Bremmer, *Acts of John*, 1-14 at 1-2.

proof thereof I cite Gregory's following words: *qui propter nimiam verbositatem a nonnullis apocrifus dicebatur*, since in the Greek text of the surviving parts of the *AA* the long speeches, to which the *nimia verbositas* refers, make up the whole of the book and are more important than the actions. From this work Gregory abstracted the miracles only, disregarding whatever would breed disgust: *praetermissis his quae fastidium generabant* (*Praef.* 8-9).

That is, he omitted the high-minded ideas of the speeches of the Greek original and chose instead the interesting actions of the miracles[4]. By so doing, he changed the intention of the Greek original which aims at teaching the Christian people the mysteries of Christian truth and life. However, Gregory wanted to entertain his readers and to teach them Christian morals, so whoever wants to amuse himself should read Gregory's epitome. On the other hand, if one wants to learn subtle ideas, one must read the speeches of the Greek original of the *AA*[5].

However, if Gregory discovered the *AA* in a Latin translation, the translator of this Latin text had probably already simplified the speeches of the Greek original and their subtle ideas, while rendering the more complicated plot of the miracle stories. We can see a similar process in the Latin text of the *APt*. We have the description of his martyrdom both in Greek and Latin, but the Latin translation is oversimplified in comparison to the Greek original. It is important to note with regard to the apocryphal writings that every copy and every translation of the same apocryphal work is in some regard different. But Gregory found even these simplified speeches too long-winded and too sophisticated, and therefore he eliminated them, while increasing the piquancy of the stories. Among the miracles of Andrew there are too many which deal with eroticism. That is the reason why I have chosen the topic of eroticism for my contribution.

The following stories contain the topic of eroticism:
1. The mother who fell in love with her own son (4).
2. The son of Gratinus in the bath of women (5).
3. The brothers who wanted to marry their cousins (11).

---

[4] Schneemelcher, *NTA* II, 106-10, 118-23; R.F. Stoops, Jr., 'Apostolic Apocrypha: Where Do We Stand with Schneemelcher's Fifth Edition?', *SBL 1993 Seminar Papers* (Atlanta, 1993) 637, 640.
[5] As is also noted by F. Bovon, 'The Words of Life in the Acts of Andrew', this volume, Ch. VII.

4. Trofima in the brothel (23).
5. Caliopa, the mistress of a killer (25).
6. *senex fornicator* (28).
7. Maximilla who would not live a normal married life with her husband (35).

It is remarkable that the first six love stories are elaborated in detail, whereas the last one is only mentioned without any comment. Let us treat them separately. The story of the mother who fell in love with her son is a cruel one. A young Christian man, Sostratus, came to the holy Andrew and informed him that his mother wanted to live with him as husband and wife. Sostratus was horrified at this crime, but his mother had gone to the proconsul and accused him of wanting to rape her. After the soldiers of the proconsul had come and placed him on trial, the proconsul had asked Sostratus whether the charge was true. The young man had remained silent because he did not want to reveal the crime of his mother. Andrew rebuked the mother, who therefore accused him, too. So the proconsul condemned both the boy and the apostle. In that situation Andrew began to pray, and God sent a big earthquake: *et omnes terrae decubuerunt; mater vero pueri percussa aruit et mortua est* (4). The proconsul was terrified and began to beg Andrew: *Miserere pereuntibus, famule Dei, ne nos terra deglutiat* (4). So the apostle began to pray, and the earthquake stopped. Andrew healed those who were wounded in the disaster. Through this act the proconsul and his people came to believe in Jesus Christ, and they were baptized by Andrew (4)[6].

This story is a famous one: the love of Phaedra for Hippolytus, or the love of Knemon's mother for her son, which contain the same plot as the preceding story[7]. In all three stories the mother is punished in the end. But there is a big difference between these two stories and ours: Hippolytus was only the stepson of Phaedra, and Knemon only the stepson of Demaenete, but Sostratus was the true son of his mother. Therefore her crime was even greater than that of Phaedra and Demaenete. This greater crime gave Andrew the possibility to

---

[6] See for a similar case *AAlat* 9.9-10, cf. D.W. Pao, 'The Genre of the *Acts of Andrew*', *Apocrypha* 6 (1995) 179-202 at 185; M. Pesthy, 'Cross and Death in the Apocryphal Acts of the Apostles', in Bremmer, *Acts of Peter*, 123-33 at 132-3.

[7] Heliodorus, *Aethiopica*, 9, cf. Prieur, *Acta Andreae*, 276 n. 4.

produce greater miracles which were the means to generate faith in Jesus Christ.

The second erotic story is that of Gratinus' son: *Gratini quoque Senopinsis filius, dum in balneum mulierum lavaretur, a daemone, perdito sensu, graviter cruciabatur* (5). In this tale, the son was possessed by a demon and went mad, while he had a wash in the bath of the women. His father and mother, too, fell ill: *Sed et ipse adpraehensus febre, graviter aegrotabat, uxor vero eius ab etrope intumuerat* (5). In fact, the whole family fell ill. The father wrote a letter to the proconsul begging him to send Andrew to his family. Upon arrival the apostle first exorcised the demon from the boy and then walked up to the bed of the ill father. He said to him: *Recte aegrotas incommode, qui, relicto proprio toro, misceris scorto. Surge in nomine domini Iesu Christi et sta sanus et noli ultra peccare, ne maiorem aegrotationem incurras* (5), and after these words he healed him. Finally he went to the bed of Gratinus' wife and said to her: *Decepit te, o mulier, concupiscentia oculorum, ut, relicto coniuge, aliis miscearis...* Then he prayed to Jesus Christ: *Certe, si scis, Domine, cuius potentia etiam futura praenoscuntur, quod se abstinere possit ab hoc flagitio, te iubente sanetur* (5). After these words he healed her and *fregit panem et dedit ei* (5), that is, he gave her the Eucharist. After that the woman believed in Jesus Christ together with her family, and they did not commit any crimes again. The family wanted to give the apostle presents (*munera*), but he did not accept them.

This erotic story is interesting from several points of view. All members of the family had committed some sexual faults. The father and mother committed adultery. Their faults are clear. But what was the fault of their son? While bathing is not a sin in itself, bathing in the bath of women (or with women) was considered a sin. The bathing place itself inflamed his sexual fantasy, and then the demon came and possessed him, causing the boy to lose his senses. Peter's daughter fell ill for the same reason[8]. The message of the scene is backed up by the symbolical meaning of water in the *AA*: the demon appears several times in connection with water and the sea[9]. But the virtuous Romans had already condemned the man who went to the

---

[8] J.N. Bremmer, 'Aspects of the *Acts of Peter*: Women, Magic, Place and Date', in Bremmer, *Acts of Peter*, 1-20 at 2.

[9] Prieur, *Acta Andreae*, 578 n. 3.

baths of women because they regarded it as immoral[10]. This is the point in the case of the boy.

The second interesting feature of this story is that Andrew gives the Eucharist only to the wife. Why? Perhaps because women play larger roles in the *AAA*, where they are always the initiators concerning the Christian religion. Gregory took over this characteristic from the *AAA*, but as a true Roman (to the Romans women were always suspicious[11]) he did not expound on it in detail because he did not want to emphasize the role of women.

The third interesting feature is that Andrew did not accept the presents from the healed family. Prieur is right when he stresses that it happens several times in the *AA*, and the reason is that, on the one hand, the apostle wants to avert the charge of magic from himself, and, on the other, he wants to stress that he detaches himself from the world[12]. This interpretation is possible, but we have to take into consideration that Gregory wrote his work at the end of the sixth century in Gaul where the bishops were very rich and lived as princes, maintaining a royal household. For example, when Venantius Fortunatus, the poet, went to Gaul, he travelled from one bishop to the other, praising them, and living in luxury as they did[13]. Although he was bishop too, perhaps Gregory wanted to call the attention of his fellow bishops to the importance of poverty in Christian life.

Let me pass on to the story of the two brothers who wanted to marry their first cousins. The scene of this story is Philippi, a city in Eastern Macedonia. In 42 BC, Philippi was the scene of the two battles in which Antony defeated Cassius and Brutus. Antony founded a colony for veterans there, and, after Actium, Octavian added more veterans as well as partisans of Antony who were evicted from Italy. There were two aristocratic brothers; one of them had two sons, the other had two daughters. They decided to marry their children to each other and appointed the day of the wedding. But after having organised this they heard the voice of God: *Nolite coniungere filios vestros, donec veniat famulus meus Andreas. Ipse enim vobis quae agere debeatis ostendet* (11). Now Andrew arrived and told them:

---

[10] Pliny, *NH* 33.153; Quintilian 5.9.14: *nam si est signum adulterae lavari cum viris...*; Martial 3. 51, 72; Bremmer, this volume, Ch. II.2.
[11] Livy 39.8-18; Minucius, *Octavius*, 8.4.
[12] Prieur, *Acta Andreae* II, 580 n. 9.
[13] G. Hasenohr and M. Zink, *Le Moyen Age* (Paris, 1992) 459f.

paenitentiam agite, quia deliquistis in Dominum, ut proximos sanguine velletis coniugio copulare (11). That is, you should not marry your sons to your daughters because you are blood relatives. The parents were moved by the words of Andrew, and they said that they did not know that marriage was forbidden between blood relatives. And they all – the fathers, the sons and the daughters – accepted the decision of Andrew, who prayed for them: *sit Deus vobiscum, et accipiatis mercedem operis vestri, id est sempiternam vitam, quae nullo clauditur fine* (11).

The story is remarkable, since it clearly shows that Gregory or the first translator changed the Greek original. According to local Greek law such a marriage was possibly legal in Philippi[14], but in the western Roman Empire it was forbidden by Roman law. Robin Lane Fox writes as follows: 'In Egypt and much of the Near East, brothers married their sisters. Whatever its origin, this custom helped family property to cohere under a system of inheritance which recognized both male and female shares'[15]. In our story one of the brothers, too, says to the other: *Filii mei accipiant filias tuas, ut opes nostrae facilius coniungantur* (11). A. Oepke stresses that such marriages also occurred among the Greeks[16]. Thus Andrew or the first translator transformed this story according to Roman law which was in harmony with the Christian moral. But there is another passage in this story which is instructive as well. When Andrew forbids this marriage he stresses that he is not against the marriage because marriage is sanctioned by God: *Non nos nuptias aut avertimus aut vitamus, cum ab initio Deus masculum iungi praecipisset et feminam, sed potius incesta damnamus* (11): he condemns only incest. In the Greek original of the *AA* encratism plays a big part, and Maximilla is a typical representative of it. Andrew or the first translator totally eliminated the doctrine of encratism in his *Liber de miraculis beati Andreae apostoli*, since encratism, which forbade married life, was not accepted by normative Christianity.

The love story of Trofima is again a famous one. Long before, but after her marriage, Trofima had been the mistress of the procon-

---

[14] Nepos, *Praef.* 4: *neque enim Cimoni fuit turpe, Atheniensium summo viro, sororem germanam habere in matrimonio, quippe cum cives eius eodem uterentur instituto.*

[15] R. Lane Fox, *Pagans and Christians* (Harmondsworth, 1986) 341.

[16] A. Oepke, 'Ehe I', *RAC* 4 (1959) 650-66 at 652.

sul. When Andrew arrived at Patras, she spent a lot of time in the house of the proconsul because she attended the speeches of Andrew. Her husband became angry with her and he said to Calisto, the wife of the proconsul, that Trofima again was the mistress of the proconsul. The wife of the proconsul became indignant with Trofima and sent her to a brothel[17]. In the brothel Trofima prayed to God and kept the book of the Gospel on her bosom. When men came to her in order to make love, they became impotent: *At illa ingressa lupanar, orabat assidue, cumque venissent qui eam contingerent, ponebat evangelium quod secum habebat ad pectus suum, et statim omnes vires perdebant accedens* [read: *accedentes*] *ad eam* (23). However, on one occasion, when a youth tore her dress, the Gospel fell down. Trofima prayed to God: *Ne patiaris me, Domine, pollui, ob cuius nomine diligo castitatem* (23). God heard her prayers and the man died. Trofima thanked God for the help and in the name of Jesus Christ she raised the young man from the dead.

Meanwhile Calisto went to the baths together with her procurator who had taken Trofima to the brothel. When they bathed together, a demon appeared to them, and they died on the spot. Everybody cried, including the proconsul. Then Andrew came and said: *Videte, dilectissimi, quantum praevalet inimicus, nam Trofime propter pudicitiam damnaverunt scorto. Nunc autem iudicium Dei adfuit, et ecce materfamilias, quae eam in lupanar poni iussit, cum lenone suo percussa in balneum, cecidit et mortua est* (23). After these words the nurse of the wife of the proconsul appeared and cried loudly. Andrew felt pity for her and asked the proconsul: 'Do you want her revived?' The proconsul answered: 'Not at all, since she has committed such a scandal in my house'. 'Don't act like that', Andrew said, and he raised the wife of the proconsul from the dead. Afterwards he told her: 'Go into your room and pray to God'. But Calisto said: 'First I would like to beg Trofima's pardon'. So it happened. After these great miracles everybody believed in Jesus Christ and everybody was happy.

Now the main topic of Trofima's love story – that is, the story of the girl who keeps her purity in the brothel – was well-known in antiquity. First it appeared under the title 'The Prostitute Priestess' in the *Controversiae* of the elder Seneca in this form: 'A virgin was

---

[17] Bremmer, this volume, 23.

captured by pirates and sold; she was bought by a pimp and made a prostitute. When men came to her, she asked for alms. When she failed to get alms from a soldier who came to her, he struggled with her and tried to use force; she killed him. She was accused, acquitted and sent back to her family. She seeks a priesthood' (1.2.1, tr. M. Winterbottom, Loeb). The same story is to be found at length in the ancient novel *Historia Apollonii regis Tyri*: the daughter of Apollonius was sold to a brothel where she kept her purity safe (33-5). It also appears in different form in the *Gesta Romanorum*, which was compiled in the late Middle Ages[18].

Why did the author of the original *AA* choose such a famous love story? Because it was interesting and suitable to illustrate the encratic ideas of the author. But Gregory or the first Roman translator again changed the religious moral of the story, trying to eliminate encratism from the original. Gregory includes it, but in an ambiguous way: Trofima *reliquid virum suum et adherebat apostolicae doctrinae et ob hoc plerumque in domo proconsulis veniebat, in quam iugiter docebat apostolus* (23). The words *reliquid virum suum* can mean that she definitively left her husband – as the encratic ladies do in the *AAA* – but it can also mean that she only left him for a while. The verbal form *veniebat* and the adverb *plerumque* can mean that she did not stay all the time in the house of the proconsul. The prayer of Trofima in the brothel (above) is ambiguous, as well. The statement *diligo castitatem* can mean that Trofima, as a married woman, will be faithful to her husband, but we can also interpret it as a declaration of encratism. Gregory does not state it clearly, and even the ambiguous wording suggests that in the original Greek text Trofima became encratic.

The motif of the Gospel is also instructive, but it carries us over to the story of the *senex fornicator*. Once, an old man, Nicolaus, came to Andrew and said to him: *Famule Dei, ecce 74 anni sunt vitae meae, in quibus non discessi ab inmunditiis et scorto ac fornicatione, plerumque praeceps deductus ad lupanar, et exercebam inlicita* (28). Three days before he had heard about the miracles of Andrew, and had decided to change his life. He got a Gospel, but he could not become better. So he went to the brothel, but the mistress (*mulier meretrix*) said to him: *Egredere, senex, egredere; angelus*

---

[18] H. Oesterley, *Gesta Romanorum* (Berlin, 1872) 153.

enim Dei es tu. Ne contingas me neque adpropinques in hoc loco; video enim in te misterium magnum (28). At first the old man did not understand what had happened, but then he realized that he himself was carrying the Gospel, which saved him with its divine power. After this incident Nicolaus requested Andrew to pray for him. Although Andrew prayed and fasted a lot, God did not respond. Finally, after five days, God said to Andrew: *Obtines, Andreas, pro sene; sed sicut tu ieiuniis fatigatus es, ita et ipse studeat ieiunium, ut salvetur* (28). So Nicolaus went home and distributed all his wealth to the poor. For six months he lived on dry bread and water and then he died (28).

In this story the motif of the Gospel is just as remarkable as in that of Trofima. In both cases the Gospel had divine power, and although the people did not see it, because it was hidden, they felt the presence of holiness in their midst. It functioned as a drug or a talisman against love. Prieur notes that such a use of a Gospel book is an anachronism and we do not know of the existence of this practice in the early church[19]. I think that this phenomenon belongs to the same category as when beasts feel the divine power of the emperors or the apostles. Holy objects can produce the same effect as holy men. Trofima and the old Nicolaus were not yet saints, therefore the Gospel, which was with them, produced this effect on the lewd young man and the mistress[20].

We find a similar case in *Abraham*, a drama of Hrotsvitha. Once upon a time there was a young girl who was devoted to Jesus Christ. A lewd man seduced her and sold her to a brothel. This young girl was the relative of a hermit whose name was Abraham. Now this Abraham decided to search for her. After three years he was informed that the girl lived in a brothel. Upon hearing this news Abraham disguised himself and as a rich soldier travelled to the brothel. The girl accepted him kindly, but she felt something strange – the holiness of the hermit – although she did not recognize him. Hrotsvitha describes the scene in the following way:

> Maria: *Quicumque me diligunt, aequalem amoris vicem a me recipiunt.*
> Abraham: *Accede, Maria, et da mihi osculum.*

---

[19] Prieur, *Acta Andreae*, 622; Bremmer, this volume, 23.
[20] T. Adamik, 'The baptized lion in the *Acts of Paul*', in Bremmer, *Acts of Paul*, 60-74 at 72-3.

Maria: *Non solum dulcia oscula libabo, sed etiam crebris senile collum amplexibus mulcebo.*
Abraham: *Hoc volo.*
Maria: *Quid sentio? quid stupendae novitatis gustando haurio? Ecce, odor istius flagrantiae praetendit flagrantiam mihi quondam usitatae abstinentiae*[21].

Just as Maria could smell the holiness of the holy hermit, so too the lewd young man felt the holiness of the Gospel.

The love story of the woman Caliopa is of another character. The first sentence of the story is important for the interpretation of the whole: *erat enim mulier Caliopa nomine, quae homicidae coniuncta, conceptum suscipit inlicitum* (25). 'There was a woman named Caliopa who married a killer, and who, consequently, became pregnant in an illegal way'. Prieur translated this sentence as: 'Il y avait une femme nommée Caliopa, marieé à un assassin, et qui s'était trouvée enceinte d'une manière illégitime'[22]. But if this is the sense of this sentence, why is the killer a part of this story? For if the killer is the husband of Caliopa, her pregnancy can be illegitimate only if she became pregnant by another man. Perhaps in this case it is not important whether she was the wife of a killer or of another man. Therefore we could interpret in this sentence the phrase *quae homicidae coniuncta* to mean that after having had sexual intercourse with a killer (a man who was not her husband but her lover), her pregnancy would be considered illegitimate. In fact, both Lucretius and Ovid use the verb *coniungere*, 'to unite sexually', in this sense.

But the remainder of the story does not allow this interpretation. When the time of labour came, the woman could not give birth to the baby. She requested her sister to call upon the goddess Diana for help. The sister did so, but at night the devil came and said to her that he could not help, therefore it would be better to call Andrew. So they called Andrew who arrived and said to the woman: *Recte haec pateris, quae male nupsisti, quae doloso concipiens, dolores intolerabiles sustines. Insuper consuluisti daemonia, quae neque ulli neque sibi prodesse possunt* (25). Now this statement shows that the interpretation is incorrect, since the verb *nupsisti* means 'you got married' and the adverb *male* is used here as a legal term: 'incorrectly, wrongly'. That is, the woman got married to a killer incorrectly.

---

[21] P. de Winterfeld, *Hrotsvithae opera* (Berlin and Zürich, 1965²) 155.13-21.
[22] Prieur, *Acta Andreae*, 630.

Why? Because according to Roman law the man who kills, as in the case of *minutio existimationis* because of *infamia*, loses his right to marry a woman who was not a case of *minutio existimationis*[23]. Thus the woman committed three sins: a) she got married to a killer illegitimately. b) consequently she became pregnant illegitimately. c) she asked for Diana's help, thereby committing idolatry, because the Christians regarded the worship of pagan gods as such.

Now the sentence of Andrew is as follows: *Crede nunc Iesum Christum, filium Dei, et proice puerperium*, 'Believe in Jesus Christ, the son of God and rid yourself of the baby' (25). The woman believed and gave birth to a dead baby, thereby ridding herself of suffering. This cruel love story shows that Gregory did not want to amuse the simple Christian people but, instead, he wanted to teach them Christian morality. These interesting love stories were meant only to arouse the interest of his readers, since Gregory knew that capturing the attention of the audience would make the teaching of Christian morality easier.

This conclusion can be supported by the last love story, which is a negative one. When Andrew arrived at Patras, Maximilla, the wife of the proconsul Aegeates, happened to be ill. Efidama, who was already Christian asked Andrew to come to her in order to cure her. After Andrew had cured her (30), Gregory speaks about another miracle of Andrew, and he returns to Maximilla's story only in *c.* 35 in which he writes as follows: Every day Maximilla called Andrew to the praetorium because the proconsul left for Macedonia. *Magna enim indignatione succensus erat contra apostolum, eo quod Maximilla, uxor eius, post acceptum salutis verbum non ei coniugebatur* (35). That is, the proconsul was angry with Andrew, since Maximilla did not live a married life with him after her conversion. And at the end of this chapter he writes once more a sentence about Maximilla: *Sed Maximilla, cum primum invenisset locum, statim veniebat ad sanctum apostolum, et suscipiens verbum Dei, regrediebatur ad domum suam* (35). Maximilla came often to the apostle in order to hear the words of God, and she always returned home. Finally, in the following chapter Gregory mentions that Andrew was crucified and Maximilla buried him. That is all about Maximilla.

---

[23] M. Kaser, *Das römische Privatrecht* I (Munich, 1955) 237.

Gregory has clearly reduced the story of Maximilla, which plays a big role in the surviving part of the *AA*. He only mentions that Maximilla did not live a married life with her husband who was therefore angry with her. He had to mention it: in this way he could suggest why Andrew was crucified by Aegeates. But he did not speak in detail about Maximilla, since he did not want to touch the question of encratism.

It is more surprising that he totally omitted the very interesting love story of Euclia while he told the above mentioned love stories in detail. He omitted this story because he regarded it as immoral; moreover, Euclia's story would show both Euclia and Maximilla to be immoral, whereas Christian morality does not allow the ruin of others in order to keep one's own purity. Moreover, if he described Euclia's story, he would have had to speak about encratism as well, which he wanted to avoid because of its heretic character[24].

Therefore we can conclude that Gregory transformed the *AA* according to his special aims[25], just as the other translators or scribes did concerning the other *AAA*[26].

---

[24] E. Junod and J.-D. Kaestli, *L'histoire des Actes apocryphes des apôtres du IIIe au IXe siècle: le cas des Actes de Jean* (Geneva, 1982) 71-2, 105-6.
[25] I. Karasszon, 'Old Testament quotations in the Acts of Andrew and John', in Bremmer, *Acts of John*, 57-71.
[26] See J.-M. Prieur, 'La figure de l'apôtre dans les Actes apocryphes d'André', in F. Bovon *et al.*, *Les Actes Apocryphes des Apôtres* (Geneva, 1981) 121-39.

IV. Aegeates, the Devil in Person

MONIKA PESTHY

The abandoned husband, betrothed or lover seeking revenge is a typical figure of the *AAA*, and Aegeates is precisely such a figure. But none of these figures plays such an important role in the *AAA* as does Aegeates in the *AA*. In fact, in these *Acts* his importance almost equals that of Andrew and Maximilla. But while much has been written about Andrew and Maximilla, Aegeates himself, as far as I know, has never received much attention. Instead, he was just 'the villain in the play' without whom no good story is conceivable. Therefore, I now propose to treat the figure of Aegeates.

In the *AA* the real adversary of the Apostle is Aegeates. The evil spirits cause him no trouble: in the extant parts of the original text, only one instance of Andrew's having to confront a demon is related, which is when the favorite slave of Stratokles is possessed by an evil spirit (5). This spirit, however, is no match for Andrew: he flees panic-stricken from the Apostle and promises never to return. As for the Devil, we have a long speech about him from Andrew (49-50), but the Apostle never has to face him openly. When fighting against Evil, Andrew has to fight against Aegeates, and it is Aegeates who represents Evil as such; he is the personification of Evil. He is absolutely and thoroughly bad, without even a chance to repent.

1. *The wickedness of Aegeates*

From the philosophical point of view, he is the precise contrary of what we should call *apathês*, 'free from passion'. Every time we meet him he is possessed by some passion or overpowering emotion: violent (and sensual) love for Maximilla, fury against Euclia, hate and thirst for revenge against Andrew, fright at hearing Andrew's speech on the cross and, finally, despair leading to suicide. He is the type of man led solely by the lowest part of the soul, by the element called *thymoeidês*, 'irascible'[1], without any control from the intellect. It is almost inevitable that he should finally fall victim to his passions.

From the Christian point of view, he incorporates almost all the mortal sins or, rather, he has within him all the sinful dispositions, such as gluttonry, fornication and wrath. From the Gnostic point of view he represents the lowest, the material nature, the type called *hylikos*. It is characteristic that in whatever situation we meet him he is always occupied with something absolutely material: in *c*. 13 he has 'an urge for a bowel movement', in *c*. 14 he wants to make love to Maximilla, in *c*. 17 he is making love to Euclia, in *c*. 18 he is drunk, in *c*. 46 he goes to a feast with his cronies and 'eats like a wild animal'. All that is spiritual is alien to him and that is why he cannot be saved.

Throughout the *AA*, one can note the tendency to identify Aegeates with the devil. It is clearly stated that his father is the devil (40), which must mean that he belongs to the devil, that the devil uses him as his instrument. But, as the plot develops, the difference between the instrument of Satan and Satan himself increasingly disappears. Thus in *c*. 16 Andrew prays to God for Maximilla with the following words: 'May your word and power be mighty in her and may the spirit that is in her struggle even against Aegeates, that insolent and hostile snake.' We can ask ourselves against whom Maximilla really has to struggle: is it against Aegeates, the human being, or against Satan? Later, in his prayer in prison, Andrew admonishes Maximilla in this way: 'Do not submit to Aegeates' threat. Do not be moved by his speech. Do not fear his disgusting schemes. Do not be conquered by his artful flatteries. Do not consent to yield yourself to his filthy wizardry. Endure each of his tortures...' (37). These words fit Satan much better than Aegeates. Aegeates only put an alternative before Maximilla, where she had to make a decision. There were no artful flatteries, no filthy wizardry and no torture at all. We have the impression that Andrew describes here the devil's machinations, not those of Aegeates.

In the same way, somewhat later Andrew warns Maximilla against the 'ambushes' (*enedrai*) of Aegeates – an expression used in

---

[1] 'That part of the soul, which is the seat of the desires and affections' (LSJ s.v.) The tripartite division of the soul originates in Plato, see e.g. Plato, *Republic*, 440.

general in connection with the devil[2]. The identification of Aegeates with the devil is made complete in Andrew's final prayer on the cross. When Aegeates tries to liberate him, Andrew exclaims: '...do not hand me over to the shameless (*anaidês*) devil, Jesus Christ, don't let your enemy (*antidikos*) unbind me, who am hanging on your grace...' (63). *Anaidês*, 'shameless' or 'void of shame' is a frequently recurring attribute of the devil in the *AAA* in general. Andrew, in his long speech concerning the nature of the devil, calls him 'entirely void of shame' (*panta anaidês*) (49), while *Antidikos*, 'the enemy', is a common name for Satan.

The *AA* is not the only work where a human being takes over the role of the devil. The same thing happens in the case of Simon the Magician in the *APt*, where Peter's whole activity is aimed at the defeating and destroying of Simon. We have a similar personality in another apocryphal work dating from the same period, the *Ascension of Isaiah*[3]. In this apocalypse, Belkira, the human agent of Satan and his master, are practically one and the same person.

This conception originates probably in the Qumranic writings where the cosmic struggle of the sons of light and the sons of darkness takes place on earth, and their respective leaders, though human beings, are the personifications of Good and Evil. In the *AA* Andrew himself is much more than a human being: he almost substitutes for Christ. Thus it is natural that his adversary also should be more than human. But the problem is that while Aegeates is considered by Andrew and Maximilla as the arch-enemy, in reality there is nothing superhuman about him. The other similar figures effectively show superhuman features: the evil teacher of the Qumranic writings, Simon the Magician, or Belkira in the *Ascension of Isaiah* all have real power, even if it is an evil one, but Aegeates has no such power at all.

In his commentary, Prieur comes to the conclusion that the author of the *AA* takes over ideas from different systems of thought (philosophical, gnostic...) and uses them in a somewhat superficial way, without really assimilating them[4]. I think that is exactly the case

---

[2] See e.g. Ignatius, *Epistula ad Trallianos* 8.1; *Epistula ad Philadelphios* 6.2.

[3] P. Bettiolo *et al*, *Ascensio Isaiae*, 2 vls (Turnhout, 1995), tr. M.A. Knibb, 'Martyrdom and Ascension of Isaiah', in J.H. Charlesworth (ed), *The Old Testament Pseudepigrapha* II (London, 1985) 143-76.

[4] J.M. Prieur, *Acta Andreae*, 2 vols (Turnhout, 1989).

with Aegeates. He becomes the Evil One in every possible respect, which makes his figure absolutely unreal and even somewhat comic. He is the cunning snake and the representative of the material nature at the same time. As a substitute for the devil, he should be superhuman, in an evil way, of course. But as a representative of earthly nature, he is rather subhuman. While Andrew speaks of his schemes, artful flatteries, filthy wizardry and ambushes (everything we could expect from a cunning snake), Aegeates himself understands nothing at all of what is going on, since he is the 'alien' one, constitutionally incapable of understanding.

2. *Aegeates, the Seducer*

Until now we have considered Aegeates in himself, now we shall turn our attention to his activities and his relation to Andrew and Maximilla. In his long speech delivered in prison, Andrew describes Maximilla and himself as a second Adam and Eve (37): they redress the fault of the first couple. It is by no means difficult to guess the nature of this fault: it must have been the sexual act, as Prieur suggests[5]. The idea that sexuality and marriage are consequences of the fall and are related to destruction and death is shared by encratics. The *Gospel of the Egyptians* quoted by Clement of Alexandria identifies the forbidden fruit of Gen 2.22 with marriage[6]. In *APt* desire is the bitter fruit of the tree of bitterness (8). Thus, according to the encratics, we must remain chaste if we want to keep ourselves free from sin. As we read in the *AP*: 'There is no resurrection for you unless you remain chaste, and do not soil your body but conserve it chaste' (12). In the *AA*, these ideas are not expressed with such clarity; nevertheless, they constitute the background of Andrew's admonitions to Maximilla.

In the light of these remarks we can better understand why Maximilla's separation from Aegeates is necessary for the salvation of Andrew and Maximilla, and further, in which way they redress the fault of Adam and Eve. The 'Return to Paradise' is through the renunciation of sexuality (not through baptism as the general faith holds – this may be the reason why baptism plays practically no part in the *AA*). The connecting of primeval sin and marriage by the

---

[5] For a different explanation see Luttikhuizen, this volume, Ch. VIII.
[6] Clement, *Stromateis* 3.66.1-2.

encratics was treated in detail by Sfameni Gasparro[7], and I have no intention here to go into any details on the subject; instead, I am interested in the role Aegeates plays in the story.

Andrew and Maximilla, as a second Adam and Eve, re-enact the primeval drama and are victorious where the first couple failed. 'For it is ordained', declares Andrew, 'that each person correct his or her own fall' (37). But the drama in Paradise was a play for three persons, and so is the play which is re-enacted. As a Seducer had to be present in Paradise so that Eve could be tempted into disregarding the Lord's command, so here, too, a Seducer must be present so that Maximilla can resist temptation. And this is the part Aegeates is to play. Thus, in this situation Aegeates takes over the role Satan played in the Genesis story: he wants to persuade Maximilla, the second Eve, to commit the sin. In this way, he becomes the seducer in two respects: as a man who wants to seduce a woman to become his lover, and as Satan who wants to induce a human being to sin. But in Andrew's conception the present situation is an exact replica of those ancient events. Therefore it seems that in Andrew's mind (or rather in the mind of the author of the *AA*) the Ancient Serpent was also a seducer in both senses[8].

The tradition is well known in which Eve, before becoming Adam's wife, had sexual intercourse with the Snake (or Satan, or one of the archons), and Cain (or Cain and Abel) was born from this union. These ideas are quite common in Gnostic writings: so we have in the *Apocryphon of John*: 'And the chief archon seduced her and he begot on her two sons;... And these he called with the names Cain and Abel with a view to deceive. Now up to the present day sexual intercourse continued due to the chief archon. And he planted sexual desire in her who belongs to Adam. And he produced through intercourse the copies of the bodies, and he inspired them with his counterfeit spirit'. Similarly in the *Gospel of Philip*: 'First adultery came into being, then murder. And he was begotten in adultery, for he was the child of the serpent. So he became a murderer, just like his father, and he killed his brother. Indeed every act of sexual intercourse which has occurred between those

---

[7] G. Sfameni Gasparo, 'Gli Atti apocrifi degli Apostoli e la tradizione dell' enkrateia', *Augustinianum* 23 (1983) 287-307.
[8] Cf. *Revelation* 12.9.

unlike one another is adultery.' More similar passages could be cited[9].

Though this idea appears mostly in Gnostic writings, it is not specifically Gnostic: we see it in Jewish sources, too. The earliest text that explicitly identifies Sammael (i. e. Satan) as the father of Cain is the *Targum Pseudo-Jonathan*. In 4.1 we read: 'Adam knew his wife Eve who had conceived from Sammael, the angel of the Lord', or it could be translated: 'Adam knew that his wife...' The belief that Cain was the child of Sammael was derived from the fact that Gen 5.3 says that Seth was in the likeness and image of Adam. Since this is not said of Cain in 4.1, the conclusion was drawn that he was not Adam's son. Ps.-Jonathan explicitly states in 5.3 that Eve bore Cain, who was not from Adam and who did not resemble him[10].

In the *AA* this thought is not clearly stated, but I think it is present in the text. It explains why the works of Cain (*ta tou Kain erga*) are mentioned and it throws light on the Andrew – Maximilla – Aegeates triangle (and it is a love-triangle all right). As Eve was first united to the snake and it was an illicit union, an adultery, so too was Maximilla's union with Aegeates. Aegeates is called the *phainomenos anêr* of Maximilla and I propose to translate *phainomenos* by 'apparent' in the sense of 'not real': he only seems to be the husband of Maximilla, just as her friends only seem to be her friends and as Satan seems to be a friend of humanity.

Prieur quotes a passage from *The Exegesis on the Soul* which I consider revelant: 'But even when she (the soul) turns her face from those adulterers, she runs to others and they compel her to live with them and render service to them upon their bed, as if they were her masters. Out of shame she no longer dares to leave them, whereas they deceive her for a long time, pretending to be faithful, true husbands, as if they greatly respected her. And after all this they abandon her and go. She then becomes a poor desolate widow...'[11]. Origen designates as 'widows' those souls who are no more living with

---

[9] J.M. Robinson (ed), *The Nag Hammadi Library in English* (Leiden, 1988³) 118-9, 146.
[10] M. Maher (transl.), *Targum Pseudo-Jonathan, Genesis* (Edinburgh, 1992) 31 and n. 2.
[11] Robinson, *Nag Hammadi Library*, 192.

their unlawful husband (i. e. the devil), but are not yet worthy of the Bridegroom (i. e. the Christ)[12].

In the *Gospel of Philip* we read: 'Indeed every act of sexual intercourse which has occurred between those unlike one another is adultery', and this is absolutely valid for our case: Maximilla as a spiritual being cannot have anything to do with Aegeates who is totally earthly, alien to everything that is spiritual. Thus Maximilla must be separated from him and united to her real husband and, as a matter of course, this will be no physical union but a spiritual one. And it is quite evident that the spiritual husband of Maximilla is Andrew, not Christ or the inner self as we should expect.

3. *Aegeates contra Andrew*

Thus, the reason for the conflict between Aegeates and Andrew concerns the possession of a woman. But Maximilla is also the second Eve, the fallen nature (see *c.* 38. and Prieur's commentary ad loc.) imprisoned in this world, and her separation from Aegeates means the liberation of nature or of the soul from its bondage and its restitution to its real self. Before meeting Andrew, Maximilla seemingly belongs to this world, the world of Aegeates. But when realising (with Andrew's help) her real nature, she passes over to Andrew's world, the spiritual one, where she belongs in reality. And Aegeates cannot follow her there, so she fully escapes him.

Aegeates and Andrew are not on the same level of existence, and Aegeates has no access to that higher level. Their confrontation is the confrontation of two worlds, the material and the spiritual. Aegeates, as representative of the material world is of course not able to realise this, and that is why his struggle is hopeless: he fights with material weapons against a spiritual power. He thinks he can imprison Andrew, who in his essence cannot be captured. He thinks he can torture him, while he can torture only his body. He crucifies Andrew in order to torture and kill him, but hanging on the cross for Andrew means being united with Christ. And finally, he wants to liberate Andrew from death, while for Andrew it is death that brings liberation, because what was prison for him was this world, as he declares in *c.* 40.

---

[12] Origen, *De principiis*, IV.2.4 (11).

Aegeates' total incomprehension is marked in every situation where he confronts Andrew or Maximilla: in *c.* 14, after his return, he thinks Maximilla is praying for him, while she is praying to get rid of him; in *c.* 23, he thinks Maximilla has an earthly lover while she is speaking about spiritual love; in *c.* 27, he does not understand why he cannot get hold of Andrew; and at the end he is totally unable to understand why Andrew does not want to escape death, and why he himself is called 'the devil devoid of shame' just because he wants to liberate Andrew – this time he is completely dumbfounded.

While Aegeates understands nothing of the motives and ambitions of Andrew and Maximilla, in their eyes he is the arch-enemy, who has to be destroyed by all possible means. Everything is permitted against him and against those who are like him. Substituting Euclia for herself, Maximilla plays him a highly devious trick which leads to the death of four persons, but the reader is not supposed to feel pity on this point for Aegeates or to lament the sad fate of those who are tortured and executed. They are not adherents of the Lord, their fate and their sufferings are of no importance at all. The words pronounced by the resurrected Christ to James in the *Second Apocalypse of James* are absolutely valid for Andrew:

> For you are not the redeemer
> nor a helper of strangers.
> You are an illuminator and a redeemer
> of those who are mine (55, 15-20)[13].

4. *Aegeates seen by Aegeates*

Finally, to do justice to Aegeates, we have to look at the events described in the *AA* from his point of view. In this way we realise that Aegeates has no intention to be evil or to do anything wicked. He lives in his world and according to the rules of that world. He serves his country, respects his gods and, above all, loves his wife. He does not want to do harm to anybody; all he wants is to get back his wife, his lawful wife according to his laws. He is even willing to forgive her infidelity, if there was any, without taking revenge on his rival. From Aegeates' point of view Andrew is the alien one, making trouble in a world where he is out of place. It is clearly stated in his words addressed to Andrew at the tribunal: 'The time to complete

---

[13] Robinson, *ibidem*, 273.

my judgement against you has arrived, you stranger, alien to this present life, enemy of my home, and corrupter of my entire house. Why did you decide to burst into places alien to you and corrupt a wife who used to please me in every way...?' (51). That is how Aegeates sees the situation. He has no idea of being the incarnation of evil from whom Maximilla, and the whole of nature has to be liberated. Andrew tells him from the cross: 'Now you look meek and peaceful, Aegeates, enemy of all of us, your audacity has disappeared. But as for me and those who are similar to me, we are hurrying to him, who belongs to us, and we let you be what you are, but what you don't know yourself' (62, end). And this is the tragedy of Aegeates: he is the devil without knowing it.

V. 'Whatever goes into the Mouth...'

ISTVÁN CZACHESZ

When the Pharisees were scandalized by Jesus' disciples not washing hands before they eat, Jesus called them hypocrites. Then he called the crowd and told them it is not what goes into a person's mouth that defiles him, but rather what comes out of it. And finally, when he was left with his disciples, he gave a still fuller explanation: 'Do you not see that whatever goes into the mouth enters the stomach, and goes out into the sewer? But what comes out of the mouth proceeds from the heart, and this is what defiles' (Mt 15.17-8)[1].

Jesus' argument is based on the fact that in terms of Jewish purity rules fecal matter may be disgusting but nevertheless it is not ritually unclean[2]. Purity laws are discussed in detail in Lev 11-15, and different sorts of bodily uncleanliness are enumerated in Lev 15. These include flux (flow or discharge), male semen, and menstruation, or the spit (in rabbinical sources also the urine) of someone having a flux, but there is no mention of excrement.

In Deut 23, among other regulations, we read the following passage: 'You shall have a designated area outside the camp to which you shall go. With your utensils you shall have a trowel; when you relieve yourself outside, you shall dig a hole with it and then cover up your excrement. Because the LORD your God travels along with your camp, to save you and to hand over your enemies to you, therefore your camp must be holy, so that he may not see anything *indecent* among you and turn away from you' (Deut 23.13-5, vv. 12-4 in NRSV, italics added). The Hebrew word translated here as 'indecent'

---

[1] Unless otherwise indicated, biblical passages in this paper follow the *New Revised Standard Version* (Grand Rapids, 1989).
[2] B.J. Malina and R.L. Rohrbaugh, *Social Science Commentary on the Synoptic Gospels* (Minneapolis, 1992) 109-10. They call Jesus' opinion a 'first-century social truism'.

is *'erwah*, which usually refers to the genital parts of the body. This regulation controls the socially acceptable behavior rather than the realm of ritual cleanness and uncleanness.

In sum, though what comes out of the stomach is unclean from the point of view of modern biology, and indecent in the public social spheres, Jesus is right when he states it is actually pure. Consequently, Jesus' argument goes, the same matter is clean also when it enters the body. Whether this means he declared all foods clean, as a late addition to Mk 7.19 concludes, is beyond our concern. Apart from this pericope, the process and matters of human metabolism are not mentioned in the New Testament. We can meet them, on the other hand, in the Old Testament and in the *AAA*.

II

In the *APt*, it is told how the senator Marcellus was misled by the tricks of Simon Magus, whom he even entertained in his own house. Upon the arrival and mighty miracles of Peter (e.g. raising a smoked tunny fish), however, Marcellus turned against his teacher, ran into his house and threw curses at his head (14). Then the servants took Simon, beat him with rods and stones, and completed the treatment by emptying chamber pots onto his head.

In my paper on the *APt* I have already discussed how these insults fulfill the role of a status degradation ritual, as a part of a deviant labeling process[3]. Now I am interested only in the final episode, the emptying of chamber pots (*vasa stercoribus plena*[4]) onto Simon's head. The word *stercus* strongly suggests that the vessels in question were not simply litter bins, as some euphemistic translations suggest ('pots full of filth', 'Gefässe von Unrats'[5]), but were actually

---

[3] I. Czachesz, 'Who is Deviant? Entering the Story World of the *Acts of Peter*', in Bremmer, *Acts of Peter*, 84-96.

[4] See *Actus Petri cum Simone* p.61 in R.A. Lipsius and M. Bonnet, *Acta Apostolorum Apocrypha* I (Leipzig, 1891, 1898, 1903, reprint Darmstadt, 1959) 45-103.

[5] So W. Schneemelcher's German translation in E. Hennecke and W. Schneemelcher (eds), *Neutestamentliche Apokryphen* II (Tübingen, 1964³) 191-221 at 203. The English rendering by R.McL. Wilson in *NTA* II, 299 follows his text.

full of human excrement (as for example, the recent Hungarian translation renders it[6]).

Another utensil of similar purpose appears in an intriguing episode of the *AA*, which is also contained in the text of Gregory of Tours. The Christian community in Patras assembled day and night in the palace of the proconsul Aegeates to listen to the teaching of the apostle Andrew. They were just celebrating the day of the Lord in the room of Maximilla, wife of the proconsul, when the servants reported the lord of the house was coming home.

Maximilla was afraid how her husband Aegeates would react to such a tumultuous jamboree in his palace, but the apostle Andrew helped her out of her embarrassment. In his prayer he asked the Lord Jesus that everyone could leave before the proconsul enters the room. And behold, Aegeates was immediately struck with diarrhea, or literally 'he was troubled by his bowels' (*hypo tês gastros ochlethê*), asked for a lavatory seat, and was sitting on it while the brothers, made invisible by Andrew, were able to steal out beside him.

The utensil what Aegeates asked for in the story is called *sella*, a Latin word in the Greek text. This may refer to the Latin *sella pertusa* and attest that the Romans were more skillful in inventing technical instruments, and the Latin names of those were used even in a Greek context[7].

But our main concern in this paper is not with the history of toilets. Rather we wish to explore the literary and theological significance of these drastic scenes, which occur rather unexpectedly in two of our *AAA*. In order to accomplish that, first we will refer to a few examples where such matters appear in Old Testament and Greco-Roman literature.

III

(1) We have already seen that in the Old Testament excrement is not ritually unclean. In the Pentateuch the dung of animals is mentioned in the sacrificial laws. Together with other parts of the animal, it is to

---

[6] *Péter Rómában* p.55, in T. Adamik and J. Dörömbözi (eds), *Az apostolok csodálatos cselekedetei* (Budapest, 1996) 41-78.

[7] As Professor Adamik suggests to me, cf. H. Blümner, *Die römischen Privataltertümer* (Munich, 1911) 49f.

be burnt outside the camp. Lev 16.28 orders that the person burning these parts washes his clothes and himself in water before returning to the camp. But the burnt matter is not waste at all! Ex 29.14 orders that the dung of the sacrifice bull (that is, the excrement found in the bowels) together with the skin and the flesh should be burnt outside the camp as a sin offering. Num 19.5ff prescribe how the skin, flesh, blood and dung of a red cow are used to prepare the water for cleansing. Though dung belongs to the menial parts of animals, it is still used for sacrificial purposes.

(2) In a large group of Old Testament passages (primarily prophetic texts) dung stands as the symbol of death and decay. God 'will consume the house of Jeroboam, just as one burns up dung until it is all gone' (1Kings 14.10). 'The corpse of Jezebel shall be like dung on the field' (2Kings 9.37). In his decree supporting the restoration of the Temple, King Darius threatens 'if anyone alters this edict, a beam shall be pulled out of the house of the perpetrator, who then shall be impaled on it. The house shall be made a dunghill' (Ezra 6.11).

Job says the sinners 'will perish forever like their own dung' (Job 20.7). The Psalmist reminds of Israel's enemies who 'were destroyed at En-dor, who became dung for the ground' (Ps 83.10). Isaiah prophesies that 'the Moabites shall be trodden down in their place as straw is trodden down in a dung-pit' (Isa 25.10). Jeremiah warns that the Lord will punish his disobedient people, the bones of the inhabitants of Juda will be brought out of their tombs and 'they shall be like dung on the surface of the ground' (Jer 8.2). 'Dung on the surface of the ground' is a recurring image of divine punishment and destruction in Jeremiah (9.22, 16.4, 25.33). Zephaniah also foretells that the flesh of sinners will be 'like dung' (1.17). All these mainly prophetic texts are characterized by a dark, pessimistic, and threatening tone.

(3) Other passages in the Old Testament talk about odd situations when excrement may represent great value. A notable story relates that Ben-hadad, king of Aram laid a siege on Samaria, and 'famine in Samaria became so great that a donkey's head was sold for eighty shekels of silver, and one-fourth of a kab of dove's dung for five shekels of silver' (2Kings 6.25). But this is not enough Two women agree to cook and eat their sons together, but the second one hides her child when her turn comes (6.28-9). Soon Elisha enters the stage and foretells that the next day 'a measure of choice meal shall be sold

for a shekel, and two measures of barley for a shekel, at the gate of Samaria' (2Kings 7.1).

This passage differs substantially from those mentioned above in that its dark colors are mixed with paradoxical and sarcastic overtones. It is evident also in the strange episode of the four lepers in the continuation of the story, who are banqueting in the empty tents of the Arameans. In a similar situation at the siege of Jerusalem, sarcasm is prevalent in the words of Sennacherib's delegate. When the leaders of Jerusalem request him to speak Aramaic so that the people in the city do not understand what they are talking about, he says he came to talk with those starers sitting on the walls who will have 'to eat their own dung and to drink their own urine' (2Kings 18.37).

(4) In the fourth group we may mention two prophetic texts. In a rather enigmatic sequel of symbolic acts, Ezekiel has to bake his bread on human dung and on cow's dung (Ez 4.12,15). Finally, in the book of Malachi God says, 'I will rebuke your offspring, and spread dung on your faces, the dung of your offerings, and I will put you out of my presence' (Mal 2.3). Again, this passage is evidently sarcastic. Moreover, this is exactly the treatment which occurs to Simon in the *APt*. Thus the idea that God's enemies get excrement in their faces is existent also in the Old Testament.

(5) One more notable text should be mentioned here finally. King Saul and his army were chasing David in the wilderness of Juda, when Saul went into a cave to relieve himself. He was not aware that David hid in the cave, and had the chance to kill Saul. But David was content with cutting off a corner of Saul's cloak (2Sam 24.3ff). This episode resembles very much to Aegeates' diarrhea. Both Saul and Aegeates are rulers, negative heroes, and enemies of God's chosen prophet (David and Andrew). In a strange situation both are occupied with 'relieving themselves', while God's people stealthily play a trick on them.

In sum, while the Pentateuch allows the conclusion that metabolic products are not unclean in themselves, in narrative and prophetic texts they usually symbolize death and destruction, and occasionally also appear as devices of irony. A certain kind of scatological humor is definitely not absent from the Old Testament, even though it is not so explicit as in Greco-Roman literature. And in a few passages this humor is turned against the enemies of God or his elect people.

IV

The inexhaustible treasury of Greek scatological humor is found in the comedies of Aristophanes. In the opening scene of *Peace*, the slaves are making cakes of dung to feed a dung-beetle so that the hero may ride up to Olympus on its back. The two servants elaborate on the subject in length. One asks for the excrement of a male prostitute (*paidos hetairêkotos*), because this is what dung-beetles are told to like most. The other one is content that nobody will accuse him of eating from what he mixes. The words of the first servant betray an important aspect of scatological humor: references to metabolic products are mixed with erotic elements. We have to conclude that the strange idea of the excrement of a male prostitute is something that ultimately pleased not only the dung-beetle but also the contemporary listener.

In the dialogues of Aristophanes, 'dung' is a most common expression (*Knights* 658, *Acharnians* 1024, etc.). For example, 'You will eat dung before I do' stands for 'You interrupted me too soon' (*Ecclesiazusae* 592). Eating dung occurs in many other phrases (*Plutus* 302-8). Smearing the faces of people with dung is also not uncommon (*Plutus* 309-15), and it may function as a punishment like in Mal 2.3 (see above).

Defecation and related phenomena are a constant source of humor in Aristophanes. People casually 'flee a fart' (*Knights* 638, *Wasps* 1177, etc.) in different situations. The sound of it may actually signify the dignity of its originator (*Wasps* 620-32). Defecation, on the other hand, seems a conventional gag to illustrate horror on the stage (*Birds* 69, *Lysistrata* 443-8).

One more passage should be mentioned at this place. In the *Wasps* (801-8), Bdelycleon brings various objects to the stage, among them a chamber pot (*amis*): 'See, here is a thunder-mug in case you have to pee; I shall hang it up beside you.' Philocleon answers: 'Good idea! Right useful at my age. You have found the true alleviation of bladder troubles.' This attests that also the objects connected with metabolic actions could be used in scatological humor. In the *APt* and the *AA* similar tools serve to ridicule Simon and Aegeates.

This is only a select illustration of Aristophanes' scatological humor[8]. As a matter of fact, Aristophanes eventually criticizes the

---

[8] For a thorough discussion se J. Henderson, *The Maculate Muse* (New York, 1991²) 187-203.

authors of the Old Comedy for using scenes like this every here and there as a cheap solution to make their audience laugh (*Frogs* 1-20). Nevertheless, he makes abundantly use of these effects.

We would miss the point if we forgot that Aristophanes' scatological humor has its religious roots. Comedies were presented at two festivals of Dionysos, the City Dionysia and the Lenaia. The Athenian Old Comedy is very likely to have developed out of the Dionysiac rites. As we know, the word *komodia* means 'the song of the *komos*', and *komos* was the communal festival of Dionysos, celebrated with dancing, singing and drinking.

The main function of the rite was probably to promote fertility through the display of health, prosperity, and virility. The costumes, the phallus, the pleasures of rural life, food, drink and marriage in the Old Comedy are all reminiscence of its Dionysian origins. Accordingly, the Aristophanic hero is usually a farmer, a typical *id* figure[9], who is interested in the material aspects of life, eating, drinking and sex. This explains why scatological humor is often mixed with eroticism, and fecal matters are referred to so frequently.

The scatological humor of the Greek Old Comedy has reappeared on the stage at several times in the later centuries. In the Roman world the most faithful disciple of Aristophanes was Plautus. Though probably not so directly as the Greek Old Comedy with the Dionysia, the Italian comedy, as well as its popular form, the *mimus*, were associated with fertility cults, the former with the yearly Saturnalia and the latter with the festivals of Flora[10]. As psychologists remark, these festivals were of vital importance for the mental health of theRomans, who had an 'overdeveloped superego'[11].

The Saturnalia gave a possibility to 'send the superego on leave'[12], and substitute Plautus' gods of pleasure (Lust, Desire, Pleasure, Charm, Delight, Love, Chat, Play, Joke, Kiss of Honey) for Cicero's virtues (modesty, prudence, steadfastness, faithfulness, piety, honor, consistency, self-restraint, justice, sobriety, power, rea-

---

[9] A. De Vito and J. Porter, 'Aristophanes and Greek Old Comedy', an electronic text found at http://www.usask.ca/classics/coursenotes/aristophanes.html.
[10] K. Dér, *Plautus világa* ('The World of Plautus': Budapest, 1989) 73.
[11] E. Segal, *Roman Laughter. The Comedy of Plautus* (Cambridge MA, 1968), cited in Dér, *Plautus*, 135.
[12] Dér, *Plautus*, 126.

son[13]). But in the comedy this break-out from the rigid norms of life, from the ever present control of the state and of public opinion is in fact left over to the actors on the stage, or better to the immoral Dionysian Greeks whom they impersonate[14].

Another late descendent of the Greek Old Comedy is the medieval farce. Like the ancient comedy, it also had its roots in the religious festivals. The passion narratives of the Gospels were dramatized, and later amplified with humorous scenes. Negative figures, Herod and devils, acted like clowns, and the mystery plays became full of scatological humor. In this form, they had to be moved out of the church buildings to the marketplace, where they were shown on huge multi-level stages. Together with ancient elements, this was the hotbed of medieval comedy.

Still later authors like Rabelais in France, Fielding and Smollett in England, went back to this tradition to scourge the hypocrisy of their societies. Though these late medieval developments lie far beyond our scope, it is worth talking a few words about Rabelais, whose art has been so brilliantly analyzed by the Russian literary critic Mikhail Bakhtin (1895-1975)[15].

Like Aristophanes and Plautus before him, Rabelais also derived vastly from the culture and language of the marketplaces of his age. But human body and its various grotesque phenomena did not remain mere artistic tools for him. While his predecessors drew on fertility rites and used popular characters and jokes in order to talk ironically about their societies, and also to achieve success with their audience, Rabelais became, so to say, an ideologist of the human body. His training in medicine (and theology) qualified him for this role.

Let us refer just two illustrative passage from Rabelais' novel *Gargantua*[16]. In the first episode (I.13), the child Gargantua reports to his father how he tried to use various objects to wipe out his bottom. The long list contains all kinds of possible and impossible things, including the silk gloves of a lady, various caps and scarves, a cat found in the bushes, many different plants, bed- and tablecloths. The ideal solution was, Gargantua reports, a downy gosling.

---

[13] Dér, *Plautus*, 136.
[14] Dér, *Plautus*, 137.
[15] M. Bakhtin, *Rabelais and His World*, tr. H. Iswolsky (Bloomington, 1984).
[16] For an analysis of these texts see Bakhtin, *Rabelais*, 368-436.

The list that Rabelais provides here, so Bakhtin argues, is part of the author's inventory of the objects of his world at the decline of a historical era and the dawn of a new one. He takes these objects out of their everyday context, and puts them into a new and grotesque situation, in order to re-qualify them. Significant is the occurrence of things which are normally related to the upper part of the body, or to the head, or directly to eating. Thus Rabelais refers the traditional grotesque view of the bottom as a comical mirror of the face.

The material quality of the things is what solely counts in this strange measurement of all products of human culture against the most primitive function of human life. This measurement establishes, to put it with M. Foucault, a new 'order of things'[17]. But when the perfect tool is found, Rabelais concludes, this action leads to the most complete satisfaction, which proceeds from the bottom through the whole body to the heart and the brain. This is recurrence to the most infantile eroticism, to the most primitive human existing in the world, where the immediate satisfaction of the primary drives does not take notion of the world out there, and thus makes impossible any kind of culture and civilization.

These pleasures are, Rabelais concludes, those which the half-gods and heroes enjoy on the Elysian fields. Thus he creates a grotesque counterpart of Christian heaven, though not directly an image of hell, as Bakhtin claims. The direct identification of fecal matters with hell can be found in another passage of the novel (III.22). When the poet Raminagrobis is dying, another character of the novel prophesies his lot, namely, that he will get into the worst place in hell, into the chamber pot of Proserpina, directly where Beelzebub does his 'hellish defecation'.

V

In a short survey, we made an attempt to understand how scatological themes were handled in Old and New Testament biblical literature, and how scatological humor pervaded the comedy of the Greco-Roman world and the Middle Ages. Now we have to answer the question how these observations help us interpreting the episode of

---

[17] I refer here to M. Foucault, *The Order of Things: An Archeology of the Human Sciences* (New York, 1971).

Simon's humiliation in the *APt* and the scene of Aegeates' diarrhea in the *AA*.

The first and most obvious conclusion is that the *AAA* used well-known literary devices to ridicule their negative protagonists. People who get the content of chamber pots on their heads and who defecate in public, just cannot be taken seriously. The reader cannot but laugh at them. They resemble the funny characters of Aristophanes, the servants who knead dung with their hands for the dung-beetle, or the Scythians who defecate from horror. The same effect is utilized to ridicule the devil in the medieval mystery plays.

There is also an important theological reason why Simon and Aegeates have to suffer this treatment. A basic idea of Old Testament theology is that the evil have to take their punishment. They will perish, they will be 'like dung on surface of the ground'. Many people rejected by God suffer a horrible death in the Old Testament (Saul, Ahab, Ahaz, Joram, Jezebel, etc.). Their death is miserable, but it is touching at the same time. In a sense, the episode of Saul and David in the cave, where Saul relieves himself, has also its pathetic overtones.

Beginning with Deutero-Isaiah, the image of the 'suffering righteous' renders obsolete the rather mechanical theory of retaliation. In the early Church, suffering is already the privilege of Christ and his martyrs. But the evil still have to be punished, and they have to reach a dreadful but nevertheless insignificant end, because significant and heroic suffering is reserved for the heroes of the Christian faith.

Thus the suffering and death of Simon is sarcastic rather than pathetic, and he wears on his head the content of chamber pots (*stercus*) rather than a crown of thorns. Aegeates receives his visitors sitting on a strange throne, a *sella pertusa*, which is a parody of royal dignity. His odd reigning may remind us to the lot of Herod Agrippa as reported in the canonical Acts (12.21-3):

> On an appointed day Herod put on his royal robes, took his seat on the platform, and delivered a public address to them. The people kept shouting, 'The voice of a god, and not of a mortal!' And immediately, because he had not given the glory to God, an angel of the Lord struck him down, and he was eaten by worms and died.

It is interesting to notice at this point, that the passion story of Jesus was originally full of acts of humiliation. But the same symbols, mainly the execution on the cross, became the signs of exaltation for his followers. Therefore, his enemies are not worthy to suffer the same tortures as he did.

Still, as A. Hilhorst noticed, 'Aegeates is the only character with a touch of individuality, and he tends to captivate the modern reader by his desperate attempts to win back Maximilla, his wife, who has embraced the ideal of chastity'[18]. No doubt, Aegeates is a remarkable figure of the *AA*, a more modern and 'round' character than the 'flat' figure of Simon in the *APt*. This lively character embodies something like the *id* personalities of the Greek Old Comedy. While Simon is a more or less abstract representation of evil (much like in a medieval allegory), Aegeates behaves like a man. He loves and hates, eats, drinks, copulates and even defecates. He embodies the Dionysian aspects of human life, which are seemingly completely denied by the encratic doctrine of the community of the *AA*.

Scatology often goes hand in hand with eroticism. This is true also in the *AAA*, and especially in the case of Aegeates. But eroticism characterizes also the thought world of the Christian protagonists[19]. The biblical metaphor of bride and groom is widely elaborated in the mystic language of the *AA*. What happens here is something that Freud called the sublimation of sexual impulses. But this is not the only way in which the *AA* balances its encratism. It also creates its Dionysian hero, who does for the Christians what they are not allowed to do themselves. Aegeates acts for the Christian listener like the Greeks of Plautus did for the Romans. The *AA* functioned much like a Christian Saturnalia, like the mystery dramas of the Middle Ages.

On the other hand, the talk about fecal matters is totally serious. It adds another twist to the 'head downward' world-view of the *APt* and forms a grotesque aspect, an interesting infernal voice in the *AA*. The enigmatic words of Peter on the cross about the necessity of turning 'what is on the right hand as what is on the left' (38) are surprisingly realized in the bottom-perspective of these 'gargantuan' heroes. The absurdly diabolic character of Simon and the vivid and realistic personality of Aegeates provide a parody of the 'upside-down' Christian world-view and its eroticism, so to say, a deconstruction of the deconstruction.

[18] A. Hilhorst, 'The Apocryphal Acts as martyrdom texts: the case of the Acts of Andrew', in Bremmer, *Acts of John*, 1-14 at 7.
[19] Adamik, this volume, Ch. III.

We have to go still one step further. The dramatization of the *id* in the *AA* is also connected with the exercise of power. This Dionysian play externalized the sexual life of the believers, and at the same time it internalized the control of the Christian community, that is, the power of the Church. The issue of sexuality was made absolutely public and common in them.

The same applies to the whole of the body. The bodies of Christians became open books when references to bodily processes were made in these Acts. Not only the 'soul' but also the *id* of the personality became the subject of public discussion. One felt x-rayed when one read these unabashed lines, and at the same time one saw x-rayed the other members of the community.

In spite of its occasional naturalism and its collective approach to human personality, this kind of x-raying is completely absent from the Old Testament. Though many areas of social life are ruled in the Pentateuch, the boundaries of the *id* body, the issues of one's natural processes are kept untouched. Only exceptional cases are controlled, e.g. when fluids are discharged which are normally not present (flux, semen, menstruation).

We may suspect some sort of Dionysian festivals in the Biblical story of the golden calf: 'And they rose up early on the morrow, and offered burnt offerings, and brought peace offerings; and the people sat down to eat and to drink, and *rose up to play*' (Ex 32.6, KJV, italics added). Something similar may have taken place during the festivals held at the holy places (shrines) of Israel, as many passages indicate in the books of Samuel and Kings (1Sam 1.12-4, 2.12-7, 9.22-4, etc.). Still the collectivization of the body, the externalization of the *id* component of personality in the *AAA* rather followed the Greco-Roman patterns, which were discussed in connection with Aristophanes and Plautus.

At the same moment when human body was 'dissected' in the *AAA*, it was alienated from the person, and controlled by the community. The whole process resembles very much the method which, according to M. Foucault[20], transformed sexuality into a thoroughly controlled discourse in Western culture. The very process that gave life to the institutional framework of the sexual discourse, confession

---

[20] M. Foucault, *The History of Sexuality, Volume 1: An Introduction*, tr. R. Hurley (New York, 1978).

(in the Roman Catholic Church), medicine, and education, provided at the same time, as Foucault remarks, a lot of incitement to sexuality.

The *AA* bear witness to the same trend in the early Christian communities with regard to the *id* aspects of personality. While the community emphasized their contempt toward anything that is material, they took pleasure in the erotic representations of faith as well as in telling stories like that of Aegeates and Maximilla, full of bodily phenomena. In sum, our survey of scatological humor and related issues in Biblical and Greco-Roman literature allowed to make important observations about the bodily images and expressions of the *APt* and the *AA*, with special regard to the episodes of Simon's chamber pots and Aegeates' diarrhea.

(1) These episodes utilize the simplest and perhaps most ancient dramatic device to make readers, onlookers and listeners laugh – namely, scatological humor. Naturalism is not alien from the Old Testament, metabolic products often appear in prophecies of judgment, and a certain irony is present in some of these passages. Still the most significant ancient resource of scatological humor is Greek Old Tragedy.

(2) Scatological humor in the *AAA* is an appropriate way to let the enemies of Christianity suffer. Serious and pathetic suffering and death is reserved for the people of God, who follow as martyrs the passion of their Master. Only insignificant and ridiculous suffering befits the negative heroes.

(3) The juicy stories of the *AAA* fulfilled the role of the ancient Saturnalia. They gave room to the imagination to indulge in mortal sins which were otherwise strictly forbidden to the believer. Like the ancient comedies, the narratives utilized negative heroes to commit drastic sins, to the horror and, at the same time, to the pleasure of the audience. Eroticism became the hotbed of Christian piety.

(4) When the *id* aspects of personality are plainly shown in the story, the bodies of the readers and listeners are x-rayed. Fleshly phenomena are made the subject of a public discourse, which at the same time controls the body down to its most hidden cells. This normative discourse provides the framework of how people of the Christian faith speak, think, and feel about their bodies. Flesh is seemingly downplayed, but in fact it becomes more important than ever.

Jesus was not concerned about 'whatever goes into the mouth'. He said it also comes out of the body and therefore it is absolutely pure in terms of religion. The biblical discourse knows about the body, but it is not obsessed with it. On the other hand, 'what goes into the mouth' and what comes out of it, and whatever is between, the human body itself, seem to have become the main concern of the Christian communities of the *AA* and the *APt*.

VI. Triangles and What is Beyond Them. Literary, Historical, and Theological Systems of Coordinates in the Acts of Andrew

JÁNOS BOLYKI

In a study published in 1995, D.R. MacDonald argued that the *Acts of Andrew* is a Christian re-evaluation of Homer's *Odyssey*, and all its components have their counterparts in Greek epic[1]. For example, Aegeates is associated with Odysseus, Stratocles with Telemachos, Maximilla with Penelope, and the apostle Andrew with Odysseus, but he is also the 'Christian Socrates'. I readily accept his thesis because it is based partly on the postscript of the *AA* itself, which begs an allegorical interpretation from the reader; moreover, in his *Address to the Greeks*, Tatian – whose encratic heresy provides the spiritual background of the *AA* – refers several hundred times to Greek artifacts of philosophy, literature and fine arts, which represent the confrontation of the Greek and Christian worlds of ideas. Also convincing is MacDonald's statement that the first readers of the *AA* could barely have understood the hidden references to the *Odyssey*.

In the following study – encouraged by the postscript of the author of the book – I will explore the association base of the *AA* not in the *Odyssey* but in the Old Testament. I will not draw mainly on the similarity of characters but rather on the structure of connections among the main protagonists. Modelled after the relationships between Aegeates, Maximilla and Andrew, I call the basic structure a *triangle-connection*. First I will study the dramatic dynamics of

---

[1] D.R. MacDonald, 'Is There a Privileged Reader? A Case from the Apocryphal Acts', *Semeia* 71 (1995) 29-43.

some Biblical triangles and then focus on those in which one protagonist becomes a martyr. Later, I draw attention to the social and historical effects of these triangles and talk about the world-view which is mirrored in them. Finally, I will apply the paradigm of the triangle to the relationship between the writer and the reader from a Christian theological point of view.

II

The Bible presents us with numerous triangle-connections, but only the situation of Joseph, Potiphar and his wife can be called a 'triangle-eternal', where somebody is lured to commit adultery. The woman wants the triangle of love, while Joseph opts for the triangle of faithfulness to his master and to God. The situation is outlined in Figure 1:

Figure 1

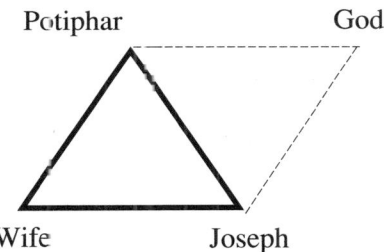

The point of the story is encratism, as always in *AA*, but here the encratic person is a man (Joseph), and not a woman (Maximilla). In the *AA* the goal of encratism is an end in itself, causing the death of two protagonists, while here its purpose is to refrain from adultery, which is richly 'rewarded' through the marriage with Aseneth, daughter of the high-priest. Joseph's story, of course, also has a historical message, demonstrating the two choices of the Jews in the diaspora: slavish and sinful assimilation on the one hand, or preserving one's identity and even gaining proselytes (Aseneth) on the other (Gen 41.50).

We have two more triangles in the stories of the patriarchs in Genesis: Abraham–Sarah–Hagar and Jacob–Leah–Rachel (Gen 16.1-16, 29.21-30). These can be conceived of as stories of families, in whose background there lies the self-identification of two sets of people in each case: Israelites and Ismaelites (Arabs?), both tracing their lineages back to Abraham: in the first, Israelites and, in the second, Transjordanian tribes (Manasseh and Ephraim). Rules of dramatic movement can be recognized in both stories. It is not the fact that Abraham loves Sarah more than Hagar and that Jacob loves Rachel more than Leah that sets the rivalry of the women, but always the birth of children. See for example Figure 2:

Figure 2

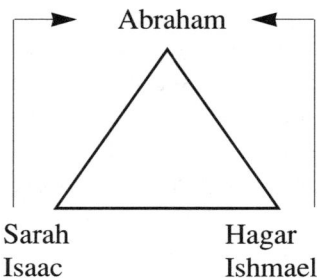

From the point of view of Biblical salvation-history ('Heilsgeschichte'), there is, of course, even more at stake than the mere self-identification of peoples. The question is which branch is going to be the receiver of the promises about revelation, the covenant and the Messiah.

Just like the triangle in the Joseph narrative, with its dramatic movements, the triangle of the Ester–Artaxerxes–Haman story also depicts the situation of the Jews in the diaspora. This might be better described as an Artaxerxes–Haman–Mordecai triangle of power, and the life-and-death struggle between Haman and Mordecai to win the king's favour. It is clear to the reader that the loser will pay with his life. Haman already seems to have won the battle, while Mordecai and the Jews seem to have lost, when Esther comes on stage taking Mordecai's side and deciding the battle for him. What Esther undertakes for her people (marriage with the pagan emperor) is not really a sacrifice, but rather a risk. She can gain or lose everything, and the story ends with the latter. This plot is just the opposite of that of the *AA*, in which the heroine – due to the influence of the apostle who is depicted as an encratist – refuses sexual intercourse with her legitimate husband, who loves her honestly.

In the Old Testament we shall finally discuss the Ahab–Jezebel–Elijah triangle. According to the laws of dramaturgy, we can take three snapshots of this narrative. The first shows Ahab's position of power (Figure 3). Elijah then has to flee from the king who is influenced by Jezebel to do what is wrong in God's eyes, and the triangle turns over (Figure 4). The third (closing) scene shows the influence of Jehu, who rebels against the foreign influence (Figure 5).

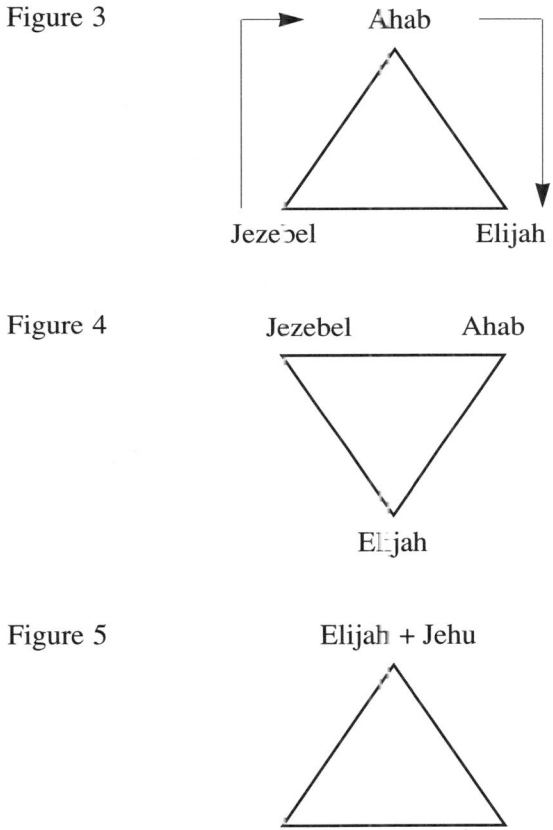

Figure 3

Figure 4

Figure 5

In addition to the dramaturgy, the historical background is also decisive: the battle between the declining kingdom and the prophetic movement which is increasing in power. The depiction of the political decline in 1Kings (ch. 22) is parallel to the *AA*: the kingdom of Israel and the Roman empire, respectively, are declining in the stories. The two heroines are, however, characterized differently. Jezebel plays a negative role while Maximilla a positive one.

In the dramaturgical movements of the five Old Testament 'triangle-stories' we can discern the following laws of dynamics: (1) a seeming balance upon the introduction of the characters; (2) the balance is shaken, due to the negative hero, while the positive hero gets into danger; (3) a new and positive power presents itself and (4) the system of power is dramatically rearranged.

III

The *AA* and the two New Testament triangles which we will present now differ from the five Old Testament examples in that their positive heroes are martyred. Let us first consider the Herod Agrippa–Herodias–John the Baptist triangle. This is very similar to the Elijah–Ahab–Jezebel story, and Jesus himself calls the Baptist Elijah (Mk 9.11-13), but the two narratives differ in that Elijah is finally taken up to heaven, while John is beheaded. Another triangle in the New Testament is found in Matthew's passion-narrative, namely in Mt 27.19, the only place where Pilate's wife is mentioned in New Testament. She sends a message to her husband sitting in the judgment seat (*bêma*) that he had better have 'nothing to do with that innocent man' (Jesus), for she has suffered much in a dream because of him[2]. The triangle here is Pilate–Pilate's wife–Jesus. In Matthew's Gospel this is only another motif for Pilate not to condemn Jesus to death, about whose innocence he is convinced. But we will see that from a theological and historical point of view this provides an important indication. John the Baptist, Jesus and Andrew were all martyred, and this is a novelty when compared with the Old Testament triangles. The laws of dramaturgy are different here. Although to the outside spectator, the hero seems to fail, in the theological drama he is victorious even when defeated. The two kings (Herod Agrippa is in fact an ethnarch) and the two governors (Pilate and Aegeates) have to face moral and/or physical annihilation, while the martyrs (John the Baptist, Jesus and Andrew) await moral and real resurrection.

---

[2] H.L. Strack – P. Billerbeck, *Kommentar zum Neuen Testament aus Talmud und Midrasch* I. 1032.

IV

But why was Andrew martyred? The twentieth-century reader, even the Christian one, cannot escape making a negative judgment at first. The main protagonist of the *AA* was not martyred for proclaiming the Gospel of Jesus Christ, as was Stephen (Acts 7) and the martyrs of the first four Christian centuries. Rather he was executed for holding and propagating encratic views[3], condemning all kinds of sexual life, inducing Maximilla to refuse sexual intercourse with her husband, and thus bringing on himself the wrath of the Roman proconsul Aegeates. Many scholars agree that the extreme views of the *AA*, disdaining matter, world and body, are not necessarily gnostic traits. They can as well reflect the merging of middle-Platonism with Christian views. No one can deny, however, that the *AA* stand under the influence of encratic heresy. Thus the Roman governor may win more sympathy from the ancient or modern reader through standing with naked sword at the bedside of his wife ready to kill himself if she dies (see the version of Gregory of Tours), requesting her so many times to resume sexual life, and confessing that he loves her so much he cannot do any harm to her, than the apostle who does not proclaim the happiness of the Good News but rather a cruel and perfectionist encratism.

The encratic sect of Christians (those 'having self-control') was founded around AD 160, and Jerome (*Praef. in Comm. ad Tit.*) calls the Assyrian (Mesopotamian) Tatian (AD 110-172) 'the patriarch of the Encratites'. He also states (*Comm. Epist. ad Gal.*) that 'Tatian... pronounces all sexual connection impure, who was also the very violent heresiarch of the Encratites'. As M. Hornschuh writes, 'E. Peterson hat auf die engen Berührungen mit der Theologie Tatians aufmerksam gemacht'[4], which originated not long after Tatian's death in 172, but by all means before 190. Its aftermath presents itself in the Pseudo-Titus epistle, written several centuries later in the Western part of Europe, which quotes the *AA* with regard to virginity: 'Als der Apostel Andreas schliesslich zu einer Hochzeit kam, um die Glorie Gottes zu zeigen, trennte er die füreinander bestimmten Gatten, Frauen und Männer voneinander und lehrte sie, heilig in Ehelosigkeit zu

---

[3] P.J. Lalleman, *The Acts of John* (Leuven, 1998) 217-44.
[4] M. Hornschuh, 'Andreasakten', in E. Hennecke and W. Schneemelcher (eds), *Neutestamentliche Apokryphen*, II. 274.

bleiben'[5]. The modern reader cannot identify with a martyr, bearing the name of an apostle, who does not bless the bride and bridegroom, but separates them from each other. He would rather subscribe to the judgement of the old Catholic church which declared both the *AA* and the encratic movement heretic, but institutionalized monasticism in which it left room for continence[6].

But the *AA* have much more to say, even about encratism. According to *Cod. Vat.* 808 (see 5 and 7) Andrew encourages Maximilla with the astounding reasoning that the sin of Adam and Eve (that is the trespassing of encratism) is within us but, if we practice encratism, we can turn around the lot of humankind which is sunk in sins[7]. Andrew thus regards himself as the second, new Adam. And though this is a gross heresy (the New Testament holds that the second Adam is Christ, 1Cor 15.22,45), it is precisely at this point that this sectarian piece of literature deserves public interest and the lot of its hero becomes universal and identical with the lot of the whole of humankind. True enough, the idea itself is still mistaken, but its point is the sacrifice undertaken in the name of humanity, which can win the sympathy of the reader of every age.

From the point of view of reader-response criticism, we are able to identify four types of readership of the *AA*: (1) the first, contemporary readers (at the end of the second century), the encratists, who found the expression of their own ideas in the text; (2) the community of Pseudo-Titus, who used the *AA* and publicized the ideal of virginity, but did not want to extend it to those already married; (3) the old Catholic Church, which answered this question by confirming the monastic way of life (fifth century) and (4) the modern reader, who is not interested in the ideal of encratism, but rather in the devotion and universal acclaim of the hero.

V

The triangles which occurred in the works in question also fulfill the role of a thermometer measuring social and historical transitions. We

---

[5] A. de Santos Otero, 'Der Pseudo-Titus-Brief', in Hennecke and Schneemelcher, *Neutestamentliche Apokryphen*, II. 104.

[6] A curious compromise between encratism and marriage: 'The Narrative of Zosimus' (before AD 250), in A. Menzies (ed), *The Ante-Nicene Fathers* X (Grand Rapids, 1974) 219-24 (222 = cap. X).

[7] Hornschuh, *ibidem*, 286-7.

have already considered the five Old Testament passages from this aspect. The John the Baptist–Herod–Herodias triangle historically indicates the end of the satellite kingdom, and the end of the historical role of Old Testament prophecy at the same time, but also illustrates the universal truth and survival of the moral message en-coded in the story. The historical background of the Jesus–Pilate–Pilate's wife and Andrew–Aegeates–Maximilla narratives is provided by the Roman Empire. What do these two triangles as thermometers signify? First of all that the position of the Roman empire is unstable in the provinces. This is proven by the crowds that fulfill such an important role in both stories. But while the crowd forces Pilate, the representative of Roman legal order, to judge against the law and sentence Jesus to death, the proconsul Aegeates is pressed to spare the life of Andrew whom he had crucified selfishly. This indicates that the destiny of the Empire will be determined in the provinces – not in Rome – by the crowds. But it also attests that the crowds, so hostile toward Christianity in the beginning, are more and more sympathetic with it at the end of the second century (the time the *AA* was written).

The female protagonists of the three triangles supply an interesting historical indication. Herodias is still the spiritual offspring of the evil Jezebel, when she intrigues against John the Baptist, the man of God. Pilate's wife, Procula Claudia (see Gnilka, *Matthäus* II, 456–7) acts on the side of Jesus, though not yet as a disciple. She follows the warning she received in a dream (cf. Mt 1.20; 2.12-13, 19), partly in a pagan way but taking the side of Jesus, whom she thinks to be a 'righteous man' (Is 9.6, 11.4f, 16.5; Jer 23.5f, 33.15. Lk 23.47). Maximilla, the wife of Aegeates, proconsul of a province, is already a full-fledged Christian at the end of the second century. She does not intervene with her husband on behalf of the apostle Andrew and is not even willing to compromise (fulfilling marital duties in return for Andrew's life, *Cod. Vat.* 804,4), but by unifying Andrew's moral power, the political power of the crowd and her own existential power, she eventually overcomes her husband who escapes into suicide. In terms of social and historical categories, the three triangles represent the relationship among household, Empire and Church. The women stand for the household, the satellite-kings for Empire, John the Baptist, Jesus and Andrew for the Church. Thus we have the following social triangle:

Figure 6

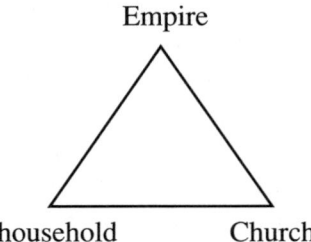

The law of motion and dynamics within the triangle is that the cooperation of two angles overcomes the third angle. In the case of John the Baptist, the family of the ruler and the power of the state together overcome the Church. Though the people support the Baptist (Mt 14.5), nevertheless they do not openly demonstrate beside him. In Pilate's dream, the household (Pilate's wife) stands up for the Church only in a dream and a timid message of a woman, thus the Empire triumphs. The Empire is represented by Pilate, not as the deputy of legal order but as one yielding temporarily to the crowd of the province incited in the defense of the Empire. The case of Andrew, however, demonstrates a historical situation where the representative of Empire is left to himself and fails against a coalition of the household (Maximilla), the crowd and the Church (Andrew). This attests to the development that the influence of the Church spreads not only to the household but also to the crowd. The crowd becomes part of the Church, and after Constantine the Great it receives a part in the ruling of the Empire. At the same time, from the point of view of theology (salvation history/'Heilsgeschichte'), the kingdom (*basileia*) means not only the satellite-kingdom but also the Kingdom of God (*basileia tou theou*), which has universal and cosmic claims.

VI

The world-view supporting this universal and cosmic claim is depicted in the Bible not through historical but through mythical triangles in Gen 1.1–3 and Rev 12. The 'tohuwabohu' and the prehistoric ocean of Genesis as well as the dragon spitting water represent chaos. In opposition to them there is the life-giving earth (cosmos, Gen 1.11,24), and the Earth ('Mother Earth') in Rev 12 which swallows the water poured by the dragon. The third point in the two myths are the first human couple and the woman clothed with the Sun, who gives life to the child (Messiah, second Adam). This is delineated in:

Figure 7

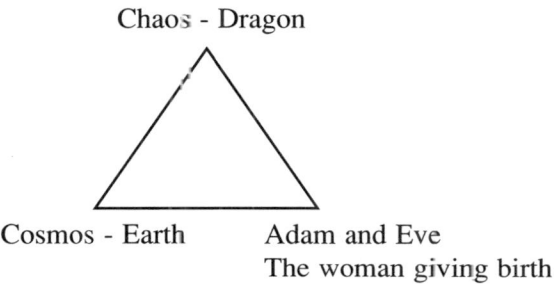

The battle in both cases is decided for humankind. In Genesis the dry earth provides a place for people to live and protects them from the chaotic dangers of the ocean and the 'waters above the dome'. In Rev 12, in turn, 'the Earth came to the help of the woman', and 'swallowed the river that the dragon had poured from his mouth' (Rev 12.16). This cosmic myth provided the basis of Jewish-Christian culture, the broadest system of coordinates supporting their world-view, by which everything else was measured, and which gave the points of orientation of the beginning and the end. But Jewish-Christian culture even stepped beyond that point, because the identification of the beginning and the end, that is, the restitution of the corrupted beginning at a higher level also gives the basis for human culture. Modern cultural anthropology does not despise myths anymore, as did enlightened rationalism which today seems to have been too naive. Moreover, at this time of ecological crisis, our culture now pays considerable attention to the threefold factors of the chaos and the earth providing a home for humankind.

VII

The triangle is, however, not only a paradigm for the dramatic relationships, a thermometer of history, a basic structure of myths and world-views, but also an authorial 'message in a bottle'. It is a message from the author's desert island to the readers of succeeding ages. Here again I refer to MacDonald's view that the first readers were unable to decode the hidden message of the *AA*. The author knows he will perhaps not be alive by the time the 'message in a bottle' he has thrown into the ocean of time reaches the reader. He also suspects that the message will be reinterpreted before the public reads it. Things he considered secondary will gain importance; important issues will become subsidiary. Perhaps the reader adds his own interpretation to the end of the message, then closes the bottle and entrusts it to the ocean of time to be taken to even farther worlds.

Given the fact that the *AA* is a Christian text, its 'message in a bottle' is more concrete than that of a general piece of literature. It is about the divine triangle, which the Christian doctrine calls the Trinity. The dynamics of the Trinity are incarnation and redemption. The Creator God becomes human in the Son, the incarnate Logos, and leads the lost humankind by the power of the Spirit to himself. In this paradigm, the triangle is not made up of a dramatic or chaotic fight between agonizing persons or powers, but the route of the descending love which allows even the defeated to triumph (*victor victus*, 'defeating defeated').

VII. The Words of Life in the Acts of Andrew

FRANÇOIS BOVON

Christianity always expressed the necessity of the proclamation of the gospel[1]. During the second century, however, the different groups and churches were not able to agree on the nature of this proclamation. For some, the apostolic witness was constituted by a memory of fundamental salvific events, namely, the birth, death, and resurrection of Christ. For others, particularly the author of the *Acts of Andrew* (*AA*) preaching the gospel meant communicating divine wisdom and proclaiming life-giving words[2].

---

[1] This paper was presented at the meeting celebrating the hundredth anniversary of the Section des Sciences religieuses at the École Pratique des Hautes Études at Paris in 1986 and was also delivered as a lecture in the same year at the Harvard Divinity School. It earlier appeared in French as 'Les Paroles de Vie dans *Les Actes de l'Apôtre André*', *Apocrypha* 2 (1991) 99-111 and in English as 'The Words of Life in the *Acts of Andrew*', *HThR* 87 (1994) 139-54. I would like to thank Ms. Jane Haapiseva-Hunter, Mr. David Warren, and Ms. Laura Nasrallah who helped me with the translation and the annotations, and the support staff of the New Testament Department for their help with word processing this article.
Abbreviation:
Leloir = L. Leloir, *Écrits apocryphes sur les apôtres. Traduction de l'édition arménienne de Venise* I (Turnhout, 1986).
[2] In the first case – the memory of salvific events – the apostle withdraws behind his message; in the other – the communication of wisdom – he tends to become a mediator of the revelation. See J.M. Prieur, 'La figure de l'apôtre dans les *Acts apocryphes d'André*'; and F. Bovon, 'La vie des apôtres: traditions bibliques et narrations apocryphes', in F. Bovon et al., *Les Actes apocryphes des apôtres: Christianisme et monde païen* (Geneva, 1981) 121-39, 141-58, respectively; H. Koester, 'La tradition apostolique et les origines du gnosticisme', *RThPh* 119 (1987) 1-16.

Two recent editions by Jean-Marc Prieur and by Dennis R. MacDonald help us to recognize this emphasis on the words uttered by the apostle in the *AA*[3]. They have brought to light large new sections of the original text even if the first parts of the work remain lost. We can only imagine the context and the sequences of these first parts through the sixth-century life of Andrew, written in Latin by Gregory of Tours[4]. Since Gregory intentionally sacrificed the apostle's speeches, however, preferring instead to summarize the apostle's activities, for our topic we must depend exclusively on what remains from the original Greek *AA*. These *Acts* are nevertheless sufficient to express their author's conviction: the apostle's words were powerful and they were able to bring life to their auditors, connecting them with God's eternal reality.

The following exposition will begin with a summary of the principle passages in the accounts of Andrew's ministry and martyrdom at Patras that are relevant to our subject. This will be followed by an analysis of the text and then I shall conclude by raising questions concerning the historical origin of soteriology by words.

Principle Passages

First meeting of Andrew and Stratocles at the house of Maximilla (6-12): Arriving at Patras, the apostle heals Alcmanes, the servant of Stratocles, the brother of the governor Aegeates. Maximilla, the wife of the governor, who has already been won to the apostle's cause, invites Andrew into her room. There, Andrew gives a speech directed to Stratocles alone; having provoked many by his miracle,

---

[3] J.-M. Prieur, *Acta Andreae*, 2 vols (Turnhout, 1989); D.R. MacDonald, *The Acts of Andrew and Matthias in the City of the Cannibals* (Atlanta, 1990). For indications on the different texts related to the apostle Andrew, see M. Geerard, *Clavis Apocryphorum Novi Testamenti* (Turnhout, 1992) 135-46.

[4] Gregory of Tours' *Liber de miraculis beati Andreae apostoli*, in W. Arndt, M. Bonnet, and B. Krusch (eds) *Gregorii Turonensis opera*, 2 vols (Hannover, 1884-85) 1.821-46; see also M. Bonnet, 'Preface', 1. 827 in the same book. The Latin text of Gregory is reprinted, along with a French translation in Prieur, *Acta Andreae*, 2.551-651. It is also in good part reedited and translated into English in MacDonald, *The Acts of Andrew*, 188-99, 205-5, 210-13, 218-41, 256-65, 268-73, 276-317.

the apostle, like a midwife, hopes for the spiritual birth of his listener. Maximilla, too, wishes the apostle to lead Stratocles to the truth. Initiated in the art of maieutics and divination, Andrew wants to awaken in Stratocles the inner man, who first is quiet and then begins to speak to the apostle (7). Thus Stratocles, the future convert, does not set forth his shameful past and his present awakening, but the apostle guesses it, through his prophetic art, and brings it to light like a mid-wife.

The effect of the speech takes place within Stratocles. Convinced of the futility of his past life, he groans like a woman giving birth and declares that he will attach himself to the apostle in order to know himself. After this Stratocles never leaves Andrew and becomes the 'true friend of the hearing of salvation' (8). Stratocles' initiation by the word continues. He passes precious moments alone with the apostle, for this is the occasion to ask questions. The apostle then introduces the questions again in the presence of the community, explaining to Stratocles 'It is not right not to expose your birth pangs with those like you' (8). Just as women 'participate in the same mysteries' (9) during childbirth (9), Andrew reveals that at a spiritual birth, 'It is also necessary for us to witness publically, your newborn being, my child, Stratocles, and not to be quiet, in order that it be recorded by the largest number of its relatives and openly put forward so as to offer liberally the saving words that I have discovered that you are a part' (9). Stratocles, 'henceforth leaning on all the words to which he was related' (10) possesses a solid soul; in faith and joy, with the title 'neophyte' (12) he participates in the life of the nascent community at Patras. Andrew seizes the opportunity for a parenetic discourse concerning the mark of God, which Andrew's disciples must protect[5]. The account of the birth of Stratocles to spiritual life ends with the two remarks by the author: Stratocles, the brother of the governor, henceforth bears the name of 'neophyte' – we should not forget the etymological sense 'newly planted' – and, lifted up to the heights of thought, he abandons all his goods 'in order to attach himself to the word alone' (12).

---

[5] To those who have been considered worthy of the seal, Andrew declares: 'My small children, if you keep this mark safe from the other seals which stamp the opposite imprint, God will approve you and welcome you amongst his goods' (11).

The meeting of Andrew and Maximilla (37-41)[6]. The second scene we shall analyze takes place later in the story[7]. Andrew is in prison and, according to their custom, Maximilla and Iphidamia visit the apostle. In ritual fashion[8], the wife of the governor presents an ethical problem to Andrew: Should she respond to the sexual demands of her husband, Aegeates? Maximilla, in asking this question, expects as an answer the opinion, the *gnômê*, of the apostle, but Andrew introduces a moral and doctrinal discourse. Andrew encourages Maximilla to refuse the advances of her husband, for by her chaste fidelity, she reserves Eve's fault and allows the apostle to reverse Adam's sin. Disobedience and obedience form the backdrop to Andrew's words: 'And what she [Eve] does not want to hear you have heard' (37). The words of the apostle, which until this moment had been moral and doctrinal, become complimentary:

> Having said these things as I have just said, I could still say the following: 'Bravo, o nature, in the process of being saved, for you did not harden your heart nor hide yourself! Bravo, soul, which shouts what you have suffered and comes back to yourself! Bravo, human being, who knows what is not your own and hurries toward what is yours! Bravo, you who listen to what is said! I know that you are greater than what is thought and said' (38).

Continuing the speech, the apostle justifies the parallel between Eve and Maximilla: 'I have said this concerning you, Maximilla, for by their power, these words are applied to you' (39). Andrew then explains that should Maximilla fall, he himself would be chastised[9]. Just as the apostle directed his words to Stratocles, here, he speaks to

---

[6] This passage has been known through the Cod. Vat. gr. 808 and was edited by Bonnet, *Acta* 2.1.39-42, where it is numbered 5-9.

[7] Between the two passages summarized here we find in particular the romanesque episode of Maximilla's substitution of her servant Euclia, cf. J.-D. Kaestli, 'Fiction littéraire et réalité sociale: que peut-on savoir de la place des femmes dans le milieu de production des *Actes apocryphes des apôtres*?', *Apocrypha* 1 (1990) 279-302 at 295-8; Bremmer, this volume, Ch. II.1.

[8] She puts the apostle's hand over her eyes, then kisses them (37).

[9] The author later mentions the effect of Andrew's words: 'For as she listened to the words which he directed toward her, they affected her in such a way that she became what the words intended. In haste, with resolution and purpose, she went to the praetorium' (46).

Maximilla, but in fact the words are offered to any attentive listener who is willing to apply them to himself or herself: 'I have said this speech for you and whoever is listening, if he or she wants to hear' (42).

The second meeting of Andrew and Stratocles (42-45): Maximilla departs, and Andrew turns to one of these listeners, Stratocles, addressing him with a long series of questions. Andrew is concerned because Stratocles is crying; he undoubtably has become aware of the imminent martyrdom of the apostle. Andrew's questions allow us to understand how the narrator visualizes the incrustation of the words of salvation in the human soul:

> Do you understand what has been said and why I pray you, my child, to be favorably disposed? Do you know to whom these words were addressed? Has each one [of these words] reached your thought? Have they touched your thinking part? Do I have you as one who has listened to me and remains [watchful]? Do I find myself in you? Is there someone who lives in you and that I can consider my own? Does he love the one who has spoken in me and does he desire to live in communion with him? (42)

The litany of questions culminates in the answer which the apostle himself gives: 'Is it not in vain that I discourse? Is it not in vain that I have spoken? No, says the man in you who has cried again, Stratocles' (42)[10]. Andrew begins a new section of this discourse by affirming Stratocles: 'Andrew then took the hand of Stratocles[11] and said: "I have the one for whom I have sought... For it is not in vain that I addressed these words to you, these words which are my relatives"' (43).

Stratocles can finally express himself:

> Do not think, blessed Andrew, that it is anything other than you which causes me sadness. For the words which you utter are like bolts of fire thrown at me, and each one hits and truly inflames and consumes me with love for you. And the affective part of my soul, which leans to what has been heard, and squeezes me with sadness, is tormented. For you are leaving, and I know well that it is good this way, but if after

---

[10] To say that Stratocles has cried 'again' probably means that he has been able to cry again for the right reasons, motivated by repentance and truth.

[11] Again we should be attentive to this gesture, as we already have noticed above Maximilla's attitude (n. 8).

> this, I seek your solicitude and tenderness, where will I find them, or with whom? I have received the seeds of the saving words and you were the sower for me. Yet for them to germinate and grow, they need you and no other, very blessed Andrew. What else do I have to say to you but this, servant of God? I need great mercy and the help which comes from you to be able to be worthy of the seeds which come from you. For they will not grow unharmed and we will not see them grow if you do not want them to and do not pray for them and for all of me (44).

Andrew can then only rejoice in the attitude by his disciple: 'This is what I also saw in you, my child, and I glorify my Lord that my thought concerning you was not useless but knew what it was saying' (45). With this, he goes toward his martyrdom.

Andrew and the gathered community (47-50): As is typical in this genre, in a first farewell speech addressed to the disciples, Andrew looks retrospectively at his activities:

> As for me, brothers, the Lord sent me as an apostle to the regions of which my Lord judged me worthy, not to teach anyone but to remind everyone related to these words that they are living in temporary evils... I deem as blessed those who have become obedient to the words preached and who through them see as in a mirror the mysteries of their own nature, for whose sake all things were built' (47).

Then he announces his martyrdom and the last interventions of the Evil One, who is angry since 'the light of the word has been shown' (50). The discourse ends with an exhortation which contains an enigmatic phrase that is important for our discussion, given the key function attributed to the word *logos* throughout the text: 'But may we all, lifted up by the whole word, welcome joyfully the end' (50)[12].

Andrew and Aegeates (51-55)[13]: The arrest of Andrew places the future martyr in the presence of his judge, the governor

---

[12] The Armenian reads: 'But raise all of you your spirit toward all these words [that I am telling you]', cf. Leloir, 236.

[13] In the narrative of the martyrdom, which begins here, I am again following the critical text established by Prieur in his *Acta Andreae*. It is a composite text established mainly from mss. *H* (Jerusalem, S. Sabas 103), *S* (Cod. Sinait. gr. 526), *C* (Ann Arbor 36), the two forms of the *Martyrium secundum*, and the Armenian version, cf. Prieur, 'Découvertes sur les Actes d'André à Patras', *Peloponnesiaca*, Suppl. 8 (1982) 321-4.

Aegeates[14]. With literary skill, the author shows that Aegeates cannot achieve a real dialogue with Andrew. Andrew makes no reply to Aegeates' attack (51), and when the apostle speaks to the governor, he does not address the latter directly but instead, referring to Aegeates in the third person, exhorts Stratocles regarding the evil nature of men like Aegeates, who are outside and foreign (53; Leloir, 239 n. 6). Between Andrew's discourse at the cross and his last sermon, pronounced while being crucified[15], Andrew again refers to Aegeates: when Stratocles asks Andrew why he is smiling, he replies that he smiles at the vain wiles of Aegeates. 'He cannot even hear, since if he could, he would have heard that the person who belongs to Jesus, having been known then by him, cannot be punished' (55).

Andrew and the crowd (56-64): In his second farewell speech, called a *koinos logos* ('common speech': 56), Andrew addresses the crowd from the cross. He invites his hearers to leave behind what is corporeal and exterior and join the soul of the apostle, which is rushing toward 'what is above the word' (57)[16]. He hopes that 'you may now see, you too, with the eyes of the soul, those things which I tell you... Clean your ears to hear what I say' (57; Leloir, 248), and he continues by saying, 'But now I know well that you are not deaf to my words. This is why men have peaceful confidence in the knowledge of our God' (58; Leloir, 248). The crowd reacts positively: 'Having heard what Andrew had said and, so to speak, held by him, the crowd did not leave the spot. And the blessed one continued to tell them even more than what he had said, so that it was fixed in the mind of those who were listening. Three days and three nights he spoke to them, and no one grew tired nor left him' (59; Leloir, 250).

Because of popular pressure, Aegeates comes to the cross to deliver the apostle, but Andrew condemns the crowd for trying to

---

[14] I shall cite all references to the Armenian version of Andrew's martyrdom from the French translation (the only one in a modern language) by Leloir, 232-57. On the great value of this Armenian version and the Greek text it presupposes, see idem, 'La version arménienne de la Passion d'André', *Handēs Amsōreay* 90 (1976) 471-4; Calzolari, this volume, Ch. XIII.
[15] For the discourse at the cross, see *c.* 54 and Leloir, 242-5; for Andrew's last sermon, see *cc.* 56-8 and Leloir, 245-50.
[16] This probably refers to the human word; see also Leloir, 245.

prevent his martyrdom. For the first time, Andrew attacks the governor directly, but not without hesitation: 'But now that Aegeates comes near to me, I will be silent and hold my children together. What I have to tell him before departing, I will tell him. Why do you return to us, Aegeates' (62; Leloir, 253)?

The author of the Acts of Andrew (65): After having told the last adventures of the martyrdom, the author surreptitiously introduces himself into the account by using 'we', thus giving a feeling of immediacy and truthfulness (64)[17]. He then summarizes Maximilla's attitude and Stratocles' decision, concluding his story with a shift to the first person singular:

> I am ending here my blessed accounts of the acts and mysteries which are difficult, if not impossible to express; may this stroke mark the end [of this book]. I will pray first for myself: that I may have heard what was truly said, and this in a clear manner, also what was not apparent, but could be caught by the thought: I will then pray for all those who were established by what has been said: may they be in communion together, God opening the ears of his hearers so that they may receive all his gifts in Jesus Christ our Lord, with whom is glory, honor and power to the Father, as well as with the very holy, good and quickening Spirit, now, always and forever and ever, amen (65)[18].

Analysis of the Acts of Andrew

Because of the relation of Andrew's inner nature with the divinity, the apostle is an indispensible intermediary. His person as well as his authority, mission, and name require that all respect him[19]. Far from hiding behind the message he proclaims, he represents it. The bonds that link him to the divine words enable his unswerving mediation of these words. The necessity of speaking weights upon him: 'I transmitted words to you which I pray are received by you in the way

---

[17] Leloir, 256. In the Armenian version, the 'we' does not appear.

[18] This is the text and translation of a Greek text constructed from mss. *H*, *S*, and *C* (see n. 13 above). The critical apparatus in Prieur's edition (*Acta Andreae*, 2.549) provides readings – which differ greatly from each other – that are found in the other manuscripts. In the Armenian version, these last lines are put on the lips of Stratocles in a similar, yet more condensed, form, cf. Leloir, 257.

[19] See n. 2.

these words themselves require' (48), Andrew explains, and he describes his words as 'what I above all had to say to you' (37). God entrusted Andrew with a mission not to teach everybody in general – perhaps an attack on the great church and its universalist mission – but to remind those who are related to these words that they are living among foreign evils (47). Indicating the divine origin of the message, the author specifies that Andrew filled others without having eaten anything (59; Leloir, 251).

With regard to the communication of the words of life, certain details in the text may reflect the cultic practices of the author's community. Maximilla takes the apostle and the future neophyte, Stratocles, by the hand and leads them into her room. The other brothers then arrive. All of them sit down and look at the apostle in the expectation of his sermon (6). A privileged hearer seizes the hands of the preacher, lifts them to her own eyes and then to her lips before explaining her problem (37)[20]. Finally, the master in turn seizes the hand of the neophyte to whom his message is addressed (43)[21].

Different types of communication and different genres of speech, moreover, are important in what we may call a rite of initiation in the AA. The seeker gains a private nocturnal meeting with the apostle; in this vein, the first meeting of Andrew and Stratocles (8-9) is similar to the meetings of Jesus and Nicodemus (John 3.1-20) or of Jesus and the young man[22]. The initiatory meeting between Andrew and Stratocles is characterized by the questions of the future initiate and the answers of the mystagogic apostle.

This private teaching, however, must be repeated in front of the gathered community. Thus the apostle avoids discrimination, and the repetition of the apostle's answers allows the disciple effectively to engrave the master's message in his or her mind. This initiation, or birth of the spiritual man or woman, is then similar to a childbirth where many are present (8-9).

The second meeting of Andrew and Stratocles (42-45), directs us toward another ecclesiastical practice, namely, the edification of a member of the community who is distressed and in a state of crisis

---

[20] See n. 8.
[21] On such a gesture see *AJ* 62 in E. Junod and J.-D. Kaestli, *Acta Iohannis*, 2 vls (Turnhout, 1983) 1.250-51 (text); 2. 436-38 (commentary).
[22] *Secret Gospel of Mark* 3.4-5, cf. M. Smith, *Clement of Alexandria and a Secret Gospel of Mark* (Cambridge MA, 1973) 99-120

because the imminent martyrdom of the leader disturbs him or her. The parenetical intervention of the apostle can be subdivided. First, a litany of rhetorical questions (42) allows the apostle to test the fidelity of the believer. Second, without waiting for the responses of the believer, the preacher presents a series of affirmations (43) which express his confidence in the positive attitude the faithful listener has made or is in the process of making. Only then can the faithful one – in this case, Stratocles – express himself (44). Stratocles celebrates both the adequacy of the words of the apostle as they relate to his own commitment to Andrew and the affective union that the words have provoked. This intervention by the master of the salvific words was doubly necessary for Stratocles. First, this speech caused the words of the apostle to be sown – this is the act of initiation, the spiritual procreation and birth. Second, the apostle's intervention caused the germination of the words – this is the moment of trial and edification. The moral aspect of the second step appears clearly in the following exclamation of Stratocles: 'I need great mercy and the help which comes from you to be able to become worthy of the seeds I have from you' (44).

In *c*. 56, we find an ecclesiastical emphasis on missionizing. The author of the *AA* notes a shift in the audience. Having formerly conversed with Stratocles privately, the apostle now addresses everyone, telling the entire public – a public made up of believers and unbelievers – to come and witness his martyrdom. Referring to Andrew's speech, the author uses the expression *koinos logos* (56)[23]. This is a significant indication for us, since with this term, the author designates the speech as a missionary sermon. From the example that we find in the *AA*, such an oratorical piece has its own structure, tonality, and themes. Andrew first unsettles his listeners with a series of hypothetical propositions that force each one to situate himself or herself personally; for example, Andrew insists. 'If you think that death is the end of the passing life, then leave this spot immediately' (56; Leloir, 246).

The discourse continues this destabilizing of the public with a brief series of questions concerning the vanity of a life that focuses on the visible and the material; Andrew states, for example. 'What is the good of possessing what is exterior, and not possessing your-

---

[23] Leloir, 245, but see also p. 146.

selves?', and then he invites each listener to change his or her life (57; Leloir, 247). For the author, this change requires the act of fleeing the world and binding one's interior being to the soul of the apostle which, thanks to his impending martyrdom, is beginning to let loose of earthly things (57; Leloir, 248). Christology is strangely absent here; the apostle alone offers a soteriological bridge. By contemplating what is taking place, the hearers attach themselves to the apostle and receive his intelligence. Thus 'another communion' (57; Leloir, 248) is established, a communion that is, without doubt, different from human sharing. The discourse ends with a promise that is Johannine in tone – 'I am going to prepare the paths over there for those who gave me their accord' (58; Leloir, 249), namely, those who accepted Andrew and his message – and with a final appeal which ends with this statement: 'O men, choose what you prefer, for the choice depends on you' (58; Leloir, 250).

Stratocles, who listens, and Aegeates, who refuses the message, represent for the author the two types of hearers who seem, paradoxically, both to determine their lives freely and to be predestined to their fate, according to their relation or lack of relation to the words of life. Aegeates, the governor, is not even able to listen (55), he is an enemy of the word, a *misologos* (42). His brother, Stratocles, on the contrary, depends upon all the related words (10) and has a part in these words of salvation (9).

The faithful in general are also characterized by their relationship to the words of salvation. They must clean their ears (57) and they know how not to be deaf (58; Leloir, 248); they are related to the words (47); they are attached to the word alone (12) and are lifted up by it (50); they are seized by the apostle (59)[24]. The word must be affirmed in the disciples (16), who are congratulated for their attention (38). The simple circuit of communication is explained in the following manner: 'The word given to me is addressed to you again, Maximilla' (40). If the author places before the hearers a real choice (58; Leloir, 250), he also seems to accept the dysphoric possibility of failing away: 'Oh! the great laziness of those I have instructed! Oh! the sudden fog which has enveloped us after so many mysteries! Oh! the discourse we have spoken until now, without being able to convince our own people!' (61; Leloir, 251-2).

---

[24] Leloir, 250, where the Armenian version seems to weaken the text.

The conclusion of the work is of great importance, for, like the Gospel of John (20.30-1 and 21.24-5), the book claims to transmit in writing the mysteries and words that the apostle communicated orally. The author, remaining anonymous, nevertheless dares to use the first person singular and states that the work is a revelation, initiation, and unveiling of the mysteries, the author's own 'blessed accounts of the acts and mysteries, which are difficult, if not impossible, to express' (65)[25]. The author announces a double prayer: first, that the text correspond to what was said and heard; and, second, that the readers might receive the gifts of the God in Christ and live in communion together after having been transformed by these words (65; Leloir, 257).

With regard to these words of life, the author sometimes uses *logos*, 'word', in the singular (12, 50), but generally prefers 'words' (*logoi*: 48), that is, maxims and discourses which confer life. The author hardly distinguishes the nature of God from the nature of the inner man and thus does not separate the word of God from the apostolic speeches which convey it. The unity of the apostle with God confers upon the apostle's words a divine effectiveness, as is seen, for example, in the divine power of Andrew's speech over Maximilla (39). Not only the effectiveness of the words is significant, but also the truth of these *logoi* (29) and the salvation that they confer (8, 9, 44).

In his Latin summary of the *AA*, Gregory of Tours places on the lips of an admirer these words: 'And now, that makes two days that I have heard your sermons full of words of life'[26]. If the apostle is the herald of these words, Jesus Christ himself is the master of them, as Andrew exclaims: 'Glory to you, Jesus Christ, master of true words and promises' (29). Thanks to the words that are proclaimed, the inner man can awaken and come to life. The words reach a privileged part of the thought (*dianoia*): They touched 'your thinking part' (42). Furthermore, a part of the soul – 'the affective part of my soul', as Stratocles says[27] – leans toward what has been heard. The divine words thus reach the cognitive and affective centers of the inner man. Just as declarations of human love provoke a good feeling of under-

---

[25] See n. 18 above and n. 33 below; Leloir, 257.
[26] *AAlat* 28: *Praedicationes tuas, quae sunt plenae verbis vitalibus.*
[27] The words 'the affective part', as well as some others prior to them, are omitted by the Cod. Vat. gr. 808.

standing and of being understood, of loving and of being loved, the saving words of the apostle arouse knowledge and love in the neophytes. The images used, such as those of embracing flames or growing seeds (44), confirm this interpretation[28].

Historical Origins of the Acts of Andrew

Having described the events of the *AA* and having presented an analysis, I may now turn to the question of the origin of this theology of the 'words'. I propose three answers, none of which excludes the other.

First, in the Jewish and Christian tradition, wisdom literature – from the Proverbs (called *logoi* in the Septuagint) to the Wisdom of Solomon, in which chapters 6-9 sing the merits and benefits of wisdom, or *sophia* – offers the reader a path toward life by means of the knowledge of and meditation on certain salvific phrases. Indeed, it seems that the author of the Gospel of John was inspired by this very idea: Peter's messianic confession of faith is transformed into an adherence to the vivifying words of Jesus: 'Lord, Simon Peter answers, to whom will we go? You have the words (*rhêmata*) of eternal life, and we believe and we know now that you are the holy one of God' (6.68-9; see also 8.51)[29]. Luke, too, may lean on this theology of the words when he proposes to Theophilus 'the assurance concerning the words (*logôn*) that you have learned' (1.4). Is the author of the *AA* also inspired by this conception? The text's silence with regard to christology and the dualistic content of its moral teachings prevent us from immediately answering the question in the affirmative.

Second, I propose that the *AA* might have found its origin in the gnostic tradition. Like the author of the Gospel of John, the authors of gnostic literature also believe that they possess words of salvation. For example, in the beginning of the *Gospel of Thomas*, we find the following statement: 'Here are the secret words which Jesus the Liv-

---

[28] On the image of the seed in Jewish and Greek traditions, see H.-J. Klauck, *Allegorie and Allegorese in synoptischen Gleichnistexten* (Münster, 1978) 189-200, 213-8, 221-7.

[29] J. Robinson, '*Logoi sophôn*: On the Gattung of Q', in J.M. Robinson and H. Koester, *Trajectories through Early Christianity* (Philadelphia, 1971) 71-113; Koester, 'La tradition apostolique' (n. 2).

ing One said and which Didymus Jude Thomas wrote. And he said: He who will find the interpretation of these words will not taste death'[30]. Unlike many gnostic texts, the *AA* do not affirm the secret character of the sayings and the privilege of an esoteric doctrine. Like the *Gospel of Thomas*, however, the *AA* particularly emphasizes the mysterious, saving, and vivifying nature of the words: 'I deem as blessed those who have become obedient to the words preached and who through them see as in a mirror the mysteries of their own nature for whose sake all things were built' (47)[31]; Andrew also cries, 'Oh! the sudden fog which has enveloped us after so many mysteries!' (61)[32]. We also recall the author's comment regarding the 'blessed accounts of the acts and mysteries which are difficult, if not impossible to express' (65)[33].

Finally, the *AA* often echoes Plato's thought. The spiritual maieutics, the invitation addressed to the soul to flee the sensual, or the correspondence of the divine truth with the human being, the emphasis on precise parts of the thought or soul[34] – all these suggest that the

---

[30] *Gos. Thom.* prologue, 1. H.-C. Puech commented at length concerning this prologue and logion 1 in his course, Explication de l'Évangile selon Thomas et recherches sur les Paroles de Jésus qui y sont réunies, at the Collège de France in 1957-58. The summary of this course appeared in Henri-Charles Puech, *En quête de la Gnose*, II, *Sur l'Évangile selon Thomas. Esquisse d'une interprétation systématique* (Paris, 1978) 74-6. This study notes several parallels to the prologue of the *Gospel of Thomas* in the ATh 10, 39 and 47f. See B. Layton (ed), *Nag Hammadi Codex II, 2-7: Together with XIII, 2*, Brit. Lib. Or. 4692(1) and P. Oxy. 1, 654, 655* (Leiden, 1989).
[31] What does the expression 'of their own nature' mean? It probably signifies the nature of the divinity, at the origin of all things.
[32] These last words, 'after so many mysteries', mean, according to the context, 'after the unveiling of so many mysteries', cf. Leloir, 251-2 (the Armenian text is rather different here); see also *c*. 9, where by childbirth the women participate in the same mysteries.
[33] See Leloir, 257. R.A. Lipsius, *Die apokryphen Apostelgeschichten und Apostellegenden*, 2 vols (Braunschweig, 1883; repr. Amsterdam 1976) 1.543-662 believed that the primitive *AA* was a gnostic text.
[34] Plato, *Tim.* 89A (*dianoêtikos*); Pseudo-Plato, *Tim. Locr.* 102E (*pathêtikos*); Albinus, *Didaskalikos*, 32; see also several scholia of Plato: W.C. Greene, *Scholia Platonica* (Haverford, 1938) s.v. *dianoêtikós*, *méros*, *pathêtikós*. Prieur called to my attention Evagrius Ponticus, *Tractatus practicus*, 78: 'The spiritual method is practical, because it purifies the

AA finds its origins in the milieu of Middle Platonism[35]. Does this mean that the idea of the words of life found in the *AA* can be explained by this source alone? This merits discussion, and it is precisely to provoke this discussion that I have presented these texts and synthesized this information, leaving to others more competent than myself the task of locating the *AA* within the religious and philosophical trends of late antiquity.

---

affective part of the soul', cf. M. Hornschuh, 'Acts of Andrew', in E. Hennecke and W. Schneemelcher (eds), *New Testament Apocrypha* II (Philadelphia, 1964) 393.

[35] J. Flamion *Les Actes apocryphes de l'apôtre André* (Louvain, 1911) 157-63 believed that the *AA*, in a form inspired by the Greek novel, communicates a Christian message sharply influenced by neoplatonism and neopythagoreanism. Hornschuh, 'Acts of Andrew', 394 prefers to speak of Middle Platonism and quotes several Platonic parallels to the *AA*.

VIII. The religious message of Andrew's speeches

GERARD P. LUTTIKHUIZEN

In the speeches of the apostle recorded in the *AA*, Andrew more than once refers to the 'inner man' of the person or persons addressed by him. This inner man, which is also designated as 'the soul within you', 'your new man', and 'the child you are bearing' (7), is supposed to suffer and to long for redemption. The apostle affirms that the individual 'souls' belong together; they are 'the race being saved' (50).

1. *The central part of Andrew's Speech to Maximilla (38)*

A concentration of these ideas can be found in the long monologue addressed to Maximilla in *cc.* 37-41, especially in *c.* 38. In the introductory sentences of *c.* 37 we are told how Maximilla visits the apostle in prison after she was pressed by her rich and powerful husband Aegeates to resume their former marital connections. Andrew's speech is a response to this situation. He strongly advises Maximilla to continue her pure and chaste life and to refuse the sexual advances of her husband. A later flashback (46) informs us that Maximilla when she heard the words of the apostle, immediately rushed out to the praetorium to announce to Aegeates that she persisted in her refusal.

The actual speech by the apostle has a concentric structure. It opens (37.5-17) and concludes (39.5-41.8) with Andrew's reaction to the attempt by Aegeates to bring Maximilla back to her former sexual life with him. Andrew strengthens Maximilla in her wish to break up with her husband[1]. After the short opening section and before the

---

[1] Chapters 40-41 can be seen as a digression (an addition to 39b). Cf. the opening words of *c.* 40: '*Once again* my speech is for you, Maximilla, do not yield yourself to Aegeates'.

comparatively long conclusion we find two clearly distinguishable sections (37.18-29 and 39.1-5), for in these two passages Andrew compares Maximilla and himself and their spiritual relationship to the first human couple, Adam and Eve[2]. Between the Adam and Eve passages is the central part of the speech (38).

This central section is expressed in more general language and seems to provide Andrew's advice to Maximilla with a philosophical background. Here, too, Andrew speaks in the second person style. However, the person addressed is not Maximilla (at least not explicitly) but what seems to be a personification of spiritual humankind[3].

The words with which the apostle introduces this more general and philosophical section clearly indicate that something extra is added: 'Having said these things as I said them, I would also say the following...' The transition from *c.* 38 to the next part of the speech, which again directly addresses Maximilla in her particular situation, is worded in the following way: 'I said these things in your presence, Maximilla, because by their power the things that have been said *also extend to you*'. The obvious suggestion is that the things in *c.* 38 said in Maximilla's presence were not said to her alone but *also apply* to her.

Chapter 38 begins with a series of exclamations in which the apostle addresses spiritual humankind as: 'nature being saved', 'soul crying out what you suffered and returning to yourself', 'man (...) longing for what is really yours'. Subsequently the hearer of his words is declared to be 'greater than what is thought or said'[4].

These phrases not only speak about the identity and the dignity of human nature but also refer to the past of spiritual humankind, to its present condition, and to its hopes for the future. Apparently, humankind, represented by individual souls, must be redeemed from the situation in which it finds itself. In the next passage of *c.* 38, 'being saved' is explained as being saved from evil powers. In a very

---

[2] For these passages see J.-M. Prieur, *Acta Andreae* (Turnhout, 1989), 204-7, and the discussion below.
[3] In the final sentence of *c.* 38 Andrew says: 'Soon you, you alone, will be acquainted with the One who was manifested to you (*i.e.* the unbegotten God)'. The exclusivity of 'you alone' hardly makes sense if the reference is just to Maximilla.
[4] Note that the masculine form *ho akouôn* is used.

concrete manner this applies to the situation of Maximilla who after all is threatened by her powerful husband, Aegeates. But in this section of his speech, as we have seen, Andrew does not address Maximilla as an individual person labouring under specific difficulties. His words have a universal application: they are directed to all those who long for redemption from the evil powers of this world. The personified collectivity of human souls is strengthened by the apostle with the following words: 'I know that you are more powerful than those who seemingly are oppressing you... who cast you down to shame... who lead you away in captivity'.

On the one hand, the idea is that human nature, as a result of some fall (see below), finds itself in the sphere of power of worldly authorities and that it suffers from their oppression; on the other hand it is emphasized that, in spite of this situation, human nature has not lost its original nobility and sublimity. Andrew reminds the soul that it is immaterial, holy, light, even heavenly and akin to the Unbegotten, *i.e.* to God himself. For this reason spiritual humankind is basically beyond all material and worldly things, all worldly powers included. At the conclusion of this central part of his speech, Andrew intimates that eventually, when the inner man has shaken off the shackles that bind him to transient things, he will be able to behold the one who manifested himself to him[5].

Our discussion of Andrew's speech to Maximilla leads to some further, more tentative observations. The first one concerns the type of rhetoric applied in this speech. This is not an unimportant issue, for it might help us to determine the rhetorical purpose of the *AA*. In this speech we find the characteristics of epideictic rhetoric as it is redefined by Ch. Perelman and L. Obrechts-Tyteca. The epideictic's function, they argue, is that it increases 'adherence to the values it lauds', and that the speaker 'tries to establish a sense of communion centered around particular values recognized by the audience'[6].

---

[5] This is another paraphrasing reference to God. In a clause (*ou genomenon*) Andrew adds that this does not mean that God is subjected to change; He has not *become* manifest.

[6] *The New Rhetoric: A Treatise on Argumentation* (Notre Dame, 1969) 50f. Cf. D.L. Sullivan, 'Establishing Authority: The Letters of Ignatius of Antioch as Epideictic Rhetoric', *Journal of Communication and Religion* 15 (1992) 71-86 at 72; R.D. Anderson, *Ancient Rhetorical Theory and Paul* (Kampen, 1996) 21.

We have seen that in *c.* 38 the hearer of Andrew's speech is ranked with nature being saved, with the soul crying out what it suffered, with man longing for what is his. This implies that at least within the narrative world of the text, Andrew's speech is meant to encourage people sharing the religious ideas of the apostle[7]. Does this give a clue to the readership intended by the author(s) of the work as a whole? Is the *AA* composed with a view to strengthening the beliefs held within a particular Christian community? It may be noted here that in his postscript (65), the author prays that all those who sympathize with what was said may have communion (*koinônia*) with each other[8]. Was it one of the purposes of the *AA* to further 'a sense of communion' around the ideas attributed to Andrew?

With respect to the content of Andrew's words I add the following observations. No doubt the view of man expressed in Andrew's speeches reminds us of Platonizing and in particular Gnostic ideas about the Godlike nature of the spiritual part of man and its descent into the phenomenal world. But how should we relate this view of man to the short statements about Adam and Eve in the direct context of *c.* 38 (37b and 39a)?

Prieur is right when he argues that the logic of our text requires that Adam and Eve are victims rather than causers of evil. Therefore I surmise that the apostle speaks about the *fate* of the first humans (not about their conduct). In *c.* 39 Andrew affirms that Adam 'died in Eve' but that he, Andrew, now lives 'in' Maximilla. This may not be a reference to sexual union and sexual abstinence, as Prieur sug-

---

[7] It should be noticed that Andrew's long speech from the cross in *cc.* 56-8 is directed explicitly to a broader audience: 'When Andrew had said these things, he addressed a general speech (*koinos logos*) to everyone, for even the gentiles had come together...' (56). Perhaps the middle part of Andrew's speech to Maximilla can be compared to the long Gnostic insertion in the *Acts of John*. As P.J. Lalleman, *The Acts of John: A Two Stage Initiation into Johannine Gnosticism* (Leuven, 1998) argues, in the *AJ* we find a combination of sections destined for a general public (the Asian episodes of the main part of the book) and a section intended for a more or less closed group of Christians who are further initiated into the mysteries of Christ (the Gospel-like insertion, *cc.* 94-102).

[8] From his cross, Andrew anticipates a future meeting (*sunodos*) of his many spiritual relatives (63.10). Does this passage refer to some kind of social (liturgical?) meeting in which the communion of souls was celebrated?

gests[9], but to the creation of Eve. The tacit supposition then is that the division of the pre-Paradisiac Adam into two human beings of different sex is the real cause of the fateful condition (the 'fall') of humankind[10]. In that case salvation could be viewed as a symbolic return to the perfect state of the first human being: as a return, that is, to asexual unity and completeness. The separation of Adam and Eve is restored by Andrew and Maximilla in as much as they make a beginning with the re-union of spiritual humankind.

Indeed it is Andrew's mission to remind the individual souls of their true nature and so to reunite them with their *suggeneis* and with God[11]. In his words his own Godlike inner man becomes transparent[12]. In effect these words are supposed to function as a mirror in which the addressees recognize their own true nature[13].

One final observation is in order. The inner man is regarded as God's gift or as a 'deposit (*parakatathêkê*)' (11-12). As such it should be protected from pollutions and abuses. So in Andrew's message the concept of the inner man includes an ethical notion: the possession of God's gift obliges man to live in conformity with this

---

[9] Prieur, *Acta Andreae*, 205.
[10] This is a well-known topic in Gnostic writings. See in particular the beginning of the *Revelation of Adam* (Nag Hamm. cod. V.5, p.64,20ff), *Gospel of Thomas*, saying 11 (cod. II.2, p.34,22-25), and *Gospel of Philip*, par. 78-79 (cod. II.3, p.60,9-22).
[11] See further Bovon, this volume, Ch. VII.
[12] In his address to Stratocles in *c*. 43, Andrew qualifies his words as 'the words which are akin (*suggeneis*) to myself'.
[13] Cf. Maximilla's reaction to Andrew' words: 'she became what the words signified' (42). Interestingly, the inner man is imagined as posing existential questions and talking to Andrew, who in affectionate words speaks about the 'child' his addressee is bearing. In *c*. 7 the apostle says to Stratocles: 'What you are birthing, I desire; what you keep to yourself, I love; what is within you, I will bring up'. In his address to Stratocles in *c*. 42, the idea of a *koinônia* of individual souls is even more strongly expressed. Here the apostle poses such rhetorical questions as: 'Do I find myself in you? Is there someone in you... whom I see as my own? Does he love the one who has spoken in me (*i.e.* Andrew's inner man) and does he wish to be in communion (*koinônêsai*) with him? Does he wish to be united with him?... Does he long to be yoked with him (*suzugênai*)?' Cf. also the conclusion of this speech, where the apostle remarks: '"No", says the man in you who once again started to weep'.

gift[14]. God's gift continues to belong to God. When it is brought back to God, He will give, in exchange for this, himself: 'I will give you myself. All that I am, I give also to my own' (12). Ideally (or in the future), therefore, the relationship with God is reciprocal: God possesses the inner man, and the inner man shall possess God. 'You have me with all that is mine and all that is mine belongs to you' (12)[15].

2. *The provenance of the inner man concept*

In ancient literature we find a few famous occurrences of the idea of an inner man: first of all, in Plato, *Politeia* IX.589A,B (*ho entos anthrôpos*); further in the New Testament, 2 Cor 4.16 and Eph 3.16 (*ho esô anthrôpos*)[16]. But it is far from plausible that the tradition included in the *AA* is directly dependent on any of these texts[17]. Theoretically, it is much more likely that this expression belonged to the Platonic *koine* of the time and as such was understandable to the audiences intended by Paul and by the author(s) of the *AA*[18].

It should be observed, however, that in the surviving texts of Middle Platonic and Stoic philosophers, the inner man terminology is strikingly absent. In fact the only philosopher of Platonic lineage who makes use of this concept is Philo of Alexandria[19]. At least this indicates that the concept of the inner man was known in Hellenistic Jewish circles in Alexandria. Actually, Philo and the author(s) of the *AA* make use of the very same variant of the Platonic expression: 'the man within you' (*AA*) and 'the man within us', 'within in each one of us' (Philo)[20].

---

[14] The same can be said about the endowment of the Lord's 'seal (*sphragis*)'. One has to keep this seal distinct from other seals (10-11).
[15] This reciprocity is already realized in Andrew who is said to possess God (*ho ton theon echôn*: 52).
[16] Cf. 1 Petr 3.4, *ho kryptos tês kardias anthrôpos* ('the hidden man of the heart').
[17] Allusions to Paul's letters and to other New Testament texts are very rare in the *AA*.
[18] Paul may have adopted the term 'inner man' from his Corinthian opponents.
[19] Th.K. Heckel, *Der innere Mensch* (Tübingen, 1993).
[20] Philo, *De Plantatione* 42, *De Agricultura* 9 and 108.

The inner man terminology occurs more frequently in Hermetic and Gnostic texts[21]. I mention two instances in the Nag Hammadi writings because these passages are particularly reminiscent of the relevant passages in Andrew's speeches. In *The Letter of Peter to Philip* the voice of the risen Jesus speaks to the disciples: 'the archons fight with *the inner man*. So you shall fight against them in this way...' From the following context it appears that the disciples should fight the evil powers by proclaiming the message of salvation in the world[22]. Just as in Andrew's speeches we find here the idea that the inner man is threatened by evil forces. Moreover, proclaiming the message of salvation in the world in fact is what the apostle Andrew is doing in the *AA*. *The Interpretation of Gnosis* teaches: 'since the body is a temporary dwelling which the rulers and [authorities] have as an abode, *the man within*, [after being] imprisoned in this fabrication, [fell] into [suffering...]'[23].

It is important to note that in the *AA* as well as in the Gnostic texts cited above we are dealing with a later development of the Platonic concept of the inner man. Plato uses the term in connection with his view of the composition of the human soul: the inner man is a metaphor of the highest, intellectual and guiding part of the soul. This is still the case in Philo's texts. In the *AA* and in Gnostic texts, however, the inner man is another word for the Godlike element in human beings. In Gnostic texts, this element in man is also imagined as a spark of divine light. In the conviction of Gnostics, salvation consists in becoming aware of one's divine nature and descent and, eventually, in the return of the light scattered in humankind to its origin in the spiritual world. Indeed several features of the inner man in Andrew's speeches come quite close to the more specific Gnostic idea of the nature and the fate of spiritual humankind. In the end, it is a question of definition whether we should label the inner man concept of the *AA* as Gnostic[24].

---

[21] Heckel, *o.c.*, 79-87. In Hermetic texts, the expression 'the inner man' alternates with 'the essential (*ousiôdês*) man', 'the real (*ontôs*) man', etc.

[22] Nag Hamm. cod. VIII,2, p. 137,20-23.

[23] *NHC* XI,1, p.6.30-35. This text is cited because of its use of the inner man metaphor. The idea of the body as a prison for the spiritual element of man was widespread in Late Antiquity.

[24] Andrew's speeches do not refer to – or presuppose – the Gnostic myth of origins. Note *e.g.* that the apostle does not allude to an inferior creator of the material universe. For a definition of 'gnosis' and 'Gnostics' see Luttikhuizen, 'A Gnostic reading of the *Acts of John*', in Bremmer, *Acts of John*, 119-152 at 123-7.

It is even more difficult to relate the relevant ideas in Andrew's speeches to other early Christian traditions. Here we have to account for our poor knowledge of the many quite diverse Christian groups and convictions in the centuries before the predominance of the great Church. Anyhow, we should be careful in relegating the impact of Platonic ideas on Christian beliefs to a relatively late period. After all, we even find clear traces of Hellenistic 'wisdom' philosophy fostered by Christian believers in Paul's first Letter to the Corinthians, one of the earliest Christian documents. But indeed the many empty spots on our map of early Christianity prevent us from determining more exactly the Christian connection of the inner man concept in Andrew's speeches.

IX. Poimandres and the Acta Andreae

JÁNOS BOLLÓK

According to the *Acts of Andrew*, when – on pressure from the people – Aegeates wanted to free the apostle who was still tied to the cross, Andrew said to the governor as he approached: 'I see you are grief-stricken, you governor, to whom I now speak, while I will disappear. I say to you: you will cry, you will beat your breast and gnash your teeth, you will grieve and despair, you will moan and mourn, and you will prepare yourself to join your relative, the sea. Can you see how madly it is weltering? It is angry that I leave you both' (62). In the apostle's flow of words there is one rather unusual phrase, 'you will prepare yourself to join your relative, the sea', which served as the incentive for writing this short study. Why and on what grounds did the author of the *AA* call him 'the relative of the sea', using the word *syggenês*?

To the best of our knowledge there have only been two attempts to explain this strange selection of words. According to the first, the writer's inventiveness was made possible by the etymological relationship between the names[1]; Aegeates' name is linked to the Aegean Sea, and Patras – the place where the apostle was executed – is located on the shores of the Aegean Sea. The other explanation asserts that the metaphor seeks to emphasize the similarity between Aegeates's state of mind and the stormy sea by making Aegeates into a relative of the sea[2]. In order to determine how well-founded these two proposed interpretations are, we must first examine the way and the contexts in which the author generally uses the word *syggenês*.

---

[1] J.-M. Prieur, *Acta Andreae* (Turnhout, 1989) 546 n. 3, but I do not think that the myth of Aegeus has exercised any influence on this part of the *AA*.
[2] T. Adamik (ed), *Az apostolok csodálatos cselekedetei* (Budapest, 1996) 223 n. 68.

At *AA c.* 4, the magi and the wizards are unable to drive out the demons from Stratocles's servant, since they are *syggeneis* of the demon. Human beings are essentially *syggeneis* 'of the Unbegotten' (38) and one who readily receives the teachings of the apostle is *syggenês* 'of the words'(47). Perhaps it is unnecessary to continue with the examples to see that in the *AA* the author uses the word which originally meant 'relative' in a peculiar way: it stands for 'essentially identical with'. The author of the *AA* proves to be consistent in using the word with this meaning, and the same can be said for the use of its opposite, the word *allotrios*[3]. The 'relative' metaphor, then, is based neither on the use of etymology nor on a similarity of moods, but on the essential identity of Aegeates and the sea. But how exactly does this identity function?

In the various *AAA*, many passages provide the impression that water is one of the demons' favorite locations. This pattern was first noticed by Prieur in a footnote to the translation of Andrew's biography by Gregory of Tours[4]. In Gregory, Gratianus's son is possessed by a demon in a bath (5); the governor and his wife are killed by a *daemon teterrimus* also in a bath (23); the youth from whom the apostle expels an evil demon emerges from a *piscina*. After expelling the demon the apostle sums up the lessons learned from the case for the youth and his companions in the following manner: 'The enemy of the human race is on the watch for us everywhere, in the baths as well as in the rivers. Therefore we should constantly call God's name to help us so that whoever wants to hatch a plot against us cannot have the power over us' (27)[5].

Other examples from *ATh* (32) and *AJ* (5, 122) make it highly unlikely that these stories are Gregory's own creations; in fact, he probably found them as existing narratives in his source or sources. It is also from a bath that the Indian woman in the *ATh* emerges when she meets the demon which will give her no peace of mind for the next five years (24). In none of the examples above is the sea mentioned in any way, but – as we stated earlier – the *balneus*, the *piscina*, the *lavacrum* and the *flumen* all involve water in some way coming into contact with the forces of evil.

---

[3] On those concepts see Prieur, *Acta Andreae*, 311-9.
[4] Prieur, *Acta Andreae*, 578 n. 3.
[5] For demons and water see also Bremmer, this volume, Ch. II.2.

These instances also suggest that the authors of the *AAA* were familiar with some kind of theory in which water – as an element – belonged to the empire of evil. We use the word 'theory', because such an idea could not have come from the field of religious rites nor from the belief of the common people, since in both of these water – including the sea – is considered to be a cleansing and purifying element. Just one example: in the mysteries of Eleusis those who were to be initiated performed their bathing rituals in the sea as well[6]. On the other hand, water, primeval water to be more precise, appears as something bad in the different cosmogonies and cosmologies. The author of Genesis for example refers to primeval water with the word *tehom*, which is etymologically related to the Tiamat of Babylonian cosmology[7]. In order to get closer to solving the secret of the *AA*'s sea metaphor we must place and examine it in a broader context. First we must look at the other metaphors or similes involving Aegeates.

In *c.* 16 the apostle prays for Maximilla: '... my God, Lord Jesus Christ... may your word (*logos*) and power be strong in her, and may the spirit in her overcome Aegeates, the insolent and hostile serpent, and may her soul remain pure, sanctified by your name... put to sleep our wild and ever untamed enemy, her visible husband'. Here Aegeates appears as a serpent, our common enemy. In a later speech – while already on the cross – Andrew calls the governor an 'impudent devil' (63). Still later again, it is not Aegeates but his father whom Andrew calls a devil and a serpent (40). Especially worthy of attention is the part where the apostle states that Aegeates is substantially identical with his (apostle's) body (39).

In the author's eyes, Aegeates is the incarnation of evil, and as such, he describes him sometimes as 'devil', sometimes as 'serpent', 'son of the serpent', 'son of the devil', 'relative of the sea' or 'substantially identical with his body'. There is nothing curious about the fact that he uses the same phrases to describe those servants who have betrayed Maximilla.

Can we identify the intellectual milieu in which to locate these ideas? In *c.* 11 Andrew gives a detailed list of the forces of evil

---

[6] R. Parker, *Miasma* (Oxford, 1983) 283.
[7] B. Alster, 'Tiamat', in K. van der Toorn *et al.* (eds), *Dictionary of Deities and Demons in the Bible* (Leiden, 1995) 1634-9.

which control people and which are also involved in their physical selves:

> If you guard this impression, my children, which does not admit of other seals that impress the opposite symbols, God will praise you and receive you to his own. When such a vision appears clearly in your souls, especially those that are released from their bodies, the punishing powers and evil authorities (*exousiai kakai*) and fiery angels (*archontes deinoi*) and wicked demons and filthy operations which cannot bear to be overtaken by you, since they do not belong to the symbol of the seal which is related to light, creep away in flight and sink down into darkness, fire and fog, that is related to them, and whatever meditates promise of punishment.

One might ask, if the elements of this list – darkness, fire and fog – are random, owing purely to the author's attraction to rhetoric, or whether they constitute some kind of order.

Two elements of the list, *exousiai* and *archontes*, can also be found in the New Testament[8]. As for the other ones, we need to look at the first piece of the *Corpus Hermeticum*, *Poimandres*, where the unknown prophet starts talking about his vision as follows:

> Having said this, it changed in appearance. Immediately, all became disclosed to me in a moment, and I saw an indeterminate vision. All turned into calm and gracious light; and seeing it, I felt a burning desire. And after a little while there was a downward-tending darkness, which had come into being in one place; it was frightful and gloomy, and was coiled like a serpent, so far as I could make out. Then the darkness changed into a kind of moist nature, which was unspeakably jumbled and gave off smoke, as from a fire. And it produced a kind of non-verbal mournful sound. Then a cry was inarticulately emitted from it, so as to seem like a voice of <fire>' (4)[9].

In this part of the firmly dualist cosmology of *Poimandres*, which deals with the birth of the principles antagonistic to Nous, 'Spirit', one can find all the basic elements – darkness, fire, serpent, steam and fog – which, according to the author of the *AA*, are related to the Evil Forces. Darkness, the oldest form of Chaos, first appears resem-

---

[8] I Cor 2.6, 15.24; Eph 1.21, 2.2; I Petr 3.22. For those powers see W. Foerster, '*exousiai*', *TWNT* II. 568-70.

[9] A.D. Nock and A.-J. Festugière, *Corpus Hermeticum* I (Paris, 1972³) 7-31, tr. B. Layton, *The Gnostic Scriptures* (New York, 1991) 452-9.

bling a serpent and, subsequently, turns into a moist nature. This in turn reemerges in Poimandres' revelation as the key element of the Empire of Death, or the flesh. '...tell me, why are those in death worthy of death?', asks the prophet (20). 'Because the prior source of each individual body is the gloomy darkness, out of which came the moist nature, out of which within the perceptible world has been put together the body, by which is fostered death' (20), answers Poimandres.

On reading the *AA*, it may be worthwhile for us to see how, according to *Poimandres*, the sea comes into being. Because of the submerging divine Logos, fire and air leave the Chaos, rise up to the Logos, and the sea and the earth remain beneath together in such a way that the earth can not be seen because of the sea.

> And from the light... holy reason (*logos*) descended upon the natural order. And unmixed fire leaped up out of the moist nature upward into the heights. It was buoyant and bright, and at the same time, active. And air, being light in weight, followed spirit, as it descended from earth and water to the fire, so that it seemed to hang from it. And earth and water were left by themselves, mixed together so that <earth> could not be contemplated apart from water' (5).

The connections of this text with the Old Testament are unimportant for our problem[10]. It is more noteworthy that in *Poimandres*' cosmology water and Logos do not even come in contact with each other. That is why water nurtures death.

Poimandres regards fire as a means of punishment via an avenging demon. According to Poimandres, the Spirit (*Nous*) is the guard of the devout, but He evades those who commit sins. The Spirit, then, stays out of the way of the avenging demon who rouses the fire in those who commit sins (23)[11].

Although they appear in both works, we will not touch on the various, well-known motifs of sleep, drunkenness, and frenzy. However, we will note two analogies that have to do with the choice of words in *Poimandres* and the *AA*. First, hanging on the cross the

---

[10] B. Pearson, 'Jewish Elements in *Corpus Hermeticum* I (*Poimandres*)', in R. van den Broek and M.J. Vermaseren (eds), *Studies in Gnosticism and Hellenistic Religion* (Leiden, 1981) 336-48.

[11] On guarding and punishing demons see A. Dieterich, *Abraxas* (Leipzig, 1891) 34-5 and *Nekyia* (Leipzig, 1905) 54-62.

apostle says to his disciples: 'If you believe that this nocturnal light (*nykterinon phôs*) is the only one that exists, and there is nothing else above that, then, truly, you are all children of this night' (56). Poimandres delivers the following words to the worthy: 'Depart from the darksome light (*skoteinou phôtos*), share in immortality, give up corruption!' (28). *Skoteinon* and *nykterinon phôs* mean the same: perceptible light as opposed to true, godly light.

Secondly, before the apostle is sentenced to death, Stratocles says to him: 'but when I seek your care and love hereafter, where or in whom am I to find it? The seeds of the saving words I have received, with you being for me the sower; but for them to sprout and grow up needs no other, than you, most blessed Andrew' (44)[12]. This utterance is generally traced back to the 'seedsower parable', but some traces of the parable can already be found in Philo Alexandrinus[13], as also in *Poimandres*. *Poimandres*'s apostle tells us that, after his enlightenment he began teaching the people: he sowed his words amongst them (29) and many people fell on their knees, asking him to teach them. As there is no such request in the New Testament, we can conclude that the *AA* is closer to *Poimandres* than to the New Testament's parable, not only in its phrasing, but also in its overall theme.

In our comparison we have concentrated only on the manifestations of evil forces, amongst which the similarities between the *AA* and *Poimandres* are conspicuous. As the *Poimandres* probably dates from the Alexandrian milieu of the first or early second century[14], its half-Platonic, half-Gnostic lines of thought clearly influenced the author of the *AA*[15]. This aspect of *Poimandres* well illustrates the colourful and multi-layered intellectual arena in which the *AAA* came into being.

---

[12] For the importance of the 'saving words' see Bovon, this volume, Ch. VII.
[13] A.-J. Festugière, *La révélation d'Hermès Trismégiste* II (Paris, 1949²) 529ff; note also A.F.J. Klijn, *The Acts of Thomas* (Leiden, 1962) 198.
[14] G. Fowden, *The Egyptian Hermes* (Princeton, 1993²) 161f.
[15] For these influences see also Bovon, this volume, Ch. VII; Schroeder, this volume, Ch. X.

X. Embracing the Erotic in the Passion of Andrew. The Apocryphal Acts of Andrew, the Greek Novel, and Platonic Philosophy

CAROLINE T. SCHROEDER

There has been a wave of recent scholarship on the social repercussions of desire in the Greek novels[1]. Classicists and historians alike have argued that in the romances of the first through third centuries, sexual desire is most successfully consummated in heterosexual relationships either within or leading to the bonds of marriage and functions to provide a sense of social stability. With marriage comes the production of children, the maintenance of lines of inheritance within a certain social class, and the prosperity of the lovers' communities. Through marriage, Longus' Daphnis and Chloe are restored to their proper heritage and the state is restored to its proper leaders. Through marriage Chariton's Chaereas and Callirhoe recon-

---

[1] D. Konstan, *Sexual Symmetry: Love in the Ancient Novel and Related Genres* (Princeton, 1994); J. Winkler, "The Invention of Romance', in J. Tatum (ed), *The Search for the Ancient Novel* (Baltimore and London, 1994) 23-38; J. Perkins, *The Suffering Self: Pain and Narrative Representation in the Early Christian Era* (London and New York, 1995) 41-76; K. Cooper, *The Virgin and the Bride* (Cambridge MA, 1996) 20-44. I rely primarily on the five major Greek novels believed to have been written during the first three centuries C.E.: Achilles Tatius' *Leucippe and Cleitophon*, Chariton's *Chaereas and Callirhoe*, Longus' *Daphnis and Chloe*, Xenophon of Ephesus' *An Ephesian Tale*, Heliodorus' *An Ethiopian Story*. English translations of these and additional novels may be found in B.P. Reardon (ed), *Collected Ancient Greek Novels* (Berkeley, 1989). All English translations cited here are taken from Reardon's volume.

cile the two leading families of their city-state. As Kate Cooper has argued, 'The love that aspired to marriage involved the temporary disruption of the social order which led to its reassertion; other forms of love might put the individual's interests against the common good'[2]. In Judith Perkins' imagery, the *concordia* of the romantic couple parallels the *concordia* of the state[3]. Desire properly expressed and properly consummated serves the stability of the society, and particularly the wealthy, propertied, high-status fraction of society. '[T]he ancient romance was designed to mobilize this complicity in desire on behalf of the social order'[4]. True love can be found only within the confines of proper, upper-class marriage, which in turn is required to ensure the equilibrium of the larger community.

The type of love that dominates the novels and drives desire is *eros*. *Eros* brings the couple together, maintains their fidelity through adventure and tragedy, and expresses itself through the marriage and passionate lovemaking of the couple. This is made most explicit at the opening of the tales. The deity *Eros* himself begins most of the novels, either by sparking the relationship or by acting as the patron god who stands as a symbol for the story as a whole. In *Chaereas and Callirhoe*, *Eros* decides to find the heroine a match (1.1). In the *Ephesian Tale*, the young Habrocomes' initial refusal to recognize *Eros* as a god prompts *Eros* to intervene in his life and cause him to fall in love with the young Anthia (1.1-2). The narrator of *Leucippe and Cleitophon* begins with an ekphrasis of a mural in Sidon, focussing on the image of *Eros* (1.1-2). Longus, also remarking on a painting depicting love, dedicates his book 'as an offering to Love (Eros), the Nymphs, and Pan' (Prologue).

Historians of early Christianity have directed their analyses of the novel toward comparisons with the *AAA*. The parallels between the two groups of literature are generally acknowledged: the hero's and heroine's desire for each other, their subsequent separation from each other, frequent travel narratives, the hero's and heroine's fidelity to each other, the high social status of the women, and the

---

[2] Cooper, *The Virgin*, 35.
[3] Perkins, *The Self*, 48.
[4] Cooper, *The Virgin*, 21.

eventual reunion of hero and heroine[5]. The *AAA* employ the same plot devices as the novels, but they center on an apostle and his convert(s) rather than a young romantic couple. Cooper and Perkins both have argued that the *AAA* use these elements of the Greek novels to subvert what the central goal of the novel: social stability. Instead of advocating marriage, they use the relationship between apostle and convert to champion sexual abstinence. Perkins has argued that the promotion of chastity in the *Acts* disrupted traditional marriage in the ancient world and implicitly challenged the social structure for which marriage was the foundation in the Greek novels[6]. The *AAA*, with their emphasis on sexual renunciation, subvert the novels' 'happy ending' of marriage and social stability. Cooper, too, has argued that they disrupt the link between the married couple and the state: 'Thus we move from a celebration of sexuality in the service of social continuity to a denigration of sexuality in the service of a challenge to the establishment'. Furthermore, Cooper regards the specific practice of sexual abstinence itself as subordinate to this larger, counter-social narrative[7].

While this kind of analysis has reanimated the study of the Greek novels and the *AAA*, it tends to neglect the erotic elements of the *Acts* and in particular the final segment of the *AA*, known as the *Passion of Andrew*[8]. For in the *Passion of Andrew*, as in the novels, only the

---

[5] The most succinct and comprehensive comparison of the novel and Apocryphal Acts can be found in J.-D. Kaestli's response to V. Burrus, *Semeia* 38 (1986) 119-31. A somewhat unconvincing counter-argument can be found in Burrus' response to Kaestli, *Semeia* 38 (1986) 132-35. Cooper and Perkins also find shared elements in these two literary forms; see Cooper, 45-46, and Perkins, 25-26. One of the earliest arguments for this connection is R. Söder, *Die apokryphen Apostelgeschichten und die romanhafte Literatur der Antike* (Stuttgart, 1932).

[6] Perkins, *The Self*, 28-29.

[7] Cooper, *The Virgin*, 55, 57.

[8] The text now called the *Passion of Andrew* circulated independently from other narratives about Andrew and contains an account of the apostle's martyrdom. Much ink has been spilled over the relationship between the *Passion of Andrew*, a presumably longer set of *AA* which includes the *Passion*, the *Acts of Andrew and Matthias*, and Gregory's epitome of the *AA*. J.-M. Prieur has argued that the *AA* and the *Acts of Andrew and Matthias* come from two separate textual traditions, whereas D.R. MacDonald has argued that the *Acts of Andrew and Matthias* originally formed a part of the text of the *AA*; but see now Hilhorst and Lalleman, this volume, Ch. I. Addition-

proper expression of love produces positive results. While Cooper may be accurate in characterizing the *AA* as a 'denigration of sexuality', one must be careful not to elide that with a denigration of love or *eros* [9]. In the *Passion of Andrew*, the *eros* of the novels becomes the Platonic *eros* – the love of beauty, the one, the divine.

The *Passion of Andrew* tells of the apostle's arrival into the town of Patras, his performance of several miracles, and his conversions of the elite Stratocles and Maximilla to an ascetic Christianity. Maximilla's close relationship with Andrew and her new adherence to sexual renunciation enrage her prominent pagan husband, Aegeates, who has Andrew killed and then kills himself. Whereas the novels always end with union of the lovers and the fulfillment of their desire, in the *Passion of Andrew*, the consummation of erotic desire appears permanently deferred. Several potential erotic couples are presented: Aegeates and Maximilla, Andrew and Maximilla, and Andrew and Stratocles. None of the couples achieve the sexual and marital union extolled in the novels; instead, the text ends with the deaths of Andrew and Aegeates and the conversion of Maximilla and Stratocles to an ascetic Christianity. Although sex is condemned in

---

ally, the existence of a lengthy *AA* that includes the martyrdom account in the *Passion of Andrew* is based solely on the existence of fragments of stories about Andrew that circulated with all or part of the martyrdom account and the existence of Gregory's epitome, which describes a larger *AA* text. No one text incorporating all of these diverse acts of Andrew survives. Since the *Passion of Andrew* circulated separately and is the most widely attested Andrew tradition, I treat it as a somewhat distinct textual unit regardless of its lost origins. For descriptions of the manuscript and textual traditions, see Prieur, in *NTA* II, 104-10; MacDonald, *The Acts of Andrew and The Acts of Andrew and Matthias* (Atlanta, 1990) 1-51. Furthermore, the *Passion of Andrew* is the most widely attested of the apocryphal legends surrounding Andrew. Almost all of the Greek texts of the *AA* include a portion or a complete version of the martyrdom account, the Latin texts all attest to the martyrdom story, and an Armenian account of the last part of the *Passion of Andrew* exists, as well, cf. *NTA* II, 104-6; J.K. Elliott, *The Apocryphal New Testament* (Oxford, 1993) 232-34; Calzolari, this volume, Ch. XIII. Unfortunately, its date and provenance are in dispute. Both Prieur and MacDonald argue that the *Acts* were written between 150 and 200, but the possibilities for its location of origin range from Greece to Syria to Egypt to Asia Minor, cf. MacDonald, *The Acts of Andrew* 55-59; Prieur, in *NTA* II, 114-15; Bremmer, this volume, Ch. II.

[9] Cooper, *The Virgin*, 55.

the *AA*, love certainly is not[10]. In fact, love, its objects, its expression, and its culmination are central elements in the text. The definition of proper love and the goals of such love, however, diverge greatly from the novels. Maximilla and Stratocles do consummate their love by the narrative's end. Neither Maximilla nor Stratocles engages in physical intercourse with their beloved, but their sojourn with Andrew does not end with tragic separation. It closes instead with joyous union, the union of the soul with the divine.

The *Passion of Andrew* presents an intriguing nexus of Greek romanticism and Platonic philosophy; it relies upon generic elements from the Hellenistic novels but reworks them using elements of Platonic philosophy to present a radically different vision of the consummation of love and desire. The erotic love of the novels is consummated in sexual passion, marriage, and procreation. Love in the *Passion of Andrew* does culminate in the heroine's union with her beloved, but the beloved is the figure of the divine, to whom both Maximilla and Stratocles are introduced by their teacher Andrew and with whom they give birth to their new, perfected selves. Andrew is the erotic stand-in for the divine lover. The results of true love and properly oriented desire in the *Passion of Andrew* are Platonic objectives: an understanding of the inner self, a unification with the divine, and a lasting sense of peace and rest. Although the relationships between the characters resemble relationships between the hero and heroines of the novels, the product of their love is a Platonic one.

Maximilla's and Stratocles' relationships with the apostle Andrew are described with language and metaphors reminiscent of the *eros* presented in the Greek novels. Although the *Passion of Andrew* rarely uses *eros*, preferring terms such as *storgê* or *agapê*, the context of the relationships parallels the novels and suggests an 'erotic' element. Yet, in the *Passion of Andrew*, true love becomes the Platonic *eros*, the love of beauty, the one, the divine. Early in the text, Stratocles first encounters Andrew when the apostle heals his

---

[10] D. Konstan, 'Acts of Love: A Narrative Pattern in the Apocryphal Acts', *JECS* 6 (1998) 15-36 also has taken to task scholars who have argued that the *AAA* uniformly critique the institutions of marriage and family, noting that the apostles frequently perform miracles that function to unite family members and loved ones rather than separate them. Of the *AA*, Konstan writes, 'The apostle does not destroy human bonds of affection, except insofar as they necessarily involve sex' (20).

servant (5)[11]. Andrew then tells Stratocles that he will assist him in giving birth to his 'new self'. Of particular interest is Stratocles' response to Andrew's gestures. In an oath similar to the oaths of fidelity the lovers in the novels swear to one another, Stratocles declares, 'I too will not separate from you', but then adds the philosophical condition, 'until I recognize myself' (8). Stratocles vows to remain with Andrew until Andrew's promise can be fulfilled. Then the story recounts: 'Stratocles was with the apostle night and day and never left him, sometimes examining, learning from, and interrupting him, and other times remaining silent and enjoying himself, having truly become enamored (*philos*) of saving attentiveness' (8). Stratocles, thus, cultivates a certain affection in the presence of Andrew. Although this emotion is not the *eros* of the novel, it is a fondness that strongly parallels the passions of the lovers of the novel: Stratocles immediately feels this attachment for Andrew after their first encounter, Stratocles avows his faithfulness to Andrew, and Stratocles spends all of his time with Andrew. Near the end of the *Passion*, Stratocles returns to this theme, naming Andrew his true love: 'I have the one I sought. I have found the one I desired (*epothoun*). I hold the one I loved' (*egapon*: 43). Yet Andrew's and Stratocles' intercourse is not passionate lovemaking but a Socratic dialogue: questioning, examining, learning.

Other characters in the *Passion of Andrew* also mistake Maximilla's relationship with Andrew for an erotic one. Maximilla's servants are aware of her and Stratocles' secret nightly visits to Andrew and threaten to tell her husband, presumably because they believe she is having a sexual relationship with Andrew (20). When Aegeates learns of Maximilla's association with Andrew, he asks her if she is having an affair. He extols her chastity and promises forgiveness if she has 'tarnished' it. He begs, 'So if you are keeping some secret from me about another man – something I never would have suspected....[O]r if there is something else even more serious than this that separates you from me, confess it and I will quickly remedy the situation' (23) Maximilla responds that she is in love with another, but that he could not understand such a love: 'I am in love,

---

[11] The edition used throughout can be found in J.-M. Prieur, *Acta Andreae*, 2 vls (Turhout, 1989). All quotations are from MacDonald's English translation.

Aegeates. I am in love, and the object of my love is not of this world and therefore is imperceptible to you. Night and day it kindles and enflames me with love (*storgê*) for it' (23). Maximilla confirms Aegeates' fears that she loves someone else, but she corrects him, as well, telling him that the *eros* of the novels is not the kind of love he must worry about. Nonetheless, Aegeates' remains enraged after his servant reports, 'My mistress...became acquainted with this stranger. She has so given way to desire for him that she loves no one more than him, including you I would say. Not only has she become intimately involved with the man, she has tied up your brother Stratocles with the same passion (*pothos*) for him that has tied her up' (25). As Cooper recognizes, Aegeates and Andrew seem to be in competition against each other for Maximilla's affection[12]. What requires further consideration, however, is the confluence of Aegeates' explicitly sexual accusations with Maximilla's distinctly philosophic discourse.

For Maximilla's association with Andrew results not in physical intercourse with the apostle but the cessation of physical intercourse with Aegeates. After baptism, Maximilla prays to be kept from his "filthy intercourse' (14). Andrew, too, prays for the preservation of Maximilla's purity: 'In particular, protect her, O Master, from this disgusting pollution. With respect to our savage and ever boorish enemy, cause her to sleep apart from her visible husband and wed her to her inner husband, whom you above all recognize, and for whose sake the entire mystery of your plan of salvation has been accomplished' (16). Andrew uses the very language of marriage to describe Maximilla's new state: she will no longer be married to Aegeates but to another, non-earthly personage. This marriage language mimics that of the Greek novels but at the same time undermines it. Maximilla's true love is not a human person, but an inner husband. But as with a corporeal husband, Maximilla wishes to unite with it: '[Y]ou cannot separate me from it, for that is impossible. Let me have intercourse (*proshomilein*) and take my rest with it alone' (23) Aegeates eventually confronts Andrew, demanding, 'Teach me too about your renown and what sort of power you have, such that you have lovers (*erastas*), so I hear, who are rich and poor, including infants, even though you appear in this manner like a simple old tramp' (26) Here the connection between Andrew and *eros* is most explicit: Aegeates only

---

[12] Cooper, *The Virgin*, 48-49.

can understand Andrew's relationships with his converts as erotic. Aegeates misunderstands the erotic element as sexual; instead, it is philosophic – the Platonic *eros* or love of the divine.

While the interactions between the main characters in the *Passion of Andrew* resemble those in the novels, they also resemble Platonic writings. Two distinct Platonic dialogues frame the entire *Passion of Andrew*. The first dialogue – as do most of the scenes between Andrew, Maximilla, and Stratocles in the first third of the *Passion* – takes place in Maximilla's bedroom, the location of previous erotic activity between her and her husband. In the beginnings of the novels, as well, the heroine's bedrooms were frequently sites of the consummation, or attempted consummation, of the lovers' desire for each other. Maximilla's bedroom, however, shifts from a location of sexual intercourse to philosophic discourse through which Maximilla and Andrew are not only converted to Christianity but somehow transformed. At the beginning of the *Passion*, Maximilla emerges from her bedroom to greet Stratocles. They enter her bedroom together and remain there for some portion of the evening[13]. Maximilla leaves her bedroom when Andrew heals Stratocles's servant (2-5). Then she leads the two of them and their companions back into her bedroom, (6) where Andrew begins the first of several dialogues that have been compared to the philosophic dialogues of Socrates[14]. Andrew tells Stratocles:

> I must bring out into the open the person now latent within you. Your total bewilderment and pondering of the source and cause of what has happened are the greatest proofs that the soul within you is troubled.... Bring to birth the child you are carrying and do not give yourself over to labor pains alone. I am no novice at midwifery or divination. I desire what you are birthing. I love what you are stifling. I will suckle what is within you....Already your new self speaks to me (7).

Andrew uses the language of birth to describe the transformative process Stratocles will undergo as a result of his conversion. As

---

[13] Immediately after reporting that Maximilla 'entered with him' into her bedroom the text reads that Maximilla was alone 'at daybreak' while Stratocles visited his friends (1).

[14] K.C. Wagener, '"Repentant Eve, Perfected Adam": Conversion in *The Acts of Andrew*', in E.H. Lovering, Jr. (ed), *SBL Seminar Papers 30* (Atlanta, 1991) 348-56 at 352-53; D.R. MacDonald, *Christianizing Homer* (New York, 1994) 252.

MacDonald has noted, the model for this dialogue seems to be Socrates' speech in Plato's *Theaetetus*. Socrates refers to himself as the son of a midwife, as well, and compares his work in eliciting the birth of the self to a midwife's work eliciting the birth of a child. In this way Andrew represents a Christianized Socrates[15]. Later, Andrew returns to the metaphor of childbirth to describe Stratocles' transformation. The apostle compares Stratocles' constant questioning of Andrew to the labor pains of a woman in childbirth and exhorts him to exhibit them publicly as if giving birth among attending women:

> It is not right for you to conceal your labor pains even from your peers. Take the example of a woman in labor: When the labor pains overcome her and the fetus is pressured by some power to come forth – not to stay within but to be squeezed outside – the fetus becomes obvious and noticeable to the attending women who take part in such mysteries....Then, postpartum, these initiates at last provide for the newborn whatever care they know, so that, insofar as it is up to them, the fetus might be born alive. Likewise, Stratocles my child, we too must not be passive but bring your embryos into the open, so that they may be registered and be brought to the donative of saving words by many kindred (9).

The product of Andrew's relationship with Stratocles parallels one of the primary products of true love in the novels: offspring. Just as the recognition of children signifies the stability of family and society in the novel, so does the recognition of Stratocles' new self signify salvific effects for him and his companions[16].

The Platonic elements of the dialogue also can be linked to the erotic themes and settings in the larger work. The birthing imagery resonates with both Platonic philosophy and the Greek novels. The dialogue is presented in Maximilla's bedroom, or *koitôn*[17]. It is situated in the same physical space as the sexual act that results in physical birth. The product of Andrew's relationship with Stratocles parallels one of the primary products of true love in the Greek novels:

---

[15] MacDonald, *Christianizing Homer*, 218-20.
[16] The communal aspect of birthing has been noted by Wagener, "'Repentant Eve, Perfected Adam",' 353.
[17] MacDonald, *Christianizing Homer*, 217 acknowledges this as one of the more sexually suggestive words that could have been used to describe her chambers.

offspring. Stratocles later reveals that it is Andrew who has inseminated him. Soon before the apostle's martyrdom, Stratocles again professes his attachment to Andrew and grieves Andrew's death. 'But after this, where and in whom will I seek and find your concern and love (*storgê*)? I received the seeds of the words of salvation while you were my sower; for them to shoot up and reproduce requires no one else but you, blessed Andrew' (44) Andrew has impregnated Stratocles, and soon Stratocles will give birth to the true self to whom Andrew alluded in his first dialogue in Maximilla's bedroom. Despite the obvious sexual overtones in all of these scenes, both desire and its effects are not of the physical realm. The *Passion of Andrew* reorients love and desire to the Platonic goals of self-knowledge, union with the divine, and the creation of the new self, away from the novels' goals of marriage, children, social stability.

Maximilla's bedroom also becomes the location of spiritual transformation in explicit contrast with Aegeates' view of the bedroom as the location of marital sexual intercourse. Aegeates returns home before Andrew and his companions have left Maximilla's bedroom. Recognizing the impropriety of the situation, Andrew miraculously covers everyone with a shield of invisibility while they exit (13). It is in Maximilla's bedroom that Aegeates approaches Maximilla for sex and is rebuffed (14). Then, it is there that Aegeates threatens to torture Andrew unless Maximilla resumes her marital obligations (36). Finally, it is in her bedroom that she recruits her slave to sleep with Aegeates in her place (17). Significantly, her slave's sexual encounters with Aegeates never occur in Maximilla's bedroom, but always Aegeates' bedroom. Maximilla's room represents a space that used to be devoted to sexual desire but has been transformed.

The second Platonic dialogue, a rewriting of the *Phaedo*, appears near the end of the text while Andrew awaits his martyrdom in prison. As MacDonald has noted, both Socrates and Andrew converse with their followers in jail before their executions, both laugh in the face of death, and both speak to their followers on the nature of death as the separation of soul and body[18]. Yet the prominence of

---

[18] See MacDonald, *Christianizing Homer*, 274 for a summary of his view of the similarities between the *Phaedo* and the *Passion of Andrew*.

love and desire in Andrew's discourse also is significant. Andrew begins his speech instructing Stratocles not to interfere in the apostle's execution and warns him not to become too 'attached to mere appearances' (53). When Andrew arrives at the cross on which he will be crucified, he addresses his followers:

> [I]f you suppose this act of dying is the end of ephemeral life, leave this place at once. If you understand the conjunction of the soul with a body to be the soul itself, so that after the separation (of the two) nothing at all exists, you possess the intelligence of animals... And if you love immediate pleasures and pursue them above all, in order to enjoy their fruits exclusively, you are like thieves... What benefit is there for you who gain for yourselves external goods but do not gain your very selves?... And why do we desire pleasure and childbearing, for later we have to separate?... Follow after my deep-seated love. Learn of my sufferings about which I am now speaking with you... I greet you with the grace of God and with love which is due him' (56-8)

Andrew's speech draws upon Socrates' exhortation to avoid the passions and his description of death as the separation of the soul from the body in the *Phaedo* (9, 13). For Socrates, the passions of the body distract the philosopher from the contemplation of the truth (10). Andrew implicitly replaces such desires with another desire – that of the soul for God. True love is the soul's contemplation of the divine. The *Passion of Andrew* deliberately combines the two themes of Platonic self-knowledge and physical procreation to introduce a decidedly Christian notion of desire: the redeployment of physical love to the divine, resulting in salvation.

Andrew instructs Maximilla, as well, to orient her love toward its proper object. She consults the apostle after Aegeates delivers an ultimatum: if she returns to her husband, resumes having sex with him, and bears his children, he will spare Andrew's life. (36) She and a friend visit Andrew in prison, and he encourages Maximilla to remain strong in her faith:

> I know that you too have been moved to resist any proposition of sexual intercourse and wish to be disassociated from a foul and filthy way of life....Do not submit to Aegeates' threat....I rightly see in you Eve repenting and in me Adam converting. For what she suffered through ignorance, you – whose soul I seek – must now redress through conversion. The very thing suffered by the mind (*nous*) which was brought down with her and slipped away from itself, I make right with you, through your recognition that you are being raised up. You healed her

deficiency by not experiencing the same passions, and I have perfected Adam's imperfection by fleeing to God for refuge. What Eve disobeyed, you obeyed; what Adam agreed to, I flee; the things that tripped them up, we have recognized. For it is ordained that each person correct his or her own fall (37).

Maximilla's rejection of sexual passion with her husband will assist her soul in its return to its true self. Because she refuses to unite her body with her husband's, her soul can unite with the divine. Andrew narrates the fall in a Platonic framework[19]. The *nous* has fallen away from its original unity with the divine into a bodily existence it then seeks to transcend in order to return to the divine. Soon after this, Andrew speaks of escaping his own body. Responding to Maximilla's grief at his impending martyrdom at the hands of Aegeates, the apostle retorts, 'So what? Let him destroy this body as he will, for it is only one body and it is akin to him [Aegeates]' (29) The return of the soul to its true self is associated with the transcendence of the soul from realm of the body and the passions.

Another frequently recurring theme in the dialogues is that of rest and motion. When Maximilla confesses her love for another to Aegeates, she wishes both to have intercourse with it and take rest in it. While urging Maximilla to preserve her chastity, Andrew exhorts Maximilla 'to pursue things that are stable, and to flee from all that undulates' (47) He recalls that everything in the current life is 'in flux'; if they maintain their faith in God they will be able to find rest (48) Immediately before his death, he returns to this theme, chastising his followers for wishing that he would not die. 'Why this excessive fondness for the flesh? Why this great complicity with it? Do you again encourage me to be put back among things in flux? If you understood that I have been loosened from ropes but tied up to myself, you yourselves would have been eager to be loosened from the many and to be tied to the one' (61) Additionally, the disorder of Aegeates household – the slave's replacement of Maximilla as Aegeates' lover, the execution of servants, Aegeates constant anger

---

[19] As Wagener, '"Repentant Eve, Perfected Adam",' 353 has observed, Maximilla and Andrew become the heirs to the first couple, Adam and Eve, whose fall away from God prefigured all others: 'For Andrew, the present scenario is a reenactment of the Paradise drama, with himself and Maximilla as the primal human beings'. For more on the neo-Platonic parallels to this account of the fall, see the discussion of Plotinus below.

over Maximilla's behavior – contrasts strongly with the peace and equilibrium in the presence of Andrew. The earthly world is connected with motion, disturbance, and the desires of the flesh. The world of the divine, in contrast, is characterized by rest, unity, and true love – the love for God. Thus, true love leads to the soul's separation from the body, its unity with the divine, and a state of rest.

The philosophy in the *Passion of Andrew* has parallels in the neo-Platonic writings of Plotinus that were composed during the period when the *Passion* began circulating widely[20]. In the *Enneads*, Plotinus writes that the good or virtuous life is 'concerned with the soul and is an activity of the soul' (1.4.14)[21], requiring a 'separation from the body and despising of its so-called goods' (1.4.14). He argues:

> Since the soul is evil when it is thoroughly mixed with the body and shares its experiences and has all the same opinions it will be good and possess virtue when it no longer has the same opinions but acts alone…and is not afraid of departing the body – this is courage – and is ruled by reason and intellect without opposition – and this is justice (1.2.3).

[20] Plotinus lived from approximately 205 to 270 C.E. The *AA* seems to have achieved popularity in the third and fourth centuries. Eusebius has knowledge of a text he calls the *AA*; the Manichean psalm-book mentions Andrew, his crucifixion, and Maximilla; Philaster of Brescia writing around 390 refers specifically to the story of Maximilla and Aegeates from the *Passion of Andrew*; Pope Innocent of Rome lists the *AA* among heretical books and attributes its authorship to Platonic philosophers in a letter dated to 405, cf. *NTA* II, 88-92 (Schäferdiek), 101-3 (Prieur); Elliott, *The Apocryphal New Testament*, 231. K. Schäferdiek, in *NTA* II, 87-100 argues that the *Acts* of Andrew, John, Paul, Peter and Thomas circulated together as one unit among Manicheans; see now J. Bremmer, 'The Novel and the Apocryphal Acts: Place, Time and Readership', in H. Hofmann and M. Zimmerman (eds), *Groningen Colloquia on the Novel* IX (Groningen, 1998) 157-80 at 163f. J.-D. Kaestli, 'L'utilisation des Actes Apocryphes des apôtres dans le Manichéism', in M. Krause (ed), *Gnosis and Gnosticism* (Leiden, 1977) 107-16 refutes the idea that the *AAA* had canonical status among the Manicheans. But despite these disagreements, the attestations demonstrate the breadth of circulation of the *AA* in some form, cf. Prieur, *Acta Andreae*, 91-128 for the most extensive account of the witnesses to the *AA*; Elliott, *The Apocryphal New Testament*, 231.

[21] All translations come from *Plotinus*, ed. and trans. A. H. Armstrong, *Loeb*, 7 vls (Cambridge MA, 1966-88).

Plotinus also describes this state as a 'likeness to God' (1.2.3); the person who achieves such a state will be 'simply god' (1.2.6). He envisions a place in which the soul might secrete itself into a 'place of its own away from the body' and 'wholly unaffected by it' (1.2.5). This separation entails a purification of the soul brought about by ridding oneself of passions and desires, especially bodily desires for food, drink, and sexual pleasure (1.2.5). Plotinus, however, remains careful not to denigrate the material world as evil. In his book *Against the Gnostics* he critiques the idea of the material world as a product of moral failure or as something inherently evil (2.9). Plotinus then connects the concepts of rest and motion with the relationship between the soul, the body, and the divine. One goal of the purified soul is to remain undisturbed; there should be no 'conflict' or 'shock' in such a soul (1.2.5).

Plotinus also writes of a system of the fall and redemption of souls similar to the account in the *Passion of Andrew*, albeit Plotinus maintains a belief in the usefulness of the material world that is less prominent in the *Passion of Andrew*. The mind has descended from the divine realm, and the soul has settled in the body. The ultimate objective of the individual soul is to become like the 'soul of the All' (4.8.2), to 'rest in the divine' (4.8.1), and to return to its original union with the divine (4.8.4). Yet the 'soul's fellowship with the body' (4.8.2) occurs for an important reason: 'The soul itself would not have known the powers it had if they had not come out and been revealed' (4.8.5). The revelation of the soul only can occur in embodied existence, and in the process of the return to the divine. This anthropology bears a striking resemblance to Andrew's speech to Maximilla on the fall of the *nous*, sexual passion, and the separation of the soul from the body.

Most importantly with respect to the *Passion of Andrew*, however, is Plotinus' treatment of *eros*. Plotinus also exhibits two understandings of *eros*. He writes, 'Now about the affection of the soul for which we make love responsible, there is no one, I suppose, who does not know that it occurs in souls which desire to embrace some beauty, and that this desire has two forms; one which comes from the chaste who are akin to absolute beauty, and one which wants to find its fulfillment in the doing of some ugly act' (3.5.1) Sexual intercourse constitutes such an ugly act for it remains embedded in a desire for 'the beauty here below" rather than the true beauty of the divine realm (3.5.1) He advocates chastity to avoid the 'error' of sexual intercourse (3.5.1). Plotinus establishes a hierarchy of the types of lovers: the lowest lover is one whose desire is directed solely towards procreation; the lover who engages in sexual intercourse but is motivated by a love of beautiful bodies rather than procreation is one step higher; the highest lovers are those who 'venerate that higher beauty, too, and do not treat this earthly beauty, either, with disrespect, since they see in it the creation and plaything of that other. These lovers, then, are concerned about beauty without any ugliness' (3.5.1). The *Passion of Andrew* and Plotinus clearly diverge in that the *Passion* never exhibits a positive valuation of the physical expression of love; Andrew presents no middle tier. The language of desire and procreation, however, is deployed in two divergent ways that resemble Plotinus' two forms: Aegeates love for Maximilla represents the lower form of love, whereas Maximilla's and Stratocles' love for Andrew and God represents the higher, truer form of love.

The *Passion of Andrew* uses these Platonic conceptions of love, rest, and the relationship between the soul and the body to present a new message. Where *eros* in the Greek novel is precisely the love expressed in sexual intercourse for the purpose of procreation and family maintenance, true love for the ideal Christian in the *Passion of Andrew* is a Platonic love, directed away from physical bodies and toward the realm of the divine. The philosophic enterprise, here, takes over the location and language of the erotic. Moreover, the *Passion of Andrew* uses the tropes of the novel to narrate its own exposition on a true love that is radically different from the true love of the novels. While the Platonic elements of the *Passion of Andrew* have been noted by other scholars[22], its Platonic formulation of love has been overlooked in efforts to characterize the text as ascetic, Encratic, or 'gnostic'[23]. The importance of the *Passion of Andrew*,

---

[22] F. Bovon, this volume, Ch. VII mentions Platonism and the importance of self-transformation and self-discovery. He and E. Junod, 'Reading the Apocryphal Acts of Apostles', *Semeia* 38 (1986) 166 only mention the Platonic elements in passing. MacDonald's discussion of Platonism in the *AA* is subordinate to his interest in the texts' parallels with Homer, and he does not mention the relationship between its Platonic elements and eroticism.
[23] On 'encratism' see Y. Tissot, 'Encratisme et Actes apocryphes' in F. Bovon *et al.*, *Les Actes apocryphes des apôtres* (Geneva, 1981) 109-20. The 'gnostic' problem seems endemic to any study of any text of the *AAA*, and I

however, lies not in its degree of asceticism, Platonism, or gnosticism, but in the early link between the ascetic way of life and Platonic philosophy. For all of its counter-social tendencies, the *Passion of Andrew* nonetheless places its ascetic agenda within a context that could be identified and understood by Christian and non-Christian readers: the philosophic school[24]. The subversive nature of Christian asceticism is couched in a recognizable discourse.

The relationship between sexual renunciation and Platonic philosophy in the *Passion of Andrew* also may be one of the earliest witnesses outside of the Nag Hammadi writings to the existence of Platonizing, ascetic Christian communities. The most notable Christian Platonist of antiquity is Origen, whose cosmology in *On First Principles* bears striking resemblance both to the *Passion of Andrew*'s and to Plotinus'. Origen's philosophy about the redemption of the soul is generally believed to have been introduced into the asceticism and monasticism of late antiquity via Platonizing monks in Egypt and Cappadocia such as Evagrius Ponticus and Gregory of Nyssa[25]. The *Passion of Andrew* presents a link between ascetic practice and a Pla-

---

have deliberately chosen to sidestep the issue of whether the text is 'gnostic' because that very category of description has been thrown into question recently. M. Williams, *Rethinking 'Gnosticism': An Argument for Dismantling a Dubious Category* (Princeton, 1996) 29-53 has adroitly demonstrated the problems of using the term to describe a particular philosophy or community. Elliott, *The Apocryphal New Testament*, 236 briefly reviews the positions of various scholars regarding the *AA*'s status as 'gnostic', 'orthodox', or something in between. Prieur, in *NTA* II, 114 craftily describes the *AA* as not 'a gnostic text in the proper sense' but instead as belonging to a 'gnosticising way of thinking'.

[24] Although J. Francis, *Subversive Virtue: Asceticism and Authority in the Second-Century Pagan World* [University Park, Penn., 1995) recently has demonstrated that ascetic tendencies in non-Christian philosophical traditions also functioned as fundamentally subversive movements, their form of social protest would have been more familiar than Christian ascetic movements.

[25] Evagrius and Gregory appear to have taken their cosmologies almost wholesale from Origen. The seminal work on Evagrius and later Origenist traditions is A. Guillaumont, *Les 'Kephalaia Gnostica' d'Evagre le Pontique et l'histoire de l'Origenisme chez les Grecs et chez les Syriens* (Paris, 1962). The most comprehensive work in English on Origenism and asceticism is E.A. Clark, *The Origenist Controversy* (Princeton, 1992).

tonic understanding of salvation that predates Origenist monasticism by centuries and Origen himself by decades. Further, Origen's *askesis* is a more intellectual exercise – contemplation and interpretation of scripture. The *Passion of Andrew* insists on a fairly strong physical ascetic practice coupled with the Platonic salvation of the soul. Its legacy for social historians is its evidence for pre-monastic, Platonic ascetic communities. The community that produced the *Passion of Andrew* can not be geographically situated[26], but the text itself and its popularity suggest the existence of ascetic Christians who understood their faith and their ascetic practices in a distinctly Platonic framework. In the West, Platonizing ascetic traditions were deemed heretical as a result of the Origenist controversies of the fourth and fifth centuries. It should not be surprising that at the beginning of the fifth century, Innocent, bishop of Rome, believed the *AA* to be written by Platonists and condemned the work as heretical[27].

---

[26] But see Bremmer, this volume, Ch. II.
[27] See note 20.

XI. Les Actes d'André et le christianisme alexandrin

ATTILA JAKAB

Nos investigations pour présenter une histoire cohérente et 'désenclavée' des origines et des premiers temps du christianisme alexandrin nous ont amené à passer en revue toutes les sources possibles et à analyser les différentes hypothèses[1]. Notre objectif est de dissiper l'obscurité qui d'un avis répandu enveloppe les origines de ce christianisme. C'est ainsi que nous avons réellement 'découvert' le champ des apocryphes et plus particulièrement les *AAA*, dont les *AJ* et les *AA*.

La difficulté majeure de notre étude a consisté dans l'insuffisance, sinon dans l'absence, des sources. Pour le premier siècle, nous n'avons pratiquement pas d'informations[2]. L'idée selon laquelle Alexandrie aurait reçu le christianisme de Palestine (ou plus exactement de Jérusalem) est généralement acceptée par les auteurs modernes (J. Daniélou[3], M. Roncaglia[4], C.H. Roberts[5], A. Martin[6] ou

---

[1] A ce sujet nous nous permettons de renvoyer à notre thèse de doctorat: *Chrétiens d'Alexandrie. Richesse et pauvreté aux premiers temps du christianisme (Ier-IIIe siècles). Essai d'histoire sociale* (Faculté de Théologie Catholique de l'Université des Sciences Humaines de Strasbourg, 1998).
[2] D'après Th.A. Robinson, *The Bauer Thesis Examined* (Leviston and Queenstown, 1988) 66-7: 'no evidence for first-century Christianity can be found for Alexandria and Egypt. (...) we believe that Alexandria did have a Christian community in the first century... but we have no solid evidence'.
[3] Voir J. Daniélou, dans *Nouvelle Histoire de l'Eglise* I (Paris, 1963) 78-9.
[4] Voir *Histoire de l'Eglise copte* I (Beyrouth, 1966) 53-60 et 126.
[5] C.H. Roberts, *Manuscript, Society and Belief in Early Christian Egypt* (London, 1979) 71.
[6] Voir 'Aux origines de l'Eglise copte...', *Revue des Etudes Anciennes* 83 (1981) 35-56, spécialement 39.

H. Koester[7]), même si les modalités – *'par qui?'*, *'quand?'* et *'comment?'* – nous échappent totalement.

Relativement à l'origine de certains documents, datés du IIe siècle et dont la localisation soulève encore des difficultés, il n'est pas rare de constater que l'avis des érudits est partagé entre la Syrie (Palestine) et l'Egypte (Alexandrie). C'est le cas notamment pour l'*Epître de Barnabé*[8] ou pour l'*Epistula Apostolorum*[9]. Parmi les textes de la bibliothèque gnostique découverte en 1945 à Nag-Hammadi (en Haute-Egypte), la Syrie est également bien représentée[10]. Les *AJ* (composé entre 150 et 200 ap. J.-C[11].) témoignent aussi de liens existants entre la Syrie et Alexandrie. Si, d'après E. Junod et J.-D. Kaestli, 'de toutes les hypothèses envisageables, celle de l'origine égyptienne (Alexandrie[12]?) paraît la moins incertaine' (du moins en ce qui concerne le 'corpus', c'est-à-dire le texte sans les *cc*. 94-102 et 109), ces éditeurs estiment également que leur texte 'a été connu et utilisé par l'auteur des *ATh*'[13]. Or ces derniers furent 'rédigés sans

---

[7] H. Koester, *Introduction to the New Testament* II (Philadelphia, 1982) 222.
[8] Voir Appendix I.
[9] C. Schmidt a découvert, en 1895 au Caire, les fragments d'une traduction copte qu'il a publiée: *Gespräche Jesu mit seinen Jüngern nach der Auferstehung* (Leipzig, 1919). Pour une version éthiopienne complète voir L. Guerrier, *Le Testament en Galilée de Notre-Seigneur Jésus-Christ* (Paris, 1913). Pour ce document, voir également M. Hornschuh, *Studien zur «Epistula Apostolorum»* (Berlin, 1965); C. Detlef G. Müller, 'Epistula Apostolorum', dans Schneemelcher, *NTA* I, 249-84; J. Hills, *Tradition and Composition in the 'Epistula Apostolorum'* (Minneapolis, 1990); J.-N. Péres, *L'Epître des Apôtres. Testament de notre Seigneur et notre Sauveur Jésus-Christ.* (Turnhout, 1994). Une nouvelle édition critique est en préparation par les soins de J.-N. Péres & J. Hills dans la collection 'Corpus Christianorum. Series Apocryphorum' chez Brepols.
[10] Voir R. Kuntzmann et J.-D. Dubois (eds), *Nag Hammadi. Evangile selon Thomas. Textes gnostiques aux origines du christianisme* (Paris, 1987).
[11] E. Junod et J.-D. Kaestli, *Acta Iohannis* II (Turnhout, 1983) 695.
[12] Nous préférerons Alexandrie à l'Egypte parce que, d'après l'état actuel de nos connaissances, il n'est pas possible de présumer l'existence d'une communauté chrétienne capable d'une production littéraire plus significative, en dehors de cette métropole, avant le milieu du IIIe siècle.
[13] Junod et Kaestli, *Acta Iohannis* I, 694, 697, 692 et n. 1.

doute à Édesse dans la première moitié du IIIe siècle'[14]. Leur idéal ascétique ressemble à celui des AA et des APt[15].

Mais, si nous admettons, avec Prieur, la possibilité que les AA dépendent des AJ[16] (= selon nous avec le 'corpus') – dont 'des similitudes ponctuelles ou thématiques' ont déjà été relevées par Junod et Kaestli[17] – et 'qu'ils doivent avoir été rédigés peu de temps après les AJ, dans la seconde moitié du IIe siècle' (ou le début du IIIe), nous ne partageons pas, en revanche, l'avis de l'éditeur quant à l'origine alexandrine du document[18].

Le christianisme de cette métropole méditerranéenne est, dans ces premiers temps, un 'mouvement[19]' (peut-on dire?) en pleine évolution, dynamique, très intellectuel et avec des aspects spirituels variés. Si le 'courant' gnostique est présent et représenté dans la communauté, il ne constitue pas pour autant sa caractéristique. D'autres 'courants' y ont également leur place, ce qui relativise l'importance généralement accordée à la 'gnosticité' du christianisme alexandrin naissant. D'ailleurs les différences intérieures ne sont pas encore tranchées et extériorisées[20].

La présence d'un 'christianisme non-gnostique' à Alexandrie, dans la seconde moitié du IIe siècle, est également confirmée par deux auteurs extérieurs à la ville: Justin et Irénée. Si ce dernier, vers 180, fait seulement mention de l'Eglise établie – entre autres – en Egypte (= Alexandrie, d'après nous) au sujet 'du contenu de la Tra-

[14] P.-H. Poirier et Y. Tissot, 'Actes de Thomas', dans F. Bovon et P. Geoltrain (eds), *Écrits apocryphes chrétiens* I (Paris, 1997) 1323.
[15] Selon J. Quasten, *Initiation aux Pères de l'Eglise* I (Paris, 1955) 159.
[16] J.-M. Prieur, *Acta Andreae* I (Turnhout, 1989) 413-4.
[17] Junod et Kaestli, *Acta Iohannis* II, 698.
[18] Prieur, *Acta Andreae* I, 414, 416.
[19] C'est-à-dire un groupement humain qui s'est formé en raison d'un lien collectif, en vue d'un objectif ou d'une action commune. Dans le cas du mouvement chrétien (d'Alexandrie) il s'agit d'une sensibilité spirituelle et religieuse partagée, sans bureaucratie fonctionnelle, ni ritualisme des devoirs religieux.
[20] J.-M. Sevrin (ed), *L'Exégèse de l'Âme (NH II, 6)* (Québec, 1983) 58. D'après l'éditeur, l'écrit 'ne se pose point de problème d'identité', ce qui 'convient tout-à-fait et à la constatation que le texte est gnostique dans son principe (et donc certainement flou sur les questions d'appartenance sociologique [du point de vue ecclésial]), et à l'hypothèse qu'il soit très ancien (et donc antérieur aux réactions hérésiologiques chrétiennes)'.

dition [qui] est un et identique' (*Adv. Haer.* 1.10.2); Justin en revanche se réfère explicitement aux chrétiens de cette ville dans sa première Apologie (29.2-3). Ce témoignage, très peu exploité par les historiens de l'Eglise pour la métropole méditerranéenne, nous révèle quelques traits du christianisme de cette cité. Il le fait avec d'autant plus de vraisemblance qu'il en parle seulement en passant, son intention n'étant nullement d'en donner une description. Outre la certitude qu'à Alexandrie, vers le milieu du second siècle, il y avait des chrétiens de qui l'écrivain de Rome pouvait se sentir très proche; nous pouvons également affirmer qu'ils appartenaient très probablement à la haute société de la ville. Mais, au-delà de son aspect social, le récit de Justin dévoile aussi cette tendance ascétique ou cette 'maîtrise de soi' – qu'évoque P.-H. Poirier au sujet de *Sentences de Sextus*[21] – et qui pouvait avoir cours dans les milieux chrétiens de la ville d'Alexandrie (pensons aussi à Origène et surtout à sa jeunesse[22]). C'est sans doute avec cette tendance que nous devons mettre en rapport la religion spiritualisée des *AJ*.

Les études menées conjointement avec beaucoup d'érudition par Junod et Kaestli au sujet des *AJ* nous permettent de dissiper un peu plus l'obscurité qui plane sur le christianisme alexandrin du second siècle[23]. Car, suivant l'opinion de ses éditeurs, 'les *AJ* (sans *cc*. 94-102 et 109[24]) ont été composés en Egypte (Alexandrie?) entre 150 et 200 par un auteur chrétien issu d'un milieu cultivé et fortement marqué par une religion païenne spiritualisée'[25].

[21] P.-H. Poirier, *Les Sentences de Sextus (NH XII, 1)* (Québec, 1983) 20.
[22] Eusèbe, *HE*. 6.3.9-12 et 6.8.1-3.
[23] E. Junod et J.-D. Kaestli, 'Les traits caractéristiques de la théologie des "Actes de Jean",' *Revue de Théologie et de Philosophie* III 26 (1976) 125-45; *Acta Iohannis*; 'Le dossier des "Actes de Jean": état de la question et perspectives nouvelles', *ANRW* II.25.6 (1988) 4293-4362.
[24] Junod et Kaestli, *Acta Iohannis*, 627 et 631-2, situe cette partie, d'origine gnostique, du texte en Syrie, au troisième quart du IIe siècle, 'dans un milieu de langue grecque vivant en contact avec des gens de culture araméenne'.
[25] Eidem, *L'histoire des Actes apocryphes des apôtres du IIIe au IXe siècle* (Genève, 1982) 4; 'Le dossier des "Actes de Jean",' 4353-4. Voir également pour le lieu d'origine (Asia Minor) et une date de rédaction antérieure à 180 P.J. Lalleman, *The Acts of John: a two-stage initiation into Johannine gnosticism* (Leuven, 1998) 256-70; J.N. Bremmer, 'The Novel and the Apocryphal Acts: Place, Time and Readership', in H. Hofmann and

Si le texte lui-même ne nous livre pas d'informations précises et concrètes sur la communauté chrétienne de la ville, il nous permet cependant de saisir, en plus de l'intention de son auteur, quelques caractéristiques de son public. 'Marqué par un spiritualisme qui affecte tout ce dont il parle', notre écrit 'ignore absolument l'enracinement du christianisme dans l'histoire d'Israël; l'Ancien Testament n'y est pas mentionné et les Juifs n'y sont pas nommés'. En plus, s'il y a une communauté de frères, elle 'semble [néanmoins] dépourvue de toute espèce d'organisation et de ministères ecclésiastiques'. 'Le texte – qui 'ne rapporte aucune célébration de baptême' – célèbre un seul Dieu, le Seigneur Jésus, immuable, bon et éternel', mais il ne fait 'aucune distinction entre le Père et le Fils, aucune référence à l'incarnation, à un ministère terrestre, à la passion et à la crucifixion', qui n'y sont pas présentes[26]. Le désir de l'auteur est tout simplement d'attirer 'l'attention du lecteur sur le vrai Dieu, la vie de l'âme et la nécessité d'une conversion spirituelle' (ce qui nous suggère inéluctablement de penser à l'intention poursuivie par Clément dans son *Protreptique*), par le biais 'd'un texte simple, plaisant, concret et dramatique'[27]. D'où la conclusion d'E. Junod et J.-D. Kaestli que la religion non-gnostique de cet écrit 'représente une forme de christianisme éminemment spiritualisé, sans lien avec la tradition juive et le judéo-christianisme[28]'. Elle 'ne s'inscrit pas [non plus] dans des formes institutionnelles, dans des rites, dans un livre', mais 'consiste [plutôt] en une conversion individuelle, dans la maîtrise de soi [présente également dans *Sentences de Sextus*] et dans un soin exclusif voué à l'âme[29].

Suivant la remarque très juste d'E. Junod et J.-D. Kaestli, 'les historiens du christianisme, à l'exception des spécialistes de la gnose, ne font pas grand cas des *AJ*'. Pourtant ce texte est issu d'une volonté identique à la littérature apologétique, littérature qui nous permet 'd'entrevoir comment des chrétiens ont été amenés non seulement à présenter et donc à penser la doctrine chrétienne à l'aide de termes, de concepts, de références empruntées à la tradi-

M. Zimmerman (eds), *Groningen Colloquia on the Novel* IX (Groningen, 1998) 157-80.
[26] Junod et Kaestli, *Acta Iohannis*, 680-1.
[27] Eidem, 'Le dossier des "Actes de Jean",' 4349.
[28] Eidem, *Acta Iohannis*, 681.
[29] Eidem, 'Le dossier des "Actes de Jean",' 4349.

tion païenne, mais encore à atténuer ou même à faire disparaître de cette doctrine les éléments susceptibles de choquer les païens'. Pareillement, les *AJ* souhaitent 'rendre le christianisme facilement assimilable', même s'ils 'le font d'une manière bien plus radicale'. En lisant cet écrit à la lumière des critiques de Celse à l'adresse des chrétiens et de leur foi, 'on s'aperçoit alors que le christianisme des *AJ* est comme vidé des traits qui scandalisaient le pamphlétaire païen. La foi au Fils de Dieu incarné, mort et ressuscité, la valeur accordée à des événements historiques et contingents, la mise en évidence de la foi au lieu de la raison, l'idée que Dieu s'intéresse en priorité à un groupe d'hommes (le peuple juif, puis les chrétiens) sont autant de points qui, aux yeux de Celse, rendent le christianisme inacceptable. Ne doit-on pas en dire autant – s'interrogent les éditeurs de ce texte – de l'auteur des *AJ* puisqu'il ne les accepte pas davantage?'[30].

A la suite des *AJ* la possibilité d'une origine égyptienne (voir alexandrine) a été également proposée pour les *AA* par Prieur dans sa publication. Ce texte – qui malgré 'certaines affinités avec le gnosticisme' n'est toutefois pas un écrit gnostique, mais relève 'plutôt d'une mentalité gnosticisante' – se situerait, selon son éditeur, dans 'une époque où la doctrine est encore flottante et l'orthodoxie mal définie, et où l'on peut exprimer des idées comme les siennes sans avoir l'intention ni de s'écarter de la pensée orthodoxe [?], ni de s'opposer à d'autres chrétiens'. L'auteur serait donc un chrétien, membre d'une 'société restreinte, à tendance élitaire' – 'une communauté peu ritualiste, dont le souci d'organisation était très faible, sinon absent, et qui cherchait à se conformer à l'idéal spirituel, éthique et communautaire formulé par les *AA*' –, qui rédigea son écrit, 'peu de temps après les *AJ*, dans la seconde moitié du IIe"siècle[31].

En ce qui concerne le lieu d'origine, à notre grand regret, Prieur ne lui consacre guère plus que quelques lignes. Il admet ne pas pouvoir 'exclure la Syrie, à cause de l'encratisme, des ressemblances avec la théologie de Tatien et de l'utilisation des *AA* par l'auteur des *ATh*, ni l'Asie Mineure' d'ailleurs; il leur préfère cependant Alexandrie en raison 'de nombreuses parentés entre les *AJ* et *AA*'. 'Alexan-

---

[30] Eidem, 4355.
[31] Prieur, *Acta Andreae*, 407-9, 412-4.

drie est le lieu – dit Prieur – où peut avoir vécu un auteur chrétien susceptible de formuler le christianisme dans les termes des *AA*'. Il juge valable l'argumentation des éditeurs des *AJ*, pour ce dernier écrit également, mais sans présenter un raisonnement plus détaillé[32]. Une localisation plus précise (ou au moins très vraisemblable) de l'écrit est pourtant indispensable pour qu'il puisse être utilisé comme source historique.

Les connexions des *AA* avec les *AJ* et avec les *ATh*, dont les rédactions se situent dans deux endroits bien distincts, sont évidentes. Pour cela il suffit de parcourir les références établies par Prieur dans les notes de son édition :

AA 2 – *AJ* 64. 5-6		*AJ* 20 – *ATh* 115
AA 3 – *AJ* 40. 16-17	*AA* 3 – *ATh* 106	*AJ* 21 – *ATh* 44
AA 7 – *AJ* 39. 6		
AJ 40.5		*AJ* 22 – *ATh* 53
	AA 9 – *ATh* 136	*AJ* 24 – *ATh* 48
AA 8 – *AJ* 54.12		
		AJ 30 – *ATh* 20
	AA 11 – *ATh* 57	*AJ* 59 – *ATh* 19 & 59
AA 13 – *AJ* 63. 1-4		*AJ* 73 – *ATh* 80; 149;
AJ 106.1-2		160; 36
AJ 46.7		
	AA 23 – *ATh* 14	*AJ* 74 – *ATh* 57
	ATh 117	
AA 24 – *AJ* 64. 3-4	*AA* 24 – *ATh* 97 & 99	*AJ* 76 – *ATh* 34; 38;
		150 & 88; 117
	AA 26 – *ATh* 106	*AJ* 81 – *ATh* 117
AA 27 – *AJ* 27. 15-16		
AA 29 – *AJ* 43. 1-2		
	AA 31 – *ATh* 152	
	ATh 95 & 97	
	ATh 134	
	ATh 137	

---

[32] Prieur, *Acta Andreae*, 414-6; 'Les Actes apocryphes de l'apôtre André: Présentation des diverses traditions apocryphes et état de la question', *ANRW* II.25.6 (1988) 4396 et 'Andrew, Acts of', dans *The Anchor Bible Dictionary* I (New York et London, 1992) 246. D.R. Macdonald, *The Acts of Andrew and The Acts of Andrew and Matthias in the City of Cannibals* (Atlanta, 1990) 59, qui voit dans cet écrit une sorte d'*Odyssée* chrétienne, suppose également la possibilité de son origine alexandrine, même s'il admet que 'other locations also are possible'.

AA 32 – AJ 115. 2
AA 34 [2] – AJ 58. 9-10
AA 37 [5] – AJ 62   AA 37 [5] – ATh 12
AA 40 [8] – AJ 49. 10
AA 42 [10] – AJ 36. 6
AA 44 [12] – AJ 108. 3-4
                          AA 46 [14] – ATh 164
AA 48 [16] – AJ 106
                          AA 49 [17] – ATh 33
AA 49 [17] – AJ 49.4   AJ 49 – ATh 33 & 74
                          AA 51 [1] – ATh 106
AA 53 [3] – AJ 23. 13
AA 56 [6] – AJ 98. 8
AA 61 – AJ 84. 2-8   AJ 84 – ATh 10 & 50
AA 62 – AJ 63. 15
AA 63 [9] – AJ 112. 17-18
            AJ 115. 15
AA 64 [10] – AJ 115. 4

En relevant ces références nous avons formulé une hypothèse de travail qui reste encore à démontrer. Ainsi les *AA* se situeraient non seulement dans le temps, mais également du point de vue géographique, dans l'intervalle existant à la fois entre la date et le lieu de rédaction des deux autres écrits: les *AJ* et les *ATh*. La perspective que les *AA* soient un texte 'intermédiaire', entre ces deux autres *Actes* apocryphes nous est aussi suggérée par l'opinion d'E. Junod et J.-D. Kaestli qui proposent, en effet, une composition et insertion syrienne des *cc.* 94-102 et 109, dans le 'corpus' des *AJ*[33], à une date proche, mais ultérieure à la rédaction de ce dernier. Le fait que les deux écrits – même en admettant l'hypothèse des témoins de courants divers – ne reflètent ni un public ni un milieu identiques (à plus forte raison celui d'Alexandrie) renforce notre conviction que les *AA* soient un texte 'intermédiaire'.

Au-delà des 'similitudes ponctuelles ou thématiques' avec les *AJ* nous devons également prendre en compte[34], outre leur diversité, les affinités que présente le texte publié par Prieur avec les *ATh*. Ainsi, la rédaction des *AA*, en raison de son contenu, tel que nous le

---

[33] Junod et Kaestli, *Acta Iohannis*, 700; eidem, 'Le dossier des "Actes de Jean".'
[34] Junod et Kaestli, *Acta Iohannis*, 698.

connaissons pour le moment, et de sa date de composition, qui, même proche de celle des *AJ*, se situerait néanmoins entre la fin du deuxième et le début du troisième siècle, nous semble plus probable dans un milieu syrien (occidental?) qu'alexandrin[35]. Dès lors, l'écrit en question pourrait être considéré davantage comme un témoin sur les liens qui existaient entre la métropole méditerranéenne et la Syrie(-Palestine). Originaires d'Alexandrie, les *AJ*, quelque temps après leur composition, ont pu être déjà connus par des chrétiens (qui les ont sans doute remaniés) de Syrie occidentale, où ils ont pu servir de 'modèle' à la rédaction des *AA* qui, par la suite, inspirera peut-être l'auteur des *ATh*. Mais pour que cette hypothèse soit confirmé ou infirmé l'histoire sociographique cohérente du christianisme à la fois d'Edesse et d'Antioche dans les trois premiers siècles ap. J.-C. nous semble indispensable.

Prieur a laissé ouvert la question de l'origine des *AA*, mais il a suggéré des perspectives de recherche. Malgré les diverses possibilités, tant que le contexte socio-historique des différents lieux proposés (Syrie, Asie Mineure) n'est pas mieux établie il ne nous semble pas possible de prendre position dans le débat. Nous pensons que les textes du christianisme ancien sont si étroitement liés à leur contexte socio-historique que sans une meilleure connaissance de la communauté où ils ont été rédigés ou remaniés la compréhension de ces écrits nous reste en partie inaccessible.

C'est dans cette perspective de meilleur connaissance à la fois des communautés chrétiennes du passé et des textes eux-mêmes que nous accordons un intérêt historique réel aux *écrits apocryphes*[36]. Dans le domaine de l'histoire sociale et institutionnelle du christianisme des trois premiers siècles cet intérêt nous semble majeur. Avec le développement des études à la fois gnostiques et apocryphes l'historien se sent interpellé pour renouveler sa réflexion. Il ne peut désor-

---

[35] Le fait que l'auteur des *AA* puisse parler de 'la cité de César' (59; cf. Prieur, 528) exclut Alexandrie – pensons-nous – comme lieu de sa rédaction. Une pareille formulation nous paraît peu cohérente pour une personne (serait-il chrétien) de l'élite grecque de cette cité qui, de surcroît, veut transmettre un enseignement à son public.

[36] Au sujet de cette appellation voir E. Junod, '"Apocryphes du Nouveau Testament": une appellation erronée et une collection artificielle. Discussion de la nouvelle définition proposée par W. Schneemelcher', *Apocrypha* 3 (1992) 17-46.

mais rien écarter *a priori* ou en vertu d'un jugement de valeur qui s'est cristalisé ultérieurement. Il n'a pas à résoudre le problème de la 'canonicité' ou de la 'non-canonicité' d'un texte, mais il doit l'analyser en fonction des renseignements qu'il peut en tirer sur les hommes (car l'écriture est l'apanage d'un petit nombre) et la situation historique que cache son document. Il lui faut donc regarder l'histoire dans son intégralité (ou dans sa globalité 'profane' et 'religieuse') s'il souhaite la comprendre réellement. C'est pourquoi tout ce qui nous reste de la production littéraire de cette période a un intérêt certain.

Les écrits apocryphes reflètent le besoin et la spiritualité du groupe qui les a produits ou seulement véhiculés. Ce sont des écrits 'communautaires' où l'auteur demeure inconnu. Ce groupe peut être 'autonome', mais il peut également faire partie d'une communauté chrétienne plus grande. En étudiant dans le contexte alexandrin les *AJ* et les *AA* notre préférance va indéniablement pour cette deuxième variante. Dès lors il nous semble pouvoir dire que les écrits apocryphes témoignent de la pluralité des tendances (ou options théologiques) et des sensibilités dans une même communauté; à savoir leur communauté d'origine. En ce qui concerne le second siècle, cette hétérogénéité du christianisme est valable non seulement pour un lieu donné (Alexandrie en l'occurrence) mais aussi pour son ensemble. En plus, ces documents apportent des éclaircissements sur les relations entre les communautés (Alexandrie et la Syrie par ex.) et contribuent à esquisser ou à améliorer la mosaïque historique et spirituelle d'une *ekklesia* bien précise.

Mais, pour pouvoir en tirer toutes les bénéfices, les écrits apocryphes doivent être resitués dans leur contexte historique de production et analysés dans leur singularité. Toute rupture opérée entre le document – pour l'étudier en soi-même et pour soi-même – et son 'environnement' initial risque de lui attribuer un sens différé. C'est ce qui se produisait, nous semble-t-il, à la suite du développement institutionnel et doctrinal du christianisme. Au fur et à mesure qu'on s'éloignait de l'époque de la production l'importance du contenu s'amenuisait en faveur du contenant. Dans le cas des *AAA* ce dernier restait comme une 'vie' pour alimenter la prédication et la piété populaire. Pourtant il est assez évident que le public des *AJ* à Alexandrie n'avait rien de populaire. Nous pensons qu'il devait être de même des destinataires des *AA*.

Pendant longtemps l'optique à travers laquelle on regardait l'histoire ancienne du christianisme était l'homogénéité du phénomène chrétien (que ce soit au niveau de l'enseignement, de l'organisation ou de l'implantation) dans la société de l'époque, jalonné par différentes formes de 'déviations', aisément qualifiées d'"hérésies"[37]. Mais la 'redécouverte' (peut-on dire), depuis un siècle ou un demi-siècle, de l'histoire ancienne en général et chrétienne en particulier, nous révèle à la fois la fluidité et la variété des aspects du christianisme primitif. Cela étant, il devient de plus en plus évident qu'il y a eu une époque où les limites étaient beaucoup moins tranchées qu'on aurait pu le supposer dans le passé[38]. C'est pourquoi nous pouvons dire que le christianisme anténicéen – en général, mais aussi par régions – présente une très grande variété[39]. L'uniformisation est bien plus un travail rétrospectif qu'une constatation des faits. En considérant donc les écrits apocryphes comme sources historiques littéraires à part entière nous pouvons non seulement éviter la schématisation et la simplification du christianisme ancien, phénomène socio-religieux complexe, mais aussi reconstituer sa diversité et sa richesse d'antan[40].

---

[37] Sur les sens de *hairesis* au premiers siècles de l'époque chrétienne, voir M. Simon, *Le Christianisme antique et son contexte religieux* = *Scripta varia* II (Tübingen, 1981) 821-36 ('From Greek Hairesis to Christian Heresy'). Voir aussi A. Schindler, 'Häresie. II: Kirchengeschichtlich', *TRE* 14 (1985) 318-41; N. Brox, 'Häresie', *RAC* 13 (1986) 248-97; A. le Boulluec, *La notion d'hérésie dans la littérature grecque. IIe-IIIe siècles* I (Paris, 1985) et 'L'émergence de la notion d'hérésie', dans *Connaissance des Pères de l'Eglise* 60 (1995) 8-11. Pour une bibliographie de la notion d'*hérésie*, voir A. Faivre, *Ordonner la fraternité* (Paris, 1992) 498-500.

[38] Voir à ce sujet H.-D. Altendorf *et al.*, *Orthodoxie et Hérésie dans l'Eglise ancienne* (Genève, Lausanne et Neuchâtel, 1993).

[39] M. Tardieu, 'Histoire du mot "gnostique",' dans M. Tardieu et J.-D. Dubois, *Introduction à la littérature gnostique* I (Paris, 1986) 21-37. Voir aussi A.F.J. Klijn, 'Jewish Christianity in Egypt', dans *The Roots of Egyptian Christianity* (Philadelphia, 1986) 161-75, spécialement 166: 'Early Egyptian Christianity is characterized by pluriformity, with both Jewish and gnostic influences'. Voir aussi F. Vouga, 'Pour une géographie théologique des christianismes primitifs', *Et. Théol. et Rel.* 59 (1984) 141-9.

[40] Cf. J.-D. Kaestli et D. Marguerat (eds), *Le mystère apocryphe. Introduction à une littérature méconnue* (Genève, 1995).

APPENDIX I: L'EPÎTRE DE BARNABÉ

D'après L.W. Barnard, 'Judaism in Egypt A. D. 70-135', dans *Studies in the Apostolic Fathers and their Background* (Oxford, 1966) 46 n. 2: 'following Clement, Origen, A.C.O. (c. AD. 300) and Codex Sinaiticus, all Egyptian witnesses, knew the Epistle. On the other hand there are no African witnesses before St. Augustine and no Syrian witnesses before the fifth century. The supposed connexions with the Odes of Solomon, Ascension of Isaiah and the Gospel of Peter are too vague to bear critical examination'; *idem*, 'The Date of the Epistle of Barnabas', *J. Egyptian Arch.* 44 (1958) 101; *idem*, 'Saint Stephen and Early Alexandrian Christianity', *NTS* 7 (1960-1961) 31-45 et 'The "Epistle of Barnabas" and its Contemporary Setting', *ANRW* II.27.1 (1993) 159-207; G. Bardy, *Littérature grecque chrétienne* (Paris, 1928) 67-8; *idem*, 'Les premiers temps du christianisme de langue copte en Egypte', dans *Mémorial Lagrange* (Paris, 1940) 203-16, spécialement 203-4 et *La question des langues dans l'Église ancienne* (Paris, 1948) 39; J. Quasten, *Initiation aux Pères de l'Église* I (Paris, 1955) 104; J. Danielou, *Théologie du judéo-christianisme* (Tournai, 1958) 46; L. Goppelt, *Les origines de l'Eglise* (Paris, 1961) 195; R. Kasser, 'Les origines du christianisme Égyptien', *Revue de théologie et de philosophie* 12 (1962) 14; M. Roncaglia, *Histoire de l'Église copte* I (Beyrouth, 1966) 148; J.J. Gunther, 'The Association of Mark and Barnabas with Egyptian Christianity', *The Evangelical Quarterly* 55 (1983) 21-9; B. A. Pearson, 'Earliest Christianity in Egypt', dans *Roots of Egyptian Christianity*, 132-59, spécialement 151 et 'Christians and Jews in first-century Alexandria', *HThR* 79 (1986) 211-4; M. Jacobs, *Das Christentum in der antiken Welt* (Göttingen, 1987) 31; B.E. Daley, *The Hope of the Early Church* (Cambridge, 1991) 11; J.J. Fernández Sangrador, *Los orígenes de la Comunidad cristiana de Alejandría* (Salamanca, 1994) 145-55; J.C. Paget, *The Epistle of Barnabas* (Tübingen, 1994) 3-9 (pour l'auteur), 9-30 (la date), 30-42 (la provenance), évoque également la probabilité d'une origine alexandrine. Aux tenants de l'origine alexandrine (égyptienne) de l'épître, dont certains se contentent d'une simple affirmation, s'opposent les auteurs attachés à une localisation en Syrie. Selon A. L. Williams, 'The Date of the Epistle of Barnabas', *JThS* 34 (1933, 337-46) 340: '... it is a vulgar error to suppose that such methods – strange as they appear to us – either originated in Alexandria or were the peculiar mark of Alexandrian Jews. The mistake arose, no doubt, from the fact that our earlier scholars who dealt with the subject could read Philo easily enough, but had no knowledge of Talmud or Rabbinic'. Voir aussi P. Prigent, *Épître de Barnabé* (Paris, 1971) 20-4; J. P. Martin, 'L'interpretazione allegorica nella Lettera di Barnaba e nel guidaismo alessandrino', *Studi Storico-Religiosi* 6 (1982) 173-85; M.B. Shukster et P. Richardson, 'Temple and "Bet Ha-midrash" in the Epistle of Barnabas', dans S.T. Wilson (ed), *Anti-Judaism in Early Christianity* II (Waterloo, 1986) 17-31, spécialement 17-20. D'après Klijn, 'Jewish Christianity in Egypt', 166: 'Barnabas's allegorizing treatment of the Old Testament is not sufficient to prove an Egyptian origin'. Pour la rédaction voir également E. Robillard, 'L'Epître de Barnabé; trois époques, trois théologies, trois rédacteurs, *Revue Biblique* 78 (1971) 184-209. Pour une bibliographie voir Fernández Sangrador, *Los orígenes*, 145 n. 1.

XII. The Acts of Andrew and the Acts of John

PIETER J. LALLEMAN

The intertextual relationships among the five most ancient *AAA* are still disputed. Together these books form a kind of corpus and the similarities among them can only mean that they are in some way related, but the exact nature of the connections is as yet a matter of dispute. One thing that seems virtually certain is that the texts are largely literary creations: the suggestion that the *AAA* originated as oral tales plays only a marginal role in contemporary European research of the narratives[1]. This means that we cannot refer to a hypothetical oral phase in the existence of the materials.

In an earlier contribution I demonstrated that the *APt* depends on the *AJ* inclusive the well-known Gnostic interpolation in *cc*. 94-102[2]. I will now investigate what kind of relationship, if any, exists between the *AA* and the *AJ*. This research is carried out against the background of the opinion of the best contemporary specialists of our texts, Eric Junod, Jean-Daniel Kaestli and Jean-Marc Prieur, who argue that the *AA* depends on the *AJ*[3]. Almost all of the points they mention are incorporated in what follows. An exception is formed by arguments based on the assumption that some extremely ascetic passages in the pseudepigraphical *Epistula Titi* formed part of the origi-

---

[1] The hypothesis is defended by V. Burrus, *Chastity as Autonomy. Women in the Stories of Apocryphal Acts* (Lewiston and Queenston, 1987).
[2] P.J. Lalleman, 'The relationship between the Acts of John and the Acts of Peter', in Bremmer, *Acts of Peter*, 161-77 (also bibliography of earlier research).
[3] E. Junod, and J.-D. Kaestli, *Acta Iohannis* (Turnhout, 1983) 698-700 and the references given there; J.-M. Prieur, *Acta Andreae* (Turnhout, 1989) 394-400 and *Actes de l'apôtre André* (s.l. [Turnhout], 1995) 52-3.

nal *AJ*, because, as I have shown elsewhere, these passages are foreign to the spirit of the second-century *AJ*[4].

1. *Generic characteristics*

In asking questions about the relationship between *AJ* and *AA*, we must keep in mind that both writings share in the characteristics which unite the *AAA* as a group. For all their individuality, the five *AAA* have important elements in common, such as the following structural resemblances:

* The *AAA* combine travelogues with narratives about the apostles' activities in certain cities. The stress falls on the individual episodes (πράξεις).
* The apostles speak about Jesus as Lord and call people to repentance. The message of the text is put into the mouth of the apostles.
* The hero-apostles are teachers, healers, miracle-workers, in fact imitators of Christ himself, but like the actors in the ancient novels they are flat characters who are little more than their roles.
* A kind of retrospective prayer is said near the end of the story (*AJ* 113, *ATh* 144-8, less certain the Bodleian Coptic Fragment of the *AA*)[5].
* The use of the we-form in part of the text, imitating the style of the canonical Acts, was originally characteristic of the five main *AAA*, as I have argued elsewhere[6]. This form is still visible in parts of the *AJ* as well as in *AAgr* 64.1, 65[7], *APt* 4, 21, *ATh* 1[8] and in the late *Acts of*

---

[4] P.J. Lalleman, *The Acts of John: a two-stage initiation into Johannine Gnosticism* (Leuven, 1998) 236-8.

[5] The first editor, J. Barns, 'A Coptic Apocryphal Fragment in the Bodleian Library', *JTS* NS 11 (1960) 70-6, rather arbitrarily suggests that the fragment stems from the beginning of the *AA*; see Prieur, in *NTA* II, 106 and *Acta Andreae*, 24-5.

[6] Lalleman, *Acts of John*, 75-81.

[7] *AAgr* = the Greek remains of the *AA*, ed. Prieur, *Acta Andreae*, 441-549; *AAlat* = the Latin epitome of the *AA* by Gregory of Tours (*ibid.*, 564-651; not in *NTA* II).

[8] See Prieur, *Acta Andreae*, 37-8, 56-7; the first person frame chosen by Gregory of Tours (*AAlat* prol., 37, 38) may still reflect the style of the underlying original. In fact the case of *ATh* 1 (only in the Greek text, which preserves the oldest form) is different because it involves only one word and because it involves no sudden change in the middle of the narrative.

Philip 3.12. Later editors of the *AAA* deleted it, presumably because they did not understand it.

Likewise, there are several literary motifs which determine the character of the *AAA* and are consequently common to *AJ* and *AA*:
* Appearances of Christ-in-metamorphosis, who sometimes takes the form of the hero-apostle of the text (*AJ* 87 and *AAgr* 46, cf. *APTh* 21 and *ATh* 11, 27, 151-153) and at other times assumes the looks of a beautiful young man (*AJ* 73, 76, 87 and *AAgr* 32, cf. *APt* 5, *AP* 7 [PH 3], *ATh* 27, 154-5).
* Miracle stories occupy a very prominent position[9]. A specific feature of these stories is that persons who have just been resurrected or converted, personally perform miracles to others (*AJ* 24, 47, 81-3 and *AAlat* 12, 15, 19, cf. *ATh* 54, 73-4).
* The words σφραγίς and σφραγίζω denote a kind of sacrament (*AJ* 115.1 and *AAgr* 10-11, 13.22, cf. *APt* 5, *APTh* 25, *APl* 4 [PHeid 29], 11.5,7, *ATh* 26-7, 49, 54, 87, 120, 131). The rite involved must have been known to the intended readers. Due to our lack of knowledge, its nature is disputed among present day scholars, although many believe that it is nothing else than Christian baptism[10]. It is even suggested that in the different *AAA* different practices are meant[11].

It will be evident that the presence of the above elements in both the *AA* and the *AJ* is not indicative of any specific relationship between these two texts. We will have to look for more specific sim-

---

[9] J.V. Hills, 'Tradition, Redaction, and Intertextuality: Miracle Lists in the Apocryphal Acts as a Test Case', in D.J. Lull (ed.), *SBL 1990 Seminar Papers* (Atlanta, 1990) 375-90; E.V. Gallagher, 'Conversion and Salvation in the Apocryphal Acts of the Apostles', *The Second Century* 8 (1991) 13-29; and F. Bovon, 'Miracles, magie et guérison dans les Actes apocryphes des apôtres', *JECS* 3 (1995) 245-59.

[10] E.g. E. Peterson, 'Bemerkungen zum Hamburger Papyrusfragment', in his *Frühkirche, Judentum und Gnosis. Studien und Untersuchungen* (Rome, Freiburg and Vienna, 1959) 190, with reference to Hermas, *Sim* 9.16; J. Ysebaert, *Greek baptismal terminology. Its origins and early development* (Nijmegen, 1962) esp. 390-5.

[11] A.F.J. Klijn, *The Acts of Thomas* (Leiden, 1962) 55-7; Prieur, *Acta Andreae*, 190-1. The fact that in *AJ* 115.1 John seals himself at the end of his life shows at least that the terminology does not always denote baptism, cf. R. van den Broek, *Studies in Gnosticism and Alexandrian Christianity* (Leiden, 1996) 110-13. L. van Kampen, *Apostelverhalen* (Diss. Utrecht, 1990) 142, points out the essentially spiritual character of the seal in the *AA*.

ilarities. In directly comparing the *AJ* with the *AA*, we will distinguish verbal, structural and ideological aspects of the texts.

2. *Verbal parallels*

A comparison on the level of the very words of the texts is no easy task, since the original wording of the *AA* has largely been lost. Nonetheless, Prieur lists the following six cases of verbal similarities between the *AJ* and *AAgr*[12]:

AJ	*AAgr*	Key words
40.1-2	2.13-4 and 3.9-10	πεπειραμένοι αὐτοῦ
43.1-2	29.1-2	ἐπαρθεὶς τὴν ψυχήν
49.4	49.8	ἀναιδέστατος
64.5-6	2.3-4	εἴθε μηδέπω εἰς πατρίδα ἐληλύθειν
106.10-13	48.4-5, 16.10	στηρίζεσθε μεμνημένοι, μυστήριον
115.1	13.22	σφραγίζω

Some of these are not really parallels and others simply reflect everyday language. In my opinion, a close parallel only exists between *AJ* 43.1-2 and *AAgr* 29.1-2: the phrases ἐπαρθεὶς τὴν ψυχὴν εἶπε πρὸς τὸν κύριον· δόξα σοι, Ἰησοῦ, and the words ἀλήθεια/ ἀληθής and μόνος (θεός) correspond. It looks as if in this particular case the one text has copied the other.

As to the Latin version, in *AAlat* 3 *primus civitatis* would seem to correspond to *AJ*'s πρῶτος τῆς πόλεως (first of the city), an expression which also occurs in the *AP*. However, the expression may also be due to the common geographical background of these *AAA*. All in all, the number of verbal parallels is small.

3. *Structural parallels*

It may be noticed that the style of prayers and speeches in *AJ* and *AAgr* is often similar, with ample use of enumerations and a repeated exclamatory ὦ. More important, a comparison of the overall structure of the *AJ* with that of the *AA* in the version of Gregory of Tours (*AAlat*, which presumably left the story line of the original *AA*

---

[12] Prieur, *Acta Andreae*. 396-7.

largely intact[13]) reveals clear resemblances. In the *AJ* John first travels to Ephesus and then stays there for a while. His stay is interrupted by a round trip through the city's environment. Likewise Andrew needs some time to come to Patras and stays twice in that city with a round trip in between[14]. The other *AAA* do not have this frame. It is not unlikely that in this respect the *AA* imitated the *AJ*.

Moreover, we can list several episodes in *AAlat* which recall scenes from the *AJ*:

AJ	*AAlat*	Subject
19	13, 22	supranatural announcement of the arrival of the apostle (double vision)
19-20	30	a man threatens to commit suicide because of the fate of his wife (similar threat in *AAgr* 2)
56	7, 14, 16, 26, 30	performance of a healing miracle in exchange for conversion
58	20	departure, sadness, farewell speech
59	21	reference to travelling companions
82-3	19, 23	a woman raises a dead person
90	20	appearance of the cross on a mountain

Some of these episodes were probably inspired by Luke's Acts of the Apostles, viz. *AJ* 19, 58 and 59, but that does not apply to all of them[15]. Those that are not dependent on Acts are possibly genuine parallels between *AJ* and *AA*. The last mentioned episode, *AAlat* 20, deserves a closer look in the category of ideological parallels below, but it also suggests a far-reaching structural parallel between our two texts. Andrew has seen a vision and tells his audience that he cannot at that moment pass on to them everything that was said; he promises that these things will become apparent at the moment of his martyrdom. This statement suggests that the account of his martyrdom will contain deeper revelations than the preceding part of the text. Is it far-fetched to think that the final part of the text will offer a deeper level of initiation? In that case the *AA* would closely parallel the *AJ*. This text also has a two-stage structure in which the second stage

---

[13] So Prieur, *Acta Andreae*, 8-12; idem, *NTA* II, 104; but L. van Kampen, '*Acta Andreae* and Gregory's *De miraculis Andreae*', *VigChr* 45 (1991) 18-26 at 22, disagrees.

[14] Prieur, *Acta Andreae*, 395; other alleged parallels are based on the debatable reconstruction of lost parts of *AJ* by Junod and Kaestli.

[15] I argue the influence of Acts on *AJ* at length in my *Acts of John*, 74-98.

contains 'stronger meat' than the first[16]. That we are probably on the right track can be seen from the author's postscript (*AAgr* 65), in which he refers his book as 'the things that were said' and 'those that were not said, (which are) only comprehensible to the intellect'.

4. *Ideological parallels*

The parallels between our two texts also pertain to their messages. Common to both is the contempt for the material world and the stress on the importance of the spiritual. The interest of both texts can be summarised as 'Care for the soul'. The Gnosticism of *AJ* 94-102 and of the *AA* is similar in that it contains no reflexion on the origin of the visible world and the constitution of the spiritual world, but is simply a way to salvation through knowledge. The only reference to cosmology in both texts is the remark that the cross separates and fastens the above and the below (*AJ* 99, *AA* Mart. Prius 14: πέπηξαι γὰρ ἐν κόσμῳ ἵνα τὰ ἄστατα στηρίξῃς)[17]. But as these functions of the cross also occur in other second-century texts, this parallel is not specifically Gnostic and less significant in the present context[18]. As in the *APt*, the *AA* regards the cross as Logos as the ordering principle of the universe[19].

The *AJ* and the *AA* are both characterised by the fact that God is not subdivided into a Father and a Son. The reader is confronted with just one divine person. The *AJ* admittedly takes more time to argue the unity of God and is therefore more clearly a representative of the docetic position that we know best from the attacks by the Johannine Epistles and Ignatius, but in point of fact the *AA* no less clearly omits

---

[16] Lalleman, *Acts of John*, 53-5.
[17] Prieur, *Acta Andreae*, 698.
[18] *Peri Pascha* 51.9, see P. Nautin (ed.), *Homélies pascales I. Une homélie inspirée du traité sur la Paque d'Hippolyte* (Paris, 1950); the Homily used to be attributed to Hippolytus of Rome, but R. Cantalamessa, *L'omelia 'In s.Pascha' dello pseudo-Ippolito di Roma* (Milano, 1967) has shown that it dates from the second century and is related to Melito's *Peri Pascha*); *Excerpta ex Theodoto* 42.1, cf. 26.2 and 35.1; Irenaeus, *Adv. Haer.* 1.3.5; Hippolytus, *Ref* 6.31.5-6.
[19] J. Bolyki, '"Head Downwards": The Cross of Peter in the Lights of the Apocryphal Acts, of the New Testament and of the Society-transforming Claim of Early Christianity', in Bremmer, *Acts of Peter*, 111-22.

Christ as a separate person[20]. Jesus' life on earth and death on the cross are never mentioned and they have no role in the salvation of the believers.

Also common to both AAA is the idea of a relation between the apostle's success and his attainment of rest[21].

A key word in the AA is 'related to' (συγγενής) which indicates the spiritual bond between believers and the divine. The same word occurs nine times in the non-Gnostic part of the AJ and always in the 'normal' sense of belonging to the same family. But its use in the AA strongly parallels its only occurrence in the Gnostic section of the AJ (101.6).

Bremmer has shown that women are depicted more favourably than men in both AJ and AA – with the natural exception of the apostle[22].

In AAlat 20 Andrew has a vision at night, in which the apostle John guides his brother Peter and himself to the top of the highest mountain. The mountain radiates with light and illuminates the whole earth. The whole scene reminds of the polymorphous appearance of the Lord to John in AJ 90. But this time the Lord is absent; instead, it is John who reveals to the two brothers that he is the 'word of the cross' (*ego sum verbum crucis*). Andrew ends his report by hinting at the fact that more was said than is reported at the time[23]. This traditional concluding sentence strongly suggests that the scene must have been part of the AA from the beginning[24], despite the fact that a few lines on the text refers to the divine Son and to the Holy Spirit, something the original AA never do.

The most remarkable aspect of the episode is the fact that of all people, it is John who is the guide, the spiritual leader of Andrew, not Christ or an angel. Also, John is taller than Andrew, which may mean that his faith or his prestige is greater than Andrew's. By pre-

---

[20] Junod and Kaestli, *Acta Iohannis*, 493, and following them Prieur, *Acta Andreae*, 365 n.2, deny that the AJ and the AA are docetic, using the same phrase 'au-delà du docétisme'.

[21] A form of ἀναπαύομαι occurs in AAgr 40, 43, and AJ 45.

[22] Bremmer, 'Women in the Apocryphal Acts of John', in Bremmer, *Acts of John*, 37-56; Bremmer, this volume, Ch. II.1.

[23] *Et multa alia mihi dixit, quae nunc silere oportet.*

[24] Cf. Sirach 43.27; 1Macc 9.22; Lucian, *Demonax* 67; O. Weinreich, *Antike Heilungswunder* (Giessen, 1909) 199-201.

senting John in this way, the author of the *AA* recognises the authority of John. In combination with the fact that the Fourth Gospel, the Gospel traditionally attributed to the apostle John, is alluded to more often than any other writing[25], the *AA* would seem to be tributary to the Johannine tradition as it is represented by the Gospel and the *AJ*.

5. *Differences*

The above similarities should not blind us to the considerable differences between *AJ* and *AA*. First of all, the polymorphy of Christ (*AJ* 82, 88-93, 97-8, cf. *APt* 20-1, *ATh* 48, 153) is conspicuously absent from the *AA*. Admittedly, the *AA* contains appearences of the Lord as Andrew and as a beautiful young man, but these are not cases of polymorphy in the strict sense because he is not seen in different ways at the same moment[26]. The reason for the absence of polymorphy in the *AA* seems to be that the text pays more attention to Andrew than to the Lord. Like the *AJ*, the *AAgr* knows no human character Jesus; in a docetic way the Saviour is merely seen as God. Such a Christology leaves the role of mediator vacant. The *AA* draws the consequences out of this state of affairs by elevating the apostle above the human level and attributing divine traits to him, as does the *ATh* (8)[27]. The *AJ*, on the other hand, never makes this move; John is no more than a very powerful messenger. I would suggest that the *AA* represents a more advanced phase of reflection.

Secondly, the spiritualism of the *AJ* has in the *AA* been changed into a rather extreme form of dualism. The *AA* has a developed theory of two classes of people, the Gnostics and the others, which has no parallel in the *AJ*. Thus the text can state that the soul of Stratocles is already related (συγγενής is the key word) to God before his conversion. The asceticism of the *AA*, which shows itself in the spheres of the Eucharist, of marriage and sexuality, of food and possesions, and which is much stronger here than in the *AJ*, is subservient to this dualism[28]. To give an example: unlike John, Andrew

---

[25] Cf. Prieur, *Actes*, 52.
[26] Cf. my 'Polymorphy of Christ', in Bremmer, *Acts of John*, 97-118.
[27] Van Kampen, *Apostelverhalen*, 157.
[28] Van Kampen, *Apostelverhalen*, 141-9; Prieur, *Actes*, 37.

prevents marriages (*AAlat* 11)[29]. The *AJ* knows no asceticism in relation to food and possessions, and only a limited restraint towards marriage.

A few minor differences may just be listed without much comment:

* Whereas the *AA* like the other *AAA* ends with the martyrdom of the apostle, John dies peacefully in the *AJ*.
* The *AAlat* is replete with stories about demons, whereas demons are virtually absent from the *AJ* (with the exception of cc.56-7, they are merely elements of the author's rhetorical vocabulary).
* More than the other *AAA*, the *AA* has a philosophical colouring.
* Prieur suggests that the *AJ* and *AA* have a similar attitude towards Scripture[30], but he overlooks the fact that the *AJ* polemises against the New Testament gospels; the *AA* does not do this because it never deals with the person of Jesus.
* In several respects the *AAlat* cannot hide the fact that it is considerably later than the *AJ* and the original *AA*. Thus *AAlat* (6) contains the doctrine of the Trinity and the appointment of a bishop. A complete copy of the *evangelium* (*AAlat* 23) was almost certainly not available to a woman (or a man) in the second century[31].

6. Conclusion

Taking all the parallels together, the thesis of Junod, Kaestli and Prieur, according to which the author of the *AA* knew and was inspired by the *AJ*, seems to hold, although they probably make too much of the ideological similarities between the two texts. In several respects, the *AA* appears to have been written later than the *AJ*.

---

[29] Not in the preserved version but in its *Vorlage*, see Junod and Kaestli, *Acta Iohannis*, 143 n. 4.
[30] Prieur, *Acta Andreae*, 397.
[31] Bremmer, this volume, Ch. II.1.

XIII. La version arménienne du Martyre d'André*

VALENTINA CALZOLARI

1. La transmission des textes apocryphes chrétiens dans les versions orientales

Le *Martyre d'André* (*MartA*) représente la section finale des *Actes d'André*[1] (*AA*), un texte apocryphe vraisemblablement écrit à Alexandrie, au IIe siècle après J.-C. Les *AA* sont mentionnés pour la première fois (à côté des *AJ* et des *Évangiles* de *Pierre*, de *Thomas* et de *Matthias*) au début du IVe siècle, par Eusèbe de Césarée. Dans son *Histoire Ecclésiastique* III, 25, Eusèbe affirme, entre autres, que la pensée et la doctrine de ces écrits s'écartent radicalement de l'orthodoxie; il les considère comme des oeuvres fabriquées par les hérétiques qui doivent être, conclut-il, absolument rejetées en tant qu'écrits absurdes et impies. La condamnation formulée par l'évêque

---

* Cet article reprend, avec quelques développements et une mise à jour de la bibliographie, mon étude parue en italien dans *Studi e ricerche sull'Oriente cristiano* 16 (1993) 3-33, sous le titre 'La versione armena del *Martirio di Andrea*: alcune osservazioni in relazione all'originale greco'. Je tiens à remercier J. N. Bremmer de m'avoir proposé de publier cet article, en traduction française, dans son volume consacré aux *Actes d'André*. Je renouvelle également les remerciements que j'avais adressés dans la première rédaction de ce travail à J.-D. Kaestli et à E. Norelli pour leurs conseils avertis.

[1] Cf. J.-M. Prieur, *Acta Andreae*, 2 vol. (Turnhout, 1989: désormais Prieur); D. R. MacDonald, *The Acts of Andrew and The Acts of Andrew and Matthias in the City of the Cannibals* (Atlanta, 1990: désormais MacDonald); à MacDonald on doit également une étude sur les sources possibles des *AA*, notamment dans la littérature grecque prophane: cf. D. R. MacDonald, *Christianizing Homer* (New York et Oxford, 1994). Les passages grecs mentionnés dans cet article seront cités selon l'édition de Prieur (P).

de Césarée inaugura une longue série d'attaques qui frappèrent les *AA* ainsi que les autres *AAA*, attaques souvent basées sur des préjugés et sur des critères d'évaluation de l'orthodoxie complètement étrangers à la période de rédaction des *AAA* les plus anciens (IIe-IIIe siècles): *AA, AP, ATh, APt, AJ*. Comme on le sait, la censure prononcée par la Grande Eglise contre les textes apocryphes chrétiens eut de lourdes conséquences sur leur diffusion et leur transmission: quelques-unes de ces oeuvres ont été complètement perdues; d'autres nous ont été conservées, mais par un nombre restreint de témoins, souvent fragmentaires; d'autres encore ont été remaniées et épurées de tous les passages considérés hétérodoxes. La réception des oeuvres apocryphes n'a toutefois pas été la même dans toute l'*oekoumène*. En effet, certains textes, condamnés en Occident par l'Eglise, ont continué en revanche à circuler dans les communautés chrétiennes orientales sous forme de traductions. Dans beaucoup de cas, le rôle joué par les versions en langues orientales, y compris l'arménien, s'est révélé fondamental.

Parmi les exemples les plus évidents, on peut citer la *Correspondance apocryphe entre Paul et les Corinthiens* (3 *Co*)[2]. Jusqu'en 1959, date de la découverte d'un témoin direct grec[3], cette *Correspondance* était connue, dans sa forme intégrale, uniquement grâce à son ancienne version arménienne[4]. Aujourd'hui encore, si le témoin direct grec reste unique, les catalogues des manuscrits permettent en revanche de repérer plus de quatre-vingts manuscrits arméniens. Dans la plupart des cas, il s'agit de manuscrits bibliques; en effet, sans doute à cause de l'influence de l'Église syrienne, pour laquelle 3 *Co*

---

[2] Cf. W. Rordorf, 'Hérésie et orthodoxie selon la Corréspondance apocryphe entre les Corinthiens et l'apôtre Paul', dans H.-D. Altendorf *et al.*, *Orthodoxie et hérésie dans l'Eglise ancienne. Perspectives nouvelles* (Genève, Lausanne, Neuchâtel, 1993) 21-63.

[3] M. Testuz, *Papyrus Bodmer X-XII* (Cologny, 1959).

[4] La version arménienne est à son tour une traduction du texte syriaque. Parmi les travaux récents sur la version arménienne de 3 *Co,* cf. P. S. Cowe, 'Text Critical Investigation of the Armenian Version of Third Corinthians', dans V. Calzolari *et al.* (éds.), *Apocryphes arméniens. Transmission, traduction, création, iconographie* (Lausanne 1999: désormais Calzolari *et al.*) 91-102. En plus de l'arménien, il convient de rappeler aussi l'importance des fragments coptes: cf. C. Schmidt, *Acta Pauli aus der Heidelberger koptischen Papyrushandschrift Nr. 1* (Leipzig, 1905^2 = Hildesheim, 1965).

a été canonique (au moins dans un premier temps)⁵, ce texte fut inséré dans la Bible arménienne. L'exemple de la *Correspondance entre Paul et les Corinthiens* démontre non seulement la complexité du processus qui conduisit à la formation du Canon du Nouveau Testament (différent en Orient et en Occident, et selon les époques), mais aussi l'importance de la connaissance des versions orientales pour l'étude de la littérature apocryphe chrétienne. C'est également un témoignage intéressant des modalités de survie des textes apocryphes chrétiens. En effet, si les *AP*, en tant qu'oeuvre intégrale, ont été irrémédiablement perdus, certaines sections du texte ont été détachées et ont eu une existence séparée. C'est le cas de 3 *Co*, du *Martyre de Paul* et des *APTh* qui, à l'origine, constituaient trois épisodes des *AP*⁶. C'est sous cette forme indépendante que ces trois textes ont été connus et traduits en arménien ainsi que dans d'autres langues orientales. Les *APTh*, en particulier, eurent une grande diffusion dans tout l'Orient et l'Occident chrétiens. Les Arméniens aussi les connurent, non pas dans le texte original grec, mais par le biais d'une ancienne version syriaque, qu'ils traduisirent probablement lors de l'âge d'or de la littérature arménienne (première moitié du Ve siècle)⁷.

Comme on le verra, la version arménienne du *MartA* se révèle fondamentale pour la restitution du texte grec; en effet, elle conserve

---

⁵ En effet, elle se trouve dans le *Commentaire aux Epîtres de Paul* d'Ephrem.
⁶ En plus de l'article sur *3 Co* cité *supra* (note 2), cf. aussi W. Rordorf, 'Tradition et composition dans les *Actes de Thècle*. Etat de la question', *Theol. Zs.* 41 (1985) 272-83. Parmi les travaux récents sur les *APTh*, cf. également J. N. Bremmer (éd.), *The Apocryphal Acts of Paul and Thecla* (Kampen, 1996).
⁷ Sur les *APTh* arméniens, cf. V. Calzolari, 'Notes sur la traduction arménienne du texte syriaque des *Actes de Thècle*', dans D. Sakayan (éd.), *Proceedings of the Fifth International Conference on Armenian Linguistics* (Delmar, NY, 1996) 233-43; Ead., 'La trasmissione dei testi apocrifi cristiani in armeno: l'esempio degli *Atti di Paolo e Tecla*', dans A. Valvo (éd.), *La diffusione dell'eredità classica nell'età tardoantica e medievale* (Alessandria, 1997) 45-58; Ead., 'De sainte Thècle à Anahit: une hypothèse d'interprétation du récit de la mort de l'empereur Valens dans les *Buzandaran Patmut'iwnk*'', dans N. Awde (éd.), *Armenian Perspectives*, (Richmond, 1997) 39-49 et 371-7; Ead, 'Un nouveau texte arménien sur Thècle: les *Prodiges de Thècle* (Présentation et analyse linguistique)', *REArm* 26 (1996-97) 249-71.

plusieurs passages vraisemblablement primitifs qui ont été perdus dans l'original grec. Le but de cette contribution est précisément d'analyser quelques-uns de ces passages conservés uniquement en arménien. Une attention particulière sera consacrée aux extraits les plus intéressants du point de vue du contenu ainsi qu'aux passages qui nous offrent un témoignage éclairant pour comprendre de quelle manière la 'censure' est parfois intervenue sur le texte original grec. L'analyse de ces extraits sera précédée par un discours général sur la technique de traduction du *MartA* arménien ainsi que sur les passages qui trahissent une intention doctrinale de la part du traducteur. La connaissance des mécanismes qui ont guidé les modifications de l'arménien par rapport à l'original est, en effet, indispensable pour distinguer les développements secondaires propres à l'arménien des possibles témoignages des passages primitifs, qui constituent le principal objet d'intérêt de cette contribution. Avant de passer à cette analyse, il me semble utile de rappeler quelques informations générales sur les *AA* grecs et sur leur version arménienne.

2. Les Actes d'André

Le texte grec
Comme on le sait, les *AA* constituent un cas exemplaire des vicissitudes vécues par les textes apocryphes au fil des siècles. En effet, jusqu'à présent, il n'existe aucun manuscrit qui contienne la rédaction complète du texte grec des *AA*. La première partie, qui décrit les pérégrinations de l'apôtre du Pont jusqu'à l'Achaïe, est connue seulement grâce à l'épitomé latin de Grégoire de Tours (mort en 593), élaboré à partir d'une version latine du texte primitif[8]. L'évêque de Tours a souvent modifié sa source, en omettant ou altérant les sections des discours jugées prolixes, hérétiques ou trop enclines au fantastique[9]. La partie des *Actes* qui concerne l'Achaïe et qui se termine par le *Martyre* à Patras nous est parvenue d'une manière très frag-

---

[8] Cf. Prieur, 551-651 et MacDonald, 179-317. Pour la partie équivalente au chapitre 18 de l'épitomé de Grégoire de Tours, nous possédons aussi le témoignage du fragment incomplet du Papyrus copte Utrecht 1, dont la première traduction, en anglais, fut publiée dans G. Quispel, 'An Unknown Fragment of the Acts of Andrew', *VigChris* 10 (1956) 129-48. Le fragment a été édité par R. van den Broek et traduit en français dans Prieur, 653-71.
[9] Cf. Prieur, 8-12, 119; MacDonald, 15-9, 181-5.

mentaire sous forme d'extraits, épitomés, remaniements, traductions[10]. Sur la base de ces témoins, directs et indirects, deux hypothèses de reconstitution du texte original grec ont récemment été proposées dans deux éditions critiques, dues respectivement aux soins de J.-M. Prieur et de D. R. MacDonald[11].

La version arménienne du Martyre d'André
La seule édition jusqu'à maintenant existante de la version arménienne du *MartA* est parue à Venise en 1904 grâce aux soins de K'. Čʻrakʻean[12]; elle est basée sur trois témoins de la Bibliothèque des Mékhitaristes de Venise[13]. L'époque de rédaction de cette version reste difficile à déterminer, faute de critères chronologiques externes précis. Rappelons que L. Leloir, à qui l'on doit une traduction française du *MartA*, considérait les traductions arméniennes des *AAA*, y compris le *MartA*, vraisemblablement postérieures à l'âge d'or et les situait au VIe-VIIe siècles après J.-C[14]. Le *MartA* arménien correspond aux chapitres 47-65 des *AA* grecs. Il n'est pas possible de préciser si le traducteur avait sous les yeux les *AA* grecs dans leur intégralité ou bien seulement le texte du *Martyre*. Une circulation et une

[10] Pour les différents témoins du texte des *AA*, cf. Prieur, 2-31, 423-35.
[11] Cf. note 1. Les deux éditions concordent généralement, sauf pour leur approche différente des *Actes d'André et Matthieu dans le pays des anthropophages*: Prieur, 32-5, en suivant J. Flamion, *Les Actes apocryphes de l'apôtre André. Les Actes d'André et de Matthias, de Pierre et d'André et les textes apparentés* (Louvain, 1911) 269-324 (désormais Flamion), les considère comme tardifs et indépendants des *AA*, alors que MacDonald, 3-47, 61-177, en publie le texte au début des *AA* et considère donc qu'ils font partie d'une seule oeuvre; à ce sujet, voir maintenant la contribution de A. Hilhorst et P. J. Lalleman dans ce volume, ch. I.
[12] Cf. K'. Čʻrakʻean, *Ankanon girkʻ aṙakʻelakankʻ* (Venise, 1904) 146-67. Les passages arméniens mentionnés dans cet article seront cités d'après l'édition vénitienne (Čʻ). L'édition de Čʻrakʻean a été traduite en français par L. Leloir, *Ecrits apocryphes sur les apôtres. Traduction de l'édition arménienne de Venise*, vol. 1 (Turnhout, 1986) 228-57 (désormais Leloir, 'Ecrits').
[13] Je prépare actuellement une nouvelle édition critique du texte arménien du *MartA* pour le *Corpus Christianorum. Series Apocryphorum*; cette édition s'appuiera sur quatorze nouveaux témoins arméniens.
[14] Cf. L. Leloir, 'Rapports entre les versions arménienne et syriaque des Actes apocryphes des apôtres', dans *Symposium Syriacum 1976* (Roma, 1978) 137-48 et notamment 138 (désormais Leloir, 'Rapports').

traduction séparées du *Martyre* ne sont pas à exclure, étant donné que dans d'autres cas aussi la section finale des *AAA* a été traduite de manière indépendante, comme nous l'avons vu à propos du *Martyre de Paul*[15].

Comme il a déjà été observé, la version arménienne conserve quelques passages absents de l'original grec[16]. L'importance de ces extraits arméniens n'a pas échappé aux derniers éditeurs des *AA* grecs: Prieur, qui en prend connaissance sur la base de la traduction française de Leloir, y consacre ses observations dans les pages du *Commentaire*; MacDonald, quant à lui, les insère dans le texte grec et, grâce à la collaboration d'un arménisant, Th. J. Samuelian, en fournit la traduction anglaise[17]. Aucun de ces extraits n'a toutefois été évalué sur la base d'une analyse directe et complète du texte arménien qui aurait pour but l'identification des caractéristiques linguistiques, stylistiques et lexicales de la version (en un mot, de l'*usus vertendi* du traducteur). La comparaison ponctuelle entre le texte arménien et le texte grec permet notamment de repérer le degré de fidélité majeure ou mineure de la version arménienne par rapport à l'original. Dans le paragraphe suivant seront exposées quelques considérations relatives aux procédés de traduction du *MartA* arménien; ne seront évidemment pas relevées les divergences qui dénoncent une probable variante grecque, ni les différences dues à l'exigence d'adapter les structures de la langue grecque à celle de langue d'arrivée. A ce propos, il suffira de remarquer que le traducteur a évité le calque des structures syntaxiques grecques étrangères à l'arménien et a préféré expliciter les tournures implicites grecques, telles

---

[15] Cf. L. Leloir, 'Les Actes apocryphes d'André', dans A. Van Tongerloo et S. Giversen (éds.), *Manichaica Selecta* (Louvain, 1991) 191-201 et notamment 193 s. (désormais Leloir, 'Actes'); M. Erbetta, *Gli Apocrifi del Nuovo Testamento*, II: *Atti e Leggende* (Torino, 1971) 397.

[16] Parmi les extraits plus étendus de l'arménien, il convient de rappeler tout particulièrement le discours sur l'oeuvre du diable, examiné *infra* (Č˚ 147, 24-149, 15; cf. P 49, 8-50, 17); l'allégorie de l'aigle, complètement absente en grec (Č˚ 152, 18-154, 22; le texte arménien se trouve en correspondance de la fin de P 53); le discours de l'apôtre à la croix (Č˚ 154, 24-156, 22) qui, en grec, peut être reconstruit uniquement sur la base de témoins indirects (le *Martyrium prius* et la *Laudatio*): cf. Prieur, 14-17, 236-65, 428-30, 673-83, 735-45.

[17] Cf. MacDonald, 322 s.; voir mon compte rendu dans *Le Muséon* 106 (1993) 198-200.

que participes, génitifs absolus, infinitifs[18]. La même comparaison entre les deux textes, élargie à toutes les variantes du grec et de l'arménien, m'a également permis de vérifier que le texte arménien présente un degré de proximité majeure avec la recension grecque que Prieur a jugée comme étant la meilleure[19]. Si cette recension grecque et la version arménienne semblent dériver d'un modèle commun, le texte arménien paraît pourtant, en beaucoup d'endroits, plus fidèle à ce modèle que la recension grecque[20].

3. *Technique de traduction du* MartA *arménien*

La comparaison entre le *MartA* arménien et l'original grec montre tout d'abord une différence entre parties narratives et discours. Dans les parties narratives, la correspondance entre les deux textes est généralement précise, alors que dans les discours on constate un grand nombre de divergences. Les deux sections, par ailleurs, révèlent l'intention du traducteur d'expliquer certains passages grecs. Cette volonté se manifeste par exemple dans le cas où: a) il explicite des adjectifs neutres, des pronoms ou des numéraux grecs; b) il utilise des périphrases; c) il ajoute des mots absents de l'original[21], comme on peut le constater dans les exemples qui suivent:

a) P 49, 2 s. πολλὰ παρέσχετο, 'il offrit *beaucoup (de choses)*': Čʿ 147, 19 *taloc' ē varjs*, 'il donnera *des récompenses*';

P 50, 19 πρὸς τὸ ἀπηλλάχθαι αὐτοῦ γιγνώμεθα, 'parvenons à nous éloigner *de lui*': Čʿ 149, 17 s. *i bazmahnar orogayt'ic' nora meržesc'uk*, 'éloignons-nous *de ses filets insidieux*';

P 55, 2 θεασάμενοι ἐκείνους, 'ayant vu *ceux-là*': Čʿ 157, 8 *teseal zdahičsn*, 'ayant vu *les bourreaux*';

---

[18] On trouvera un examen de la langue du *MartA* arménien dans V. Calzolari, 'Particolarità sintattiche e lessicali della versione armena del *Martirio di Andrea*, messa a confronto con Teone armeno', *Le Muséon* 106 (1993) 267-88.

[19] Pour un classement des manuscrits grecs, cf. Prieur, 431-5.

[20] Les résultats de cette analyse ont été exposés dans V. Calzolari, 'La versione armena del *Martirio di Andrea* e il suo rapporto con la tradizione manoscritta dell'originale greco', *Le Muséon* 111 (1998) 139-56 (désormais Calzolari).

[21] Beaucoup moins fréquents sont les cas où la traduction arménienne présente un texte plus court qu'en grec: cf. Čʿ 167, 15 face à P 54, 18; Čʿ 158, 1 s. face à P 56, 8 s.; etc.

P 55, 4 s. προσεδόκουν τι πάλιν ἀκούσεσθαι παρ ' αὐτοῦ, 'ils espéraient entendre encore *quelque chose* de *lui*': Čᵉ 157, 10 s. *akn unēin zi ayl ews luic'en bans i surb beranoy nora*, 'ils espéraient entendre encore d'autres *mots* de *sa sainte bouche*';
P 51, 11 ἑπτὰ μάστιξιν ἐκέλευσεν αὐτὸν μαστιχθῆναι, 'il ordonna qu'il soit fouetté avec *sept* fouets': Čᵉ 150, 12 s. *hramayeac' tanǰel zna gawazanōk', minč'ew poxec'an eōt'n ayr harkanel zna*, 'il ordonna de le torturer avec des bâtons, *jusqu'à ce que sept hommes se relayassent pour le frapper*';

b) P 51, 16 ὁ ξένος, 'l'étranger': Čᵉ 150, 19 s. *or i heṙust... ekeal ē*, 'celui qui est venu de loin';
P 47, 8 ἠθῶν ἀνθρωπίνων, 'les *coutumes* humaines': Čᵉ 146, 11 s. *xorhurdk' ew bank' mardkan sovorut'eambn handerj*, '*les pensées et les mots* des hommes *avec le concours de l'habitude*';
P 47, 4 s. ταῖς ... φαντασίαις, 'les fantaisies': Čᵉ 146, 6 *or aṙač῾ōk' erewin*, '(les choses) qui apparaissent devant les yeux', (interprétation étymologique);

c) P 51, 4 ἐκ τοῦ δεσμωτηρίου, 'de la prison': Čᵉ 150, 2 *i bandēn kapanac'*, 'de la prison *des liens*', (interprétation étymologique de δεσμωτήριον < δεσμός, 'liens');
P 62, 23 βρύξῃ, 'tu grinceras': Čᵉ 165, 7 *krčesc'es zatamuns k'o*, 'tu grinceras *des dents*'[22] (le traducteur reprend ici l'expression *krčel atamanc'*, 'grincer des dents', par laquelle est traduit Mt 8, 12 ὁ βρυγμὸς τῶν ὀδόντων = Mt 13, 42 et 50; 22, 13; 24, 51; 25, 30; Lc 13, 28; cf. aussi Mc 9, 18; Ac 7, 54[23]).

Le traducteur du *MartA* arménien n'est donc pas un traducteur servile, mais un écrivain qui se sent suffisamment maître de la langue grecque pour pouvoir s'affranchir parfois des structures de la langue de départ, dans le but de mieux exprimer en arménien le contenu de l'original. La maîtrise du grec du traducteur est également attestée par sa capacité de reconnaître et de rendre les verbes grecs rares, comme dans les deux exemples suivants:

a) dans P 47, 12, on lit une forme du verbe ὀπτρίζομαι, qui est un *hapax* absolu qui signifie 'voir comme dans un miroir'[24]. Le traduc-

---

[22] Le *Thesaurus* de la langue arménienne (G. Awetik'ean *et al.*, *Nor Baṙgirk' Haykazean Lezui* [Venise, 1836]) signale que le verbe arménien *krčem*, utilisé de manière absolue, équivaut au gr. βρύχομαι avec le sens de 'grincer des dents'. L'adjonction de *zatamuns k'o*, 'tes dents', est donc une hyperdétermination du sens.

[23] Les passages bibliques sont cités d'après Y. Zōhrapean, *Astuacašunč῾ Matean Hin ew Nor Ktakaranac'* (Venise, 1805).

[24] Cf. Prieur, 500, note 2.

teur a saisi le champs sémantique de ce verbe et l'a traduit par le verbe arménien *tesanem*, 'voir' (Č' 146, 17), probablement sur la base de κατοπτριζόμενοι de 2 Co 3, 18 (traduit en arménien par la périphrase *ibrew and hayeli teseal*, 'en voyant comme dans un miroir');

b) P 53, 22 conserve une forme du verbe grec στερρύνω (cf. στερρόω, 'solidifier, fortifier', στερρότης, 'fermeté, solidité', στερρός, 'solide, dur, fort') qui n'est pas citée dans les lexiques de la langue grecque et qui constitue donc une forme rare[25]; ce verbe a été compris par le traducteur qui l'a traduit par l'expression *zōrac'eal linim*, 'devenir fort' (Č' 152, 14).

On notera toutefois quelques erreurs, comme dans les deux cas où le traducteur ne reconnaît pas le verbe ἀνιάω, 'affliger, tourmenter', et le traduit par arm. *t'olum*, 'laisser', qui correspond plutôt au gr. ἐάω ou ἀνίημι[26]. Il convient également de rappeler que, dans les sections qui contiennent les discours de l'apôtre, les divergences entre les deux textes sont parfois tellement grandes qu'elles rendent impossible l'établissement d'un parallèle entre les deux textes. Dans ces cas, il est difficile de préciser si les divergences sont entièrement imputables au traducteur, étant donné que, dans le cadre de la tradition directe aussi, les discours sont les parties les plus remaniées et souvent transmises sous une forme incomplète[27].

Tels sont brièvement évoqués les procédés de traduction du *MartA* arménien. Reste maintenant à mettre en évidence les points qui trahissent une intention doctrinale de la part du traducteur.

4. Extraits du MartA *arménien qui trahissent une intention doctrinale de la part du traducteur*

Comme première remarque d'ordre général, on peut observer que le traducteur arménien tend à interpréter le texte grec à la lumière de réminiscences bibliques[28], comme dans les passages suivants:

[25] J'ai pu consulter les dictionnaires et les concordances usuels ainsi que le TLG informatisé.
[26] Cf. P 54, 17 ἀνιᾶσαι, 'affliger': Č' 157, 4 *t'olul*, 'laisser', et P 62, 24 ἀνιάσῃ, 'tu t'affligeras': Č' 165, 8 s. *t'oc'es*, 'tu laisseras'.
[27] Cf. Prieur, 5 s.
[28] La série des allusions bibliques, surtout néotestamentaires, attestées dans le *MartA* arménien a été signalée dans Leloir, 'Ecrits', notes à sa traduction française. Sur les citations bibliques des *AA*, voir aussi Prieur, 404 s.; L. Leloir, compte rendu de Prieur, dans *RHE* 85 (1990) 361 s.; Leloir, 'Actes', 197 s.

P 64, 17 s. Τὰ σά ... ἅμα σοὶ πορευέσθω, 'que tes biens viennent avec toi': Č⁽ᶜ⁾ 167, 14 s. *inč'k' k'o ənd k'ez ełic'i i korust*, 'que tes biens viennent avec toi *dans la perdition*', qui rappelle Ac 8, 20 τὸ ἀργύριόν σου σὺν σοὶ εἴη εἰς ἀπώλειαν = arm. *arcat' k'o ənd k'ez lic'i i korust*, 'que ton argent vienne avec toi dans la perdition';

P 55, 11 οὐκ ἔχει τὸ ἀκούειν, 'il ne peut pas écouter': Č⁽ᶜ⁾ 157, 19 s. *oč' uni akanǰs lseloy*, 'il n'a pas d'oreilles pour écouter', qui rappelle Mt 11, 15; 13, 9 et 43; etc. ὁ ἔχων ὦτα ἀκουέτω, traduit en arménien par *or unic'i akanǰs lseloy luic'ē*, 'celui qui a des oreilles pour écouter, qu'il écoute';

P 52, 10 φέρειν τὰ ἐπαγόμενα, 'supporter ce qui a été infligé': Č⁽ᶜ⁾ 151, 7 s. *baṙnal zbeṙn irerac'*, 'supporter les poids des uns et des autres', qui est semblable à Ga 6, 2 ἀλλήλων τὰ βάρη βαστάζετε, traduit en arménien par *zmimeanc' beṙn barjēk'*, 'supportez les poids des uns et des autres'.

Une deuxième particularité de la version est représentée par le rôle fondamental attribué aux 'commandements' de Dieu. Alors qu'en grec il y a une seule référence au 'commandement du Seigneur' (τὴν τοῦ κυρίου ἐντολήν, P 39, 4)[29], l'arménien insiste plusieurs fois sur la nécessité d'accomplir les 'commandements' de Dieu, qui sont au fur et à mesure qualifiés de 'doux', 'délicieux', 'lumineux', 'bienheureux', 'désirables', et qui sont considérés comme l'ornement naturel de l'âme[30]. L'importance accordée par le traducteur aux commandements divins est claire dans le *desinit* du *MartA*: le grec ἐνταῦθά που τὸ τέλος τῶν μακαρίων μου διηγημάτων ποιήσαιμι καὶ πράξεων καὶ μυστηρίων δυσφράστων ὄντων, ἵνα μὴ καὶ ἀφράστων εἴπω, 'que j'achève ici mon récit bienheureux des actes et des mystères qui sont difficiles, sinon impossibles à exprimer' (P 65, 1-3), a été traduit en arménien par *ayl inj ełic'i yaysmhetē xokal yeraneli ew i c'ankali patuirans Teaṙn or ančaṙk' en ew anhasanelik'*, 'mais qu'il soit désormais pour moi temps de penser aux com-

---

[29] Cf. Prieur, 490, note 2.

[30] Voir les passages suivants, tous absents en grec: Č⁽ᶜ⁾ 148, 16 s. *zi zna siresc'uk' ew zpatuirans nora arasc'uk'*, 'afin que nous l'aimions (*scil.* Dieu) et accomplissions ses commandements', (cf. 1 Jn 5, 2); Č⁽ᶜ⁾ 152, 21 s. *yałags k'ałc'r ew hešt patuiranac'n Astucoy*, '(les démons... se disputent avec nous) quant aux doux et délicieux commandements de Dieu'; Č⁽ᶜ⁾ 153, 8 s. *zardaric'emk' zmez luselēn patuiranawn ew hogełinac'n aṙak'inut'eambk'*, 'nous nous parons du commandement lumineux et des vertus spirituelles'.

mandements bienheureux et désirables du Seigneur, qui sont indicibles et inaccessibles' (Čᵉ 167, 20 -22).

Dans certains passages, le traducteur semble avoir soumis le texte grec à une révision, dans le but de supprimer toute ambiguïté d'interprétation. Il semble avoir intentionnellement modifié l'original dans les passages suivants:

a) après avoir constaté l'instabilité des hommes et de leurs coutumes, André explique que cela arrive διὰ τὴν ἀπαίδευτον ψυχὴν τὴν εἰς φύσιν πλανηθεῖσαν, 'à cause de l'âme inéduquée qui s'est fourvoyée dans la nature' (P 47, 9 s.), c'est-à-dire, comme l'explique Prieur, dans le corps et ses liens[31]. Le grec a été traduit en arménien par *anxrat anjin or iwrov isk kamōk' molorec'an*[32], 'l'âme inéduquée qui, *par sa propre volonté*, s'est fourvoyée' (Čᵉ 146, 13 s.). On peut supposer que le traducteur arménien a aperçu la possibilité d'une interprétation déterministe de l'expression εἰς φύσιν, considérée comme l'équivalent de κατὰ φύσιν ou πρὸς τὴν φύσιν, 'par nature, selon (sa) nature', et a donc corrigé de manière intentionnelle le passage, en 'traduisant' le gr. εἰς φύσιν par le pronom réfléchi *iwr*, 'propre', et le substantif *kamk'*, 'volonté', à l'instrumental[33].

b) Face à P 49, 8 ὁ ... διάβολος τὰ ἴδια τέκνα ὁπλίσει, 'le diable armera ses fils', en arménien on lit *bansarkun zor xotorec'uc'eal yAstucoy arar iwr ordis, zineal varē*, 'le diable, après les avoir armés, stimule ceux dont il a fait ses fils, en les éloignant de Dieu' (Čᵉ 147, 25 s.); la proposition relative a pour fonction de pré-

---

[31] Cf. Prieur, 333.
[32] Sur la base de la comparaison avec le grec, je suis la variante du ms. 731 de Venise *molorec'an*, 'elle s'est égarée', (cf. gr. πλανηθεῖσαν, 'égarée') à la place de la leçon retenue par Čʿrak'ean *molic'in*, 'elle est devenue folle'.
[33] Augustin, *Contra Felicem* II, 6, rappelle différentes expressions des *AA* (cités comme 'Actes écrits par Leucius') qui font allusion aux hommes qui vivent dans l'erreur à cause de l'influence nuisible du monde sensible (*per se ipsum deterior factus est per seductionem*). Augustin modifie le sens de la source d'une manière semblable à celle du traducteur arménien et l'utilise pour mettre en évidence le libre arbitre de l'homme, concept qui est absent du texte original. Cf. E. Junod et J.-D. Kaestli, *L'histoire des Actes apocryphes des apôtres du IIIᵉ au IXᵉ siècle: le cas des Actes de Jean* (Genève, Lausanne, Neuchâtel, 1982) 64: 'Pour Augustin, la phrase de Leucius signifie clairement que l'homme est pécheur non par nature, mais par volonté... en cédant à la séduction du Diable' (désormais Junod et Kaestli).

ciser le sens de l'expression 'fils du diable'[34]. Dans ce cas aussi, le traducteur souligne le fait qu'on n'est pas 'fils du diable' par nature, mais qu'on le devient si l'on cède à l'action du Malin. Le texte arménien est plus riche que le grec d'expressions indiquant l'oeuvre du diable[35]. Ces expressions contribuent à dessiner d'une façon plus nette l'idée de l'oeuvre mauvaise du démon qui intervient parmi les hommes pour les amener à accomplir ce qu'il souhaite. Il est intéressant de relever que de très nombreux verbes transitifs actifs ont comme sujet le diable et comme objet les hommes. Ces derniers subissent donc son action. En effet, Satan 'fait éloigner les hommes de Dieu... les mène à la perdition... lutte contre ceux qui aiment la paix... les soustrait à la vie éternelle... lutte contre ceux qui ne sont pas les siens... trompe leurs pensées... les fait tomber... en fait ses enfants'. La lutte menée par le diable contre ceux qu'il n'arrive pas à ramener dans ses rangs est décrite par de nombreux termes appartenant au langage militaire[36]. Seule l'illumination qui vient de la Parole

---

[34] Sur les 'fils du diable', cf. 1 Jn 3, 10 et Mt 13, 38.

[35] Sur la figure du diable et sur les puissances démoniaques dans les *AA*, cf. Prieur, 367-72.

[36] Voir la série d'expressions arméniennes qui font allusion à l'oeuvre du diable. Elles sont a) sans équivalent en grec; b) amplifiées ou légèrement modifiées par rapport à l'original: a) Č^c 148, 3 s. *zi korusc'ē zmardik or yastuacut'enēn*, 'pour conduire à la perdition les hommes (qui ont été créés) par la divinité'; Č^c 148, 7 *paterazmi ənd sirołs patueal xałałut'ean*, 'il lutte contre ceux qui aiment la paix et l'honorent'; Č^c 148, 23-25 *a) i xotorec'uc'aneloy yararč'ēn mermē Astucoy. ew hanic'ē yawitenakan kenac'n*, 'pour éloigner (les hommes) de Dieu notre Créateur et pour les soustraire à la vie éternelle'; b) Č^c 147, 26 *zineal vařē*, 'après les avoir armés, il incite', (cf. P 49, 8 ὁπλίσει); Č^c 148, 8 *ənd aynosik martnč'i or oč' iwrn en*, 'il lutte contre ceux qui ne sont pas siens', (cf. P 49, 12 τὸν μὴ ἴδιον); Č^c 148, 10 *patrē zmits aynoc'ik or oč'n čanač'en zAstuac*, 'il trompe la pensée de ceux qui ne connaissent pas Dieu' (cf. P 49, 13 s. καὶ μηδέπω δυνάμενον γνωρίζεσθαι); Č^c 148, 19 s. *oč' erewec'uc'anēr ziwr t'oynsn nengawors*, 'il ne montrait pas ses poisons insidieux' (cf. P 49, 19 ἐχθρὸς μὲν οὐκ ἐδείκνυτο); Č^c 148, 20-22 *i sērs anařaks ew i č'aris płcut'ean zmardik arkanelov*, 'en faisant tomber les hommes dans des amours luxurieuses et dans le mal de l'impureté' (cf. P 49, 17 s. ὑποβάλλων γὰρ αὐτῷ τὰ ἴδια πολλάκις διέγραψεν ἐνήδονα ὄντα καὶ ἀπατηλά); Č^c 148, 22 s. *zi i mořac'ut'iwns ew i hełgut'iwns acc'ē zmardik*, 'pour conduire les hommes à l'oubli et à la négligence', (cf. P 50, 1 s.... ὡς εἰς λήθην).

réfléchissant la volonté et le dessin divins permet aux hommes de prendre conscience qu'ils sont 'dominés' par les flatteries du Malin, comme on peut le lire dans P 50, 3-5 (cf. Č' 148, 25-28). Après avoir souligné le rôle de la révélation divine, le texte continue par une série de pronoms réfléchis renvoyant au démon qui se voit désormais méprisé et qui voit ses dons ridiculisés. Le processus de prise de conscience des hommes grâce à la révélation a pour conséquence le fait que le diable, d'abord agent, se voit lui-même disqualifié pour devenir l'objet de l'action des autres.

Le texte arménien se distingue également de l'original par sa différence d'attitude vis-à-vis de la sotériologie. Si le grec ne développe aucune réflexion sur l'action salvatrice du Christ[37], l'arménien contient, au contraire, de nombreuses allusions à la venue du Seigneur et à l'oeuvre de Rédemption réalisée grâce à la Passion. La question sotériologique est présente notamment dans le discours d'André sur l'oeuvre du diable, dans un passage qui compte parmi les plus épineux des *AA* grecs et qui soulève la question de l'identification de l'*anarchos*. La comparaison directe entre l'original grec et la version arménienne permet d'éclaircir, du moins partiellement, cette section du *MartA* qui, en raison de son importance, mérite d'être examinée ici dans un paragraphe indépendant.

5. *L'antithèse entre l'oeuvre du Christ et le 'prince des anges'*

Le passage en question appartient au dernier discours qu'André adresse aux disciples en privé. Après avoir annoncé son martyre désormais imminent – conséquence de l'hostilité du diable envers tous ceux qui aiment Jésus – l'apôtre commence une digression sur le diable et son oeuvre[38], où est introduit le terme ἄναρχος (*anarchos*), 'sans-commencement', qui a fait l'objet d'interprétations controversées. Prieur a déjà évalué l'importance de la comparaison avec l'arménien pour la compréhension de cet extrait obscur et, dans les pages de son commentaire, il a proposé un tableau synoptique entre le grec et la traduction française de l'arménien par Leloir[39]. Toutefois, l'analyse directe du texte arménien comparé avec l'original démontre qu'il est possible de repérer des parallèles plus précis entre les deux textes

---

[37] C'est l'opinion de Prieur, 301, 365 *et passim*.
[38] Cf. P 49, 8-50, 17 e Č' 147, 24-149, 15.
[39] Cf. Prieur, 218-26, 208 s.

et de corriger le tableau comparatif de Prieur. Cela implique aussi, évidemment, une hypothèse d'interprétation différente. Pour permettre aux lecteurs de mieux saisir les différences, je donnerai ci-dessous: 1) le tableau synoptique de Prieur pour le passage en question[40]; 2) les modifications que j'ai jugées nécessaires.

1)
P 49, 11-14
ἀπὸ μὲν τῆς πάντων ἀρχῆς,
καὶ εἰ δεῖ λέγειν, ἐξ οὗπερ ὁ
ἄναρχος τῇ ὑπ' αὐτὸν ἀρχῇ
κατῆλθεν ἀπωθῆσαι <...> [41]

ὁ πολέμιος
εἰρήνης ἀλλότριος,
τὸν μὴ ἴδιον, ἀλλὰ μόνον τινὰ
τῶν ἀσθενεστέρων καὶ <μὴ>
περιφανῆ καὶ μηδέπω δυνάμε-

LELOIR, *Ecrits*, p. 234 s.
Comme il était prince des anges et créé avant tous <les autres>, s'il est nécessaire de <le> dire, il est tombé des cieux comme l'éclair, afin de perdre les hommes <créés> par la divinité. Aussi le Seigneur de gloire, éternel et incorruptible, est-il venu sur terre, pour le chasser du <milieu de> nous et <le> perdre, <lui> qui lutte continuellement avec ceux qui aiment <et> honorent la paix. Lui-même, en effet, est étranger à la paix, et il lutte avec ceux qui ne sont pas siens; alors qu'il est lui-même faible, impuissant et invisible d'aspect, il séduit

---

[40] Cf. Prieur, 219 s.
[41] Les crochets obliques indiquent la lacune déjà devinée par M. Bonnet dans M. Bonnet, *Acta apostolorum apocrypha* II, 1 (Leipzig, 1898 = Darmstadt, 1959) 45, 2 (désormais Bonnet) et supposée par Prieur, dans Prieur, 502, note 4 en correspondance de l'objet de ἀπωθῆσαι, 'écarter', et du verbe dont ὁ πολέμιος, 'l'ennemi', est le sujet et τὸν ἴδιον, 'celui qui n'est pas sien', l'objet direct. Face à la lacune grecque, l'arménien a l'accusatif du pronom personnel *zna*, suivi par la proposition relative *or yamenayn žam paterazmi ənd siroɫs xaɫaɫut'ean patueal*, 'lui, qui à chaque heure lutte contre ceux qui aiment la paix et l'honorent'. Le témoignage de l'arménien, toutefois, ne peut pas nous aider dans la restitution du texte grec, étant donné que, comme on l'a vu, le *MartA* arménien développe les allusions à l'oeuvre de Satan davantage que le grec.

νον γνωρίζεσθαι.	les ésprit de ceux qui ne
Καὶ διὰ τὸ μηδὲ αὐτὸν ἐπίσ-	connaissent pas Dieu.
τασθαι, ...	

Probablement induit en erreur par la traduction de Leloir, Prieur place le passage grec sur l'ἄναρχος face au passage arménien sur le 'prince des anges... créé avant tous <les autres>', c'est-à-dire le diable. Ce choix présuppose que le traducteur arménien aurait interprété la descente de l'ἄναρχος (le 'sans-commencement') comme la chute de Satan et qu'il aurait interpolé l'allusion à la venue du Christ, 'Seigneur de gloire' et Sauveur du genre humain, peut-être pour une question d'orthodoxie[42]. Ce que Prieur n'a pas vu, c'est que l'adjectif arménien *anskizbn* (composé signifiant littéralement 'sans-commencement') est l'exact équivalent du grec ἄναρχος. Il a probablement été trompé par la traduction française qui rend cet adjectif arménien par 'éternel'. Cela l'a empêché de saisir la correspondance précise qui existe entre le passage grec sur l'ἄναρχος, 'sans commencement', et le passage arménien sur le 'Seigneur incorruptible et *sans-commencement*' et non pas entre l'ἄναρχος et le 'prince des anges créé avant tous les autres'. On peut par conséquent modifier le tableau synoptique de la manière suivante:

2)

P 49, 11-12	Č' 148, 1-11
	k'anzi hreštakapet ēr ew
ἀπὸ μὲν τῆς πάντων ἀρχῆς,	yaṙaǰ k'an zamenesean naxastełc,
καὶ εἰ δεῖ λέγειν,	et'ē part ic'ē asel,
	vasn oroy ankawn yerknic' ibrew zp'aylakn, zi korusc'ē zmardik or yastuacut'enēn.
ἐξ οὕπερ ὁ ἄναρχος	vasn oroy anskizbn ew anełc Tērn p'aṙac'
τῇ ὑπ' αὐτὸν ἀρχῇ κατῆλθεν	ekn yerkir,
ἀποθῆσαι <...>	zi zna meržesc'ē i mēnǰ, ew korusc'ē, or yamenayn žam paterazmi ənd siroł patueal xałałut'ean.

---

[42] Cf. Prieur, 222.

ὁ πολέμιος
εἰρήνης ἀλλότριος,

τὸν μὴ ἴδιον,
ἀλλὰ μόνον τινὰ
τῶν ἀσθενεστέρων
καὶ <μὴ> περιφανῆ

καὶ μηδέπω
δυνάμενον
γνωρίζεσθαι.

k'anzi ew ink'n
ōtar ē i xałałut'enē,
ew ənd aynosik martnč'i
or oč' iwrn en.
zi ink'n
tkar ē ew anzōr
ew anerewoyt' tesleamb.
patrē zmits aynoc'ik
or oč'n

čanač'en
zAstuac:

Traduction du texte grec

Depuis le commencement de toutes choses et,

s'il faut (le) dire,

depuis que le *sans-commencement*

descendit

vers le commencement (qui est) au-dessous de lui
pour écarter
<...>

l'ennemi,
étranger à la paix

celui qui n'est pas sien,

Traduction du texte arménien
Comme c'était un archange et avant toutes choses

créé-avant,
s'il faut (le) dire,
pour cette raison, il tomba des cieux comme l'éclair, pour perdre les hommes qui (furent créés) par Dieu;
pour cette raison, le *sans-commencement*
et incorruptible Seigneur de gloire
vint
sur la terre

pour l'écarter
de nous et le perdre, lui qui à chaque heure lutte contre ceux qui aiment la paix et l'honorent.
Car il (*scil.* le diable) est lui-même étranger à la paix,
et il combat contre
ceux qui ne sont pas siens.

mais seulement quelqu'un des plus faibles, \<in\>visible	Puisque lui-même est faible et impuissant et invisible à la vue, il trompe les esprits de ceux qui ne
et ne pouvant pas encore être connu/se connaître.	connaissent pas Dieu.

Analyse formelle des deux textes
Le deuxième tableau synoptique permet de mettre en évidence la proximité formelle entre l'expression temporelle grecque ἀπὸ μὲν τῆς πάντων ἀρχῆς, 'depuis le commencement de toutes choses', et l'arménien *yaṙaǰ kʿan zamenesean*, 'avant toutes choses', dépendant de l'adjectif composé arménien *naxastełc*, 'créé-avant', qui se réfère à l'archange tombé des cieux. Le tableau permet de remarquer également une proximité formelle entre la relative-explicative grecque ἐξ οὗπερ, 'pour cela, pour cette raison', (préposition + pronom relatif au génitif) et l'arménien *vasn oroy*, 'pour cela, pour cette raison', (préposition + pronom relatif au génitif). L'arménien est suivi par l'adjectif *anskizbn*, 'sans-commencement', qui est formé par le préfixe négatif *an-* et le substantif *skizbn*, 'commencement' (= gr. ἀρχῇ) et qui représente donc un calque du grec ἄναρχος. Dans le texte arménien, l'adjectif a la fonction d'épithète du 'Seigneur de gloire' (*Tērn pʿaṙacʿ*), qui est défini également comme *anełc*, 'incorruptible' (citation de Jc 2, 1 et de 1 Co 2, 8 [43], absente en grec). Il faut donc placer en face du texte arménien 'le sans-commencement vint… pour écarter…' le grec ὁ ἄναρχος … κατῆλθεν ἀπωθῆσαι, 'le sans-commencement… descendit… pour écarter…'. Cela permet de corriger Prieur qui pense que le traducteur aurait compris le thème de 'l'abaissement de l'ἄναρχος comme la chute du prince des anges'[44]. La dernière partie du texte grec, qui est visiblement corrompue, a été interprétée par Prieur comme une série d'épithètes se référant à

---

[43] Cf. aussi *Tʿagawor pʿaṙacʿ*, 'Roi de gloire', de Ps 23; 7; 8; 9; 10 (bis) et d'Is 33, 17; *Astuac pʿaṙacʿ*, 'Dieu de gloire', de Ps 28, 3 et Ac 7, 2; *Hayr pʿaṙacʿ*, 'Père de gloire', d'Ep 1, 17 (la même expression se trouve dans Čʿ 148, 15, toujours à l'intérieur du discours sur l'oeuvre du diable, dans un passage absent en grec).
[44] Cf. Prieur, 222.

l'ἄναρχος, qui serait défini ainsi comme 'faible... invisible et ne pouvant pas encore être connu'[45]. Dans le texte arménien, au contraire, il est évident que ces épithètes se réfèrent au diable et non pas au 'sans-commencement'. Le traducteur a notamment traduit les adjectifs grecs à l'accusatif par une série de nominatifs qui se réfèrent au pronom personnel *ink'n,* 'lui-même' (*scil.* Satan), sauf pour l'accusatif gr. τὸν μὴ ἴδιον, 'celui qui n'est pas sien', qui a été traduit en arménien par un accusatif, objet direct du verbe *martnč'i*: 'il combat contre ceux-qui ne sont pas siens'. Finalement, malgré la différence de diathèse, on peut signaler la proximité entre les formes verbales arméniennes *oč'n čanač'en,* 'ils ne connaissent pas', et grecque μηδέπω ... γνωρίζεσθαι, 'ne (pouvant) pas encore être connu'. Cette proximité rend vaine l'hypothèse d'une coïncidence entre ces mots arméniens et le début de la période suivante du texte grec (καὶ διὰ τὸ μηδὲ αὐτὸν ἐπίστασθαι..., 'et c'est parce qu'il ne le connaissait pas...'), comme le présuppose le tableau de Prieur. Le texte arménien insiste sur l'idée que la tromperie du démon exerce son pouvoir surtout sur 'les esprits de ceux qui ne connaissent pas Dieu'[46], ce qui justifie le fait que la révélation et l'illumination divines, qui réveillent la conscience de l'homme, permettent de démasquer l'oeuvre du diable, comme on le lit aussi dans P 50, 3-5. Après avoir mis ainsi en évidence les parallélismes principaux entre les deux textes, grec et arménien, il convient de rappeler les hypothèses d'interprétation qui ont été déjà exprimées à propos du passage sur l'ἄναρχος.

Interprétation du passage
Ce passage attira l'attention de E. Hennecke, qui proposa d'identifier le 'sans-commencement' avec Dieu, sur la base de Tatien, *Oratio ad Graecos* 4 et de Platon, *Leges* 4 (*ap.* Hippolyte, *Refutatio* 1, 19)[47]. A ces citations, nous pouvons ajouter les suivantes: Héraclide, cité par Origène dans le *Dialogus cum Heraclide* 2; Hymenaeus *et al., Epistula ad Paulum Samosatenum* 2; Jean Crysostome, *Homiliae in Col.*

---

[45] Cf. Prieur, 222 et 225.
[46] Cf. P 47, 9 où, comme on l'a vu, l'ignorance de l'âme inéduquée est responsable de l'égarement de l'âme elle-même.
[47] Cf. E. Hennecke, *Handbuch zu den neutestamentlichen Apokryphen* (Tübingen, 1904) 555 s. Hennecke pensa à une allusion au péché original et à Gen 3.

5, 3. Prieur n'est pas du même avis que Hennecke. En effet, il écrit: 'L'ἄναρχος représente l'élément spirituel qui, au commencement de toutes choses, s'est abaissé dans ce qui a un commencement (ἀρχή). Il s'agit, en d'autres termes, de la venue de l'âme dans le corps'[48]. L'adjectif ἄναρχος pourrait indiquer – soutient Prieur – le νοῦς de P 37, 22 s. ou l'ἄνθρωπος auquel se réfèrent les passages P 7, 2; 7, 11; 7, 19. Prieur rapproche notamment le motif de l'abaissement de l'ἄναρχος de celui de la chute du νοῦς entraîné vers le bas par Eve (P 37, 22 s.) et de celui de l'égarement de la ψυχή inéduquée dans la nature (P 47, 9 s.). D'après Prieur, il s'agit de trois façons différentes d'indiquer 'l'union d'un élément supérieur et spirituel au monde matériel et inférieur'; c'est la situation profondément négative du devenir, de la γένεσις. Remarquons que dans aucun des passages choisis par Prieur pour éclaircir le concept d'ἄναρχος ne se trouve attesté un lexique commun à celui du passage en question; ces extraits ne peuvent donc pas être considérés comme des *loci similes* dans le vrai sens du terme. Quant à la présence dans d'autres textes que les *AA* du thème de la descente de l'ἄναρχος dans ce qui a un commencement, Prieur cite le *Corpus Hermeticum* IV, 8, où on lit que le bien est sans-commencement (ἄναρχον), même s'il nous semble en avoir un (ἀρχὴν ἔχειν), et Plotin, *Ennéades* V, 1, 2, qui fait allusion à l'âme[49].

A l'ἄναρχος s'oppose l'ennemi' (πολέμιος), c'est-à-dire le diable. L'appellation du Malin en tant qu'ἐχθρός, 'ennemi', est attestée dans le Nouveau Testament, dans Mt 13, 39 (qui reprend Mt 13, 25) et dans Lc 10, 19. Le terme ἐχθρός est utilisé pour indiquer le diable également dans les textes pseudépigraphiques juifs (par exemple dans le *Testament de Dan* 6, 3 s.; dans l'*Apocalypse de Moïse* 2, 4; 7, 2; 25, 4; 28, 4; dans la *Vie d'Adam* 17; dans *Apocalypse de Baruch* grecque 13, 2); dans les textes apocryphes chrétiens (par exemple dans les *AA* 49, 19; 16, 8; 45, 6; dans les *ATh* 39; dans les *Actes d'André et Matthieu* 20; dans les *AJ* 83; 84; 112 et dans les *Actes de Philippe* 38); dans l'*Homilia in Passionem Christi* 102 de Méliton de Sardes; etc. Le terme πολέμιος est employé pour indiquer le démon dans le *Contra Celsum* 5, 48; 6, 28 et dans les *Homiliae in Jer.* 5, 17 d'Origène, ainsi que dans les *Commentarii in Pss.*

---

[48] Cf. Prieur, 208, note 3 et 225.
[49] Sur l'ἄναρχος et les thèmes apparentés, cf. Prieur, 207-9.

108, 6 et dans l'*Historia Ecclesiastica* 5, 39, 11 de Théodoret de Cyr. Dans 1 P 5, 8, le διάβολος est appelé ἀντίδικος, adjectif qui revient avec le même sens d'"ennemi" également dans les *AA* 63, 6 et dans les *AJ* 108. Les *AJ* 66 et l'*Ascension d'Isaïe* 11, 19 conservent en outre l'adjectif ἀλλότριος, 'étranger', qui revient dans les *AA* au passage P 49, 12[50].

L'oeuvre de l'ennemi est décrite comme un piège. Le diable ne manifeste pas ouvertement son action méchante, mais flatte les hommes et cherche de s'emparer de leurs esprits en feignant d'être leur ami. Le motif de la séduction du diable se trouve dans le Nouveau Testament par exemple dans Lc 22, 31; Rm 16, 17-20; 2 Co 2, 11; 14-16 et 11, 3-15. Au sujet des pièges et des ruses du démon, Prieur rappelle les *Leçons de Sylvain*, NHC VII, 4; les *Odes de Salomon* 38; Porphyre, *De abstinentia* II, 40, 1[51]. Le dévoilement de l'oeuvre frauduleuse du diable est accompli par la révélation (cf. P 50, 3 s.). A ce propos, Prieur explique que la conception du salut des *AA* doit être interprétée comme l'effet de la révélation que les disciples reçoivent à travers les miracles et la parole de l'apôtre[52]. Il s'agirait de la même conception que dans les *AJ* [53].

Après avoir rappelé ces commentaires modernes[54], il est intéressant d'examiner comment ce passage a été interprété dans l'Antiquité, notamment par le traducteur arménien. Comme on l'a dit, le deuxième tableau synoptique permet de comprendre que le traducteur a identifié l'ἄναρχος avec le Seigneur qui est venu sur terre (qui 'descendit', selon le texte grec). Les raisons de sa venue sont expliquées par le passage précédent, où l'arménien fait allusion au thème de l'archange 'tombé des cieux comme l'éclair' (*ankawn yerknic' ibrew zp'aylakn*, citation de Lc 10, 18 *tesanēi zsatanay ankeal yerk-*

---

[50] Cf. G. J. M. Bartelink, "Ἀλλότριος und *alienus* als Teufels- und Dämonenbezeichnung', *Glotta* 58 (1980) 266-79.
[51] Cf. Prieur, 371, note 3.
[52] Cf. Prieur, 226, 293-5. Sur les paroles d'André dans les *AA*, cf. aussi l'article de F. Bovon dans ce volume, ch. VII.
[53] Cf. E. Junod et J.-D. Kaestli, *Acta Iohannis*, vol. 2 (Turnhout, 1983) 681. Sur la théologie des *Actes de Jean*, cf. aussi E. Junod et J.-D. Kaestli, 'Les traits caractéristiques de la théologie des Actes de Jean', *Revue de Théologie et de Philosophie* 26 (1976) 125-145.
[54] Cf. aussi L. Van Kampen, *Apostelverhalen: doel en compositie van de oudste apokriefe Handelingen der apostelen* (Utrecht, 1990) 148 s.

nic' ibrew zp'aylakn, 'je voyais Satan tomber des cieux comme l'éclair'[55]). A l'intérieur de ce passage, on peut repérer deux tournures parallèles, introduites par *vasn oroy*, 'donc', et suivies par une proposition finale, avec répétition du même verbe *korusc'ē*, '(pour)... perdre', ayant comme sujet respectivement l'"archange' et le 'Seigneur de gloire'. Le traducteur a vraisemblablement voulu faire précéder le thème de la venue du Christ par une adjonction explicative dans le but de rendre plus compréhensible un texte très énigmatique: c'est parce que Satan est d'abord tombé des cieux pour perdre les hommes que le Christ, à son tour, est venu sur terre pour l'écarter et le perdre. A propos de l'allusion à l'oeuvre salvatrice accomplie par le Christ, Prieur affirme: 'alors que les *AA* sont centrés sur la lutte du démon contre l'ἄναρχος et sur la dialectique ignorance/connaissance qui caractérise cette lutte, la *Passion arménienne* introduit le thème, beaucoup plus orthodoxe, de l'incarnation du Christ venu pour révéler Dieu et vaincre le diable'[56]. Prieur appuie cette hypothèse sur la conviction erronée que le passage arménien sur la venue du Christ est un ajout de l'arménien complètement depourvu de correspondant en grec. En réalité, comme on l'a vu plusieurs fois, c'est le motif de la chute du diable qui reste sans correspondant dans l'original. Un indice du caractère secondaire de ce dernier extrait est par ailleurs constitué par la présence de la citation de Lc. En effet, dans d'autres endroits aussi de la traduction arménienne du discours sur l'oeuvre du diable, dépourvus de parallèle en grec, l'arménien déploie une série d'allusions ou citations bibliques. En plus de Lc 10, 19, on peut citer également Jn 12, 31; 1 Jn 5, 2 et 1 Jn 2, 26[57].

---

[55] Cf. aussi Is 14, 12-15. Sur la chute de l'ange, cf. J.-M. Rosenstiehl, 'La chute de l'ange. Origines et développement d'une légende. Ses attestations dans la littérature copte', dans *Ecritures et traditions dans la littérature copte* (Louvain, 1983) 37-60.

[56] Cf. Prieur, 223.

[57] Cf. Jn 12, 31 *ayžmik datastan ē ašxarhis aysorik. ayžmik išxan ašxarhis aysorik ənkesc'i artak's*, 'c'est maintenant le jugement de ce monde; maintenant le prince de ce monde sera jeté dehors', repris dans Č' 148, 12 s. *ew ənkēc' i p'aṙac' ew yišxanut'enēn*, 'et il (le) fit précipiter (litt. 'jeter') de la gloire et de la principauté'. Cela rappelle aussi Jn 16, 11 et 1 Jn 5, 2 *yoržam zAstuac siresc'uk' ew zpatuirans nora arasc'uk'*, 'lorsque nous aimons Dieu et accomplissons ses commandements', repris mot à mot dans Č' 148, 16 s. *zi zna siresc'uk' ew zpatuirans nora arasc'uk'*, 'afin que nous aimions (Dieu) et accomplissons ses commandements', suivi par Č' 148, 17 *ew es*

L'impression générale qui ressort de ce passage est donc la suivante. Le traducteur arménien a certainement réécrit l'extrait grec sur l'oeuvre du diable, si obscur, en cherchant à le rendre plus compréhensible et, dans ce but, il s'est servi, entre autres, d'éléments bien connus tels que les citations bibliques. Néanmoins, le parallélisme, dans les deux langues, entre les phrases sur le 'sans-commencement' reste un fait important. On ne saurait non plus négliger le fait que la version arménienne conserve un texte cohérent là où, comme le remarque Prieur, l'original grec est trop mutilé pour être compris exactement[58]. En outre, le fait que le texte original grec soit à cet endroit conservé par un seul manuscrit, de plus corrompu, incite à garder au moins une attitude 'ouverte' à l'égard des deux textes. Malgré les remaniements évidents du texte arménien, il me semble toujours possible de repérer, en partie, le grec sous-jacent et de penser que, dans ce passage, ce texte grec était meilleur que celui dont nous disposons aujourd'hui[59]. Sur la base de toutes ces constatations, et contrairement à ce que Prieur avait affirmé, retenons surtout qu'on ne peut pas exclure d'une manière absolue l'absence de toute allusion à l'oeuvre de Rédemption du Christ dans les *AA* primitifs.

6. *Deux passages à tendance encratite du* MartA *arménien*

Le *MartA* arménien se prête à un commentaire hétérogène: à côté d'un langage riche d'allusions aux Ecritures, à l'incarnation du Christ, aux commandements – allusions qui s'insèrent bien dans un contexte 'orthodoxe' –, il présente en d'autres endroits un texte auquel, comme

---

jez bazum angam grec'i, 'et moi, je vous ai écrit plusieurs fois...' (cette allusion à des écrits antérieurs d'André n'est pas justifiable sur la base de la narration des *AA*), qui rappelle 1 Jn 2, 26 *zays grec'i jez*, 'je vous ai écrit cela'. Prieur pense que le traducteur arménien veut faire d'André une sorte de Paul qui écrit aux Eglises qu'il a fondées: cf. Prieur, 222, note 1.
[58] Cf. Prieur, 225.
[59] D'autres indices textuels démontrent aussi la fiabilité du texte arménien. Par exemple, la leçon εἰ δεῖ, 's'il faut', de P 49, 10, supposée dans Bonnet, 45, 1 et retenue par Prieur au lieu de la leçon ἤδη (conservée dans le seul manuscrit grec à disposition pour ce passage), est confirmée par l'arm. *et'ē part ic'ē*, 's'il faut'; la négation grecque μή de P 49, 13, supposée dans Bonnet, 45, 3 et retenue par Prieur avant περιφανή, est confirmée par l'arménien *an-erewoyt'*, 'in-visible', avec préfixe négatif *an-*; etc.

l'avait souligné Leloir, 'les retouches d'orthodoxie ont été épargnées, du moins partiellement. D'où son intérêt'[60]. C'est le cas des passages à tendance encratite qui seront examinés ci-dessous[61].

Ces extraits font partie d'un discours de prédication missionnaire, dans lequel André commence par condamner ceux qui ne saisissent pas le vrai sens de la mort comme libération de l'âme du corps et de la vie terrestre, et qui continuent, au contraire, à rester liés aux plaisirs temporels, au corps, au monde sensible et aux biens matériels (P 56-58)[62]. Le fait que ces passages appartiennent à un discours de l'apôtre plutôt qu'à une section narrative augmente leur valeur critique, comme on peut le déduire des paroles suivantes de Prieur: 'Les *AA* gr. sont très prolixes; ils contiennent en particulier de nombreux et longs discours. L'évolution textuelle... s'est effectuée, non dans le sens de l'amplification d'un texte de base bref, mais dans celui de l'abréviation d'un long texte original. Ce sont les discours qui, se prêtant le mieux à ce travail et jugés sans doute d'une ampleur excessive, ont fait les frais de cette opération'[63]. La probabilité est donc grande que les passages arméniens qui n'ont pas de correspondant en grec constituent des parties des *AA* primitifs, perdues dans la tradition directe. L'analyse du lexique et de la structure nous permet de le vérifier.

A) Le premier passage (Č‛ 158, 16-21) se trouve après la traduction de P 56, 18 s. (καὶ εἰ τὰ ἐκτὸς ὑμῶν εὐτυχήματα μακαρίζει ὑμᾶς, ὄντως ἐστὲ ἀθλιώτατοι, 'si vous vous réjouissez de vos succès extérieurs, vous êtes vraiment bien misérables'):

> ew et'ē amusnut'ean heštut'iwnk' ew xaṙnakut'iwnk' uraxac'uc'anē zjez, ew or i noc'anē aṙtetut'iwnn ē, li c'awovk' trtmec'usc'ē[64] zjez.

---

[60] L. Leloir, 'La version arménienne de la Passion d'André', *Handēs Amsōreay* 41 (1976) 471-4 et notamment 471.
[61] Je remercie A. M. Mazzanti qui, à l'occasion d'une conversation privée, m'avait permis de mieux comprendre certains aspects de l'encratisme.
[62] Cf. Prieur, 172-4, 265-73, 295-7.
[63] Cf. Prieur, 8.
[64] Je suis la variante arménienne *trtmec'usc'ē* (subjonctif aoriste attesté dans les manuscrits 731 de Venise, 178 de la Bibliothèque Nationale de Paris, 1-d de Jérusalem et 1325 du Maténadaran d'Erevan) à la place de la leçon retenue par Č‛rak'ean *trtmec'uc'anē* (présent indicatif), par analogie avec les subjonctifs aoristes (*nełesc'ē* et *naxatesc'ē*) des phrases successives, ayant une structure proche de celle de la phrase en question.

ew et'ē snndean bazum ordeac' c'ankanayc'ēk' ew or i noc'anē janjrali t'šuaṙut'iwnn cnanic'i jez, nełesc'ē zjez.

'Et si vous vous réjouissez des plaisirs et des accouplements du mariage, au contraire (litt. et), que la souillure qui en résulte, pleine de douleurs, vous attriste;

et si vous désirez la naissance[65] de beaucoup d'enfants et la souffrance pénible qui sera engendrée pour vous par eux, qu'elle vous opprime'.

Analyse du lexique

Du point de vue du lexique, on observe une grande concordance par rapport au répertoire lexical du *MartA* arménien ainsi que par rapport au vocabulaire des *AA* grecs. Considérons seulement les mots les plus significatifs: arm. *heštut'iwn*, 'volupté, plaisir, délice', est utilisé dans Č 159, 9; 159, 23 et 161, 4 face au gr. ἡδονή, 'plaisir', et dans Č 158, 3 (au pluriel) face au gr. τὰ ἡδέα, 'douceurs, délices'. Dans Č 148, 29, on lit *hešt c'ankut'iwn*, 'douce volupté', face au gr. ἡδονή. Arm. *heštut'iwn* est également attesté dans Č 152, 14 face au verbe gr. ἥδω ayant le même radical que le substantif ἡδονή; dans Č 158, 22 face au gr. ἰδίους, qui a été probablement confondu avec une forme dérivée de ἡδύς à cause d'une lecture par itacisme de la lettre η, et dans Č 158, 27, qui n'a pas de correspondant en grec. Arm. *xaṙnakut'iwn*, 'accouplement, union', équivaut au gr. μῖξις et au gr. συνουσία avec le sens d''union sexuelle'. Les deux termes grecs sont attestés, avec la même connotation négative que le mot arménien, dans trois passages des *AA*: P 14, 15 et 21, 14 (μῖξις); P 37, 7 (συνουσία). Arm. *ałtełut'iwn*, 'souillure, impureté, turpitude', a le même radical que l'adjectif *ałteli*, 'impur', qui équivaut au gr. ῥυπαρός; cet adjectif grec est attesté dans trois passages des *AA*, parmi lesquels P 37, 8, où l'adjectif grec est utilisé pour qualifier d''impure' la vie consacrée à la συνουσία. Arm. *ałteli* équivaut également au gr. αἰσχρός, qui est attesté dans les *AA* quatre fois, notamment dans P 21, 14, où il est suivi par le substantif ἔργον, employé avec le sens de μῖξις. Arm. *trtmec'uc'anem*, 'attrister', est attesté dans Č 162, 8 face au gr. λυπέω, 'affliger, chagriner'; la forme intransitive *trtmim*, 'être triste', quant à elle, est attestée dans Č 165, 8 face au passif du même verbe grec. Arm. *c'ankanam* (ou *c'ankam*),

---

[65] Littéralement le substantif *snund* signifie 'nourriture, subsistance' (cf. gr. τροφή).

'désirer', est employé dans Č⁺ 166, 17 face au gr. ποθέω, ayant le même sens, ainsi que dans deux autres passages sans correspondance en grec. Pour finir, arm. *amusnut'iwn*, 'mariage', qui est utilisé également dans Č⁺ 159, 16 (passage sans correspondant en grec), équivaut sémantiquement au gr. γάμος, 'mariage', qui se trouve au passage P 36, 2 des *AA* grecs.

Analyse de la structure
En ce qui concerne la structure, on peut relever que les deux périodes hypothétiques présentent une grande ressemblance avec la série de propositions hypothétiques du texte grec qui les précède, toutes introduites par καὶ εἰ, 'et si' (P 56, 5-19)[66]. En plus, les propositions relatives des deux protases arméniennes rappellent la relative d'une des périodes hypothétiques arméniennes précédentes, qui traduit, elle, une tournure implicite grecque, selon un procédé de traduction typique de la version arménienne du *MartA*[67]; cela suggère que face aux relatives du passage arménien examiné ici il y avait peut-être en grec aussi des propositions implicites. La comparaison avec la période hypothétique qui suit cet extrait arménien absent en grec permet les considérations les plus intéressantes; ce passage est attesté en grec aussi:

> P 56, 19 s. καὶ εἰ τὰ λοιπὰ ὑμῶν κτήματα ἰδίους ἐπαίρει ἑαυτοῖς, τὸ πρόσκαιρον αὐτῶν ὀνειδιζέτω ὑμᾶς
> 'et si vos autres richesses vous attirent à elles comme leurs biens, que leur caractère éphémère vous outrage'.
> Č⁺ 158, 21-23 ew et'ē zawelstac'ut'ean mecut'iwnr. heštut'eamb siric'ēk' apakanut'ecmbn iwrov, naxatesc'ē zjez
> 'et si vous aimez avec volupté la grandeur du recevoir-en-abondance, avec son caractère éphémère (litt. sa corruption), qu'elle vous outrage'.

Comme on peut le constater, le verbe de l'apodose grecque est à l'impératif de la troisième personne du singulier (ὀνειδιζέτω, 'qu'il outrage') et il a été traduit en arménien par un subjonctif aoriste avec valeur exhortative-impérative (*naxatesc'ē*, 'qu'elle outrage')[68]. La

---

[66] Pour le texte, je renvoie à l'édition de Prieur.
[67] Cf. P 56, 15 s. et Č⁺ 158, 10 s.
[68] Cf. aussi Č⁺ 147, 17 *mi xrovec'usc'ē*, subjonctif aoriste arménien par lequel a été traduit l'impératif grec de la troisième personne du singulier de P 49, 1 s. μὴ ...ταρασσέτω.

possibilité de cette comparaison nous permet d'éclaircir la valeur des subjonctifs aoristes du passage attesté seulement en arménien (*trtmec'usc'ē*, 'qu'elle attriste', et *nełesc'ē*, 'qu'elle opprime'). Ils doivent sans doute être interprétés comme des subjonctifs exhortatifs-impératifs et, très vraisemblablement, ils présupposent des impératifs grecs. Cette interprétation affaiblit l'hypothèse de Prieur, fondée sur la traduction française de Leloir qui a considéré les deux formes verbales avec valeur de futur ('... une plénitude de malheurs vous attristera... la misère... vous attristera'[69]), également possible pour le subjonctif aoriste arménien; peut-être sur la base du futur grec, Prieur pense en effet que le traducteur a edulcoré la phrase sur le mariage, en lui conférant un sens moralisateur: il ne faut pas se réjouir des voluptés et des accouplements du mariage parce qu'ils *engendreront* tristesse et souffrance; il ne faut pas désirer la naissance de beaucoup d'enfants, parce que la misère qu'ils apportent *opprimera*[70]. En réalité, l'expression arménienne '*qu'elle* (*scil.* la souillure qui dérive du mariage et des accouplements) *vous attriste*' fait partie de la condamnation radicale de l'apôtre, de même que les mots '*qu'elle vous opprime*', prononcés par André à propos de la souffrance engendrée par le fait d'avoir beaucoup d'enfants[71].

B) Le deuxième passage à tendance encratite examiné (Č⁰ 158, 27-159, 3) se trouve après la traduction de P 57, 2 s. (ἢ τίς ἐκ τοῦ ἐκτὸς γένους ἔπαρσις, τῆς ἐν ὑμῖν ψυχῆς αἰχμαλώτου ταῖς ἐπιθυμίαις πεπραμένης;, 'ou quel orgueil tirez-vous de la race extérieure, alors qu'en vous l'âme est prisonnière, vendue aux désirs?'), à l'intérieur d'une série d'interrogatives directes qui condamnent tout ce qui est extérieur:

> *ew zinč' heštut'ean ew ordecnut'ean c'ankal yoržam yetoy bažanel unimk' ews i mimeanc'?*
> *k'anzi ew oč' gitē ok' zinč' aṙnē.*
> *kam ov knoj iwrum xnam tanic'i zbałeal tṙp'anōk' c'ankut'ean?*
> '... et pourquoi désirer le plaisir et la procréation, quand nous devons, ensuite, nous séparer les uns des autres?
> En effet, personne ne sait ce qu'il fait.

---

[69] Cf. Leloir, 'Ecrits', 247.
[70] Cf. Prieur, 270.
[71] Sur la souffrance qui dérive de la procréation, cf. Prieur, 226, note 4 et 324-6.

Ou bien qui prendra soin de sa femme, étant donné qu'il s'y est intéressé par amour de concupiscence?'.

Analyse du lexique et de la structure
Du point de vue lexical, en plus des mots déjà rappelés *heštut'iwn*, 'plaisir', et *c'ankal*, 'désirer', on peut relever également arm. *xnam*, 'soin, sollicitude', qui équivaut au gr. ἐπιμέλεια de P 57, 4 et 64, 5 (cf. aussi P 44, 8); la périphrase arménienne *xnam tam*, 'prendre soin de', équivaut sémantiquement au gr. ἐπιμελέομαι, qui est attesté dans P 13, 17. Quant à la structure du passage, on remarque que la première période est introduite par le syntagme arménien *ew zinč'*, 'et pourquoi...?', qui rappelle *ew zinč'*, 'et pourquoi...?', (cf. P 57, 1 τί γάρ) et *ew kam zinč'*, 'ou pourquoi...?', (cf. P 57, 2 ἢ τίς) des passages précédents, ainsi que *kam zinč'*, 'ou pourquoi...?' (cf. P 57, 3 ἢ τίς) du passage suivant. La première interrogative est suivie par une proposition subordonnée temporelle, introduite par la conjonction *yoržam*, 'quand'; elle est semblable à la proposition temporelle de la phrase précédente, qui explicite le génitif absolu grec[72]. La deuxième phrase, introduite par la conjonction explicative *k'anzi*, 'puisque, car', a été considérée par Prieur comme une glose[73]. En effet, elle casse la série d'interrogatives directes et s'éloigne de la structure du contexte narratif dans lequel elle s'insère. Je serais plus prudente dans le fait de considérer comme une glose également la troisième phrase, introduite par les mots *kam ov*, 'ou qui?'.

La cohérence structurale des deux passages arméniens avec le contexte, l'homogénéité lexicale par rapport au reste du *MartA* arménien et, surtout, la possibilité d'apercevoir un lexique grec sousjacent bien attesté dans d'autres passages des *AA* grecs, laisse supposer que les deux extraits arméniens sont primitifs[74]. Est-il possible de comprendre les raisons qui en ont provoqué la perte dans la tradition directe grecque? Est-ce le fruit d'un simple accident de la transmission manuscrite grecque, ou bien la conséquence d'une intervention doctrinale de la part d'un copiste grec? L'examen du contenu nous permet de vérifier que la deuxième hypothèse s'impose comme étant la plus vraisemblable.

[72] Cf. P 57, 2 s. et Č' 158, 25 s.
[73] Cf. Prieur, 267.
[74] Cf. Prieur, 267.

Interprétation des passages

Le contenu de ces deux passages est caractérisé par le refus du mariage et de la procréation qui constitue l'élément fondamental du *kerygma* encratite[75]. Certains mots, en particulier, sont très explicites de ce point de vue: arm. *ałtełut'iwn* 'souillure, impureté' – dit des plaisirs et des accouplements du mariage – rappelle le gr. ῥυπαρός qui est utilisé pour qualifier l'acte sexuel dans les *ATh* 12 aussi, dont le caractère encratite est admis par les savants[76]. Une telle connotation du mariage rappelle la formule du *Encratitarum patriarches* [77], Tatien, qui identifie le γάμος avec πορνεία, 'fornication', et φθορά, 'corruption'[78]. Est également significatif le terme *c'ankut'iwn*, 'volupté', équivalent au gr. ἐπιθυμία, qui pour Jules Cassien (champion de l'encratisme comme Tatien) est responsable de la déchéance de l'âme vers le 'devenir' (γένεσις) et la 'corruption' (φθορά)[79]. Dans les *APt* 8, la *concupiscentia* constitue l'instrument de séduction du 'fruit complètement amer de l'arbre de l'amertume', c'est-à-dire du diable[80]. Relevons que dans les *AA* 16, le proconsul grec Egéate

---

[75] Le concept d''encratisme' doit être distingué de celui de 'tradition de l'*enkrateia*'. Comme le précise U. Bianchi, alors que le terme simple *enkrateia* '... ne dénomme autre chose que la 'continence', sexuelle et alimentaire, dans un milieu parlant grec...' et constitue 'le mot clé d'un courant idéologique... qui valorise... un régime abstentionniste concernant la sexualité et les aliments...', le terme 'encratisme', en revanche, indique la forme radicale de l'*enkrateia*, caractérisée par le rejet du *gamos*, comme l'avaient précisé déjà les hérésiologues anciens: cf. U. Bianchi, 'Le thème du colloque en tant que problème historico-religieux', dans U. Bianchi (éd.), *La tradizione dell'enkrateia. Motivazioni ontologiche e protologiche* (Roma, 1985) 1-32 et notamment 1 (désormais Bianchi). Sur la distinction entre 'encratisme' et 'tradition de l'*enkrateia*', cf. aussi 'Documento finale del colloquio. Proposte concernenti l'uso dei termini encratismo ed enkrateia', dans Bianchi, XXIII-V.

[76] Cf. notamment Y. Tissot, 'L'encratisme des Actes de Thomas', dans *ANRW* II. 25. 6, 4415-30 (désormais Tissot, 'Actes de Thomas').

[77] Cf. Jérôme, *Prol. com. in ep. ad Titum* 685 (*PL* 26, 590).

[78] Cf. Irénée, *Adv. Haer.* I, 28, 1, *ap.* Eus., *HE*, IV, 29, 3. La formule de Tatien est mentionnée dans Clément d'Alexandrie, *Strom.* III, VI, 49, 1.

[79] Cf. Clément d'Alexandrie, *Strom.* III, XIII, 93, 3.

[80] La définition du démon comme 'arbre amer', également commune aux *ATh* 44, rappelle la βοτάνην, τὴν ... πικρίαν ἔχουσαν (qui fait allusion à la sexualité et à la γένεσις) dont le Seigneur invite à s'abstenir dans

est considéré comme un obstacle à l'accomplissement des propos de son épouse, Maximille, de s'éloigner de la 'répugnante souillure' et, pour cette raison, il est appelé 'serpent effronté et hostile' (P 16, 4 s.), 'ennemi sauvage et à jamais incorrigible' (P 16, 7 s.); par ces appellations, Egéate est ainsi apparenté au diable[81]. Le troisième terme significatif est arm. *ordecnut'iwn*, 'procréation d'enfants', équivalent au gr. παιδοποιΐα, qui est attesté dans le premier énoncé de la doctrine encratite réfuté par Clément d'Alexandrie, consistant précisément dans le rejet du γάμος et de la παιδοποιΐα, dans le but de ne pas offrir 'une nourriture à la mort'[82]. Sur la base de ces constations, il est possible d'affirmer que les passages arméniens examinés attestent une terminologie fortement connotée d'un point de vue encratite.

Comme on le sait, depuis l'Antiquité on a insisté sur l'encratisme des *AAA*. En particulier, Epiphane de Salamine nous informe que les Encratites connaissaient et utilisaient les *AA*, les *AJ* et les *ATh*[83], et que les Apotactites (ou Apostoliques) utilisaient à leur tours

---

l'*Evangile des Egyptiens* (cf. Clément d'Alexandrie, *Strom*. III, IX, 66, 1, 226, 15 s.). Selon Clément d'Alexandrie, *Strom*. III, IX, 63, 1, 25, 1-4, c'est sur cette oeuvre que les encratites appuyaient leurs argumentations. Dans l'*Epître des presbytres et diacres d'Achaïe* 5 (oeuvre élaborée au VIe siècle sur la base de la fin des *AA* primitifs), on trouve une allusion au *lignum concupiscentiae* goûté par Adam qui est opposé au bois de la croix du Christ. L'origine juive de ce concept est attestée par exemple dans l'*Apocalypse de Moïse* XIX, 3, où l'ἐπιθυμία est τὸν ἰὸν τῆς κακίας ... κεφαλὴ πάσης ἁμαρτίας, 'le poison de la méchanceté... commencement de tous péchés'. Le contexte évoqué par ces extraits nous renvoie à la motivation protologique de l'*enkrateia*, comme l'a remarqué G. Sfameni Gasparro, 'Le motivazioni protologiche dell'*enkrateia* nel Cristianesimo dei primi secoli e nello gnosticismo', dans Bianchi, 149-237 et notamment 153-5 (désormais Sfameni Gasparro, 'Motivazioni protologiche'). Sur le thème de l'amertume associé à celui de la concupiscence, cf. aussi R. Cantalamessa, *L'omelia 'in S. Pascha' dello Pseudo-Ippolito di Roma. Ricerche sulla teologia dell'Asia minore nella seconda metà del II secolo* (Milano, 1967) 288-91.

[81] Le rapport de filiation d'Egéate par rapport au diable est souligné dans P 40, 3 s.; 40, 14 s.; 42, 20.

[82] Cf. Clément d'Alexandrie, *Strom*. III, VI, 45, 1. Comme l'explique Sfameni Gasparro, il s'agit d'une allusion à l'*Evangile des Egyptiens*: cf. Sfameni Gasparro, 'Motivazioni protologiche', 153.

[83] Cf. *Pan*. 47, 1, 5.

les *AA* et les *ATh*[84]. On connaît bien, pourtant, la maigre objectivité des témoignages sur les textes apocryphes offerts par les auteurs ecclésiastiques anciens, qui sont très souvent tendancieux et exagérés dans l'identificatiae des éléments 'hérétiques'. Comme cela a été souligné, parfois cette condamnation des textes apocryphes est basée sur un préjudice qui fait que, 'puisque les textes canoniques sont la source de l'orthodoxie, les textes apocryphes deviennent automatiquement associés à l'hérésie'[85].

Une vigoureuse remise en question de l'interprétation encratite courante des *AAA* a été effectuée au début de notre siècle par J. Flamion, pour lequel l'exaltation de la continence sexuelle de ces *Actes* est simplement une convention littéraire, héritée du roman hellénistique, qui ne répond pas à une réelle pratique populaire. Flamion remarque que de nombreuses occasions offertes par la narration de développer un enseignement encratite n'ont pas été exploitées dans les *AAA* et que les allusions à la continence sont plus abondantes dans les parties narratives que dans les sections qui se prêteraient mieux à exprimer la doctrine de l'apôtre, à savoir les discours. Flamion considère en outre la condamnation radicale du mariage comme l'expression d'une idéalisation des temps apostoliques[86].

Les objections de Flamion ont été réfutées par Prieur[87], qui considère les *AA* comme une oeuvre encratite[88]. Le rejet de la sexua-

---

[84] Cf. *Pan.* 61, 1, 5. Le témoignage d'Epiphane fait allusion aux mouvements encratites du IVe siècle mentionnés également par Amphiloque d'Iconium, *Fragmenta* X, 1-3. Cf. Junod et Kaestli, 23-34.

[85] Cf. E. Junod, 'Actes apocryphes et hérésie: le jugement de Photius', dans F. Bovon *et al.*, *Les Actes apocryphes des apôtres. Christianisme et monde païen* (Genève, 1981) 11-24 et notamment 24, ainsi que 22 à propos du jugement de Photius sur la tendance encratite des *AAA*.

[86] Cf. J. Flamion, 'Les Actes apocryphes de Pierre', *RHE* 10 (1909) 14-20.

[87] On trouvera la critique que Prieur adresse aux objections de Flamion dans Prieur, 323 s.

[88] Cf. Prieur, 321-4 et notamment 323. La même opinion est partagée par G. Sfameni Gasparro qui souligne les motivations protologiques de l'*enkrateia* radicale des *AA*. Le contexte protologique est évoqué par l'allusion au *lignum concupiscentiae* de l'*Epître des presbytres et diacres d'Achaïe* 5 et par le parallèle, renversé, qui est suggéré entre le couple Adam-Eve et le couple André-Maximille; dans ce parallèle, le deuxième couple rétablit

lité, liée à l'"homme extérieur" et à la chair, est pour Prieur une conséquence logique de la pensée des *AA*, qui font de la découverte et de la possession stable de l'"homme intérieur" le contenu même du salut[89]. Prieur se réfère à la définition d'encratisme proposée par Y. Tissot: 'nous définirons l'encratisme comme une tendance faisant de la continence sexuelle une exigence de la foi'[90]. En particulier, pour Tissot les *AAA* peuvent être dits encratites 'quand leur auteur traite le récit de martyre sous la forme encratite du mariage rompu, avec une insistance montrant qu'il s'agit là de sa conviction, surtout si sa conviction est confirmée ailleurs'[91]. La narration du *Martyre* à laquel il fait allusion présente le schéma suivant: 1. conversion de la femme d'un homme notable qui refuse de continuer sa vie conjugale; 2. réaction de l'époux qui menace et fait jeter en prison l'apôtre, responsable de la conversion de la femme; 3. fermeté de la femme, exhortée et soutenue par l'apôtre; 4. martyre de l'apôtre[92].

Les traces les plus nombreuses d'épisodes caractérisés par ce schéma se trouvent dans l'épitomé latin de Grégoire de Tours. Elles ne sont pas évidentes, à cause de la révision orthodoxe de Grégoire; on peut seulement les reconstruire par supposition[93]. Dans les *AA*

---

l'état des protoplastes antérieur au péché, c'est-à-dire antérieur à l'accomplissement du γάμος: cf. G. Sfameni Gasparro, 'Gli Atti apocrifi degli Apostoli e la tradizione dell'*enkrateia*. Discussione di una recente formula interpretativa', *Augustinianum* 23 (1983) 287-307 et notamment 300-2 (désormais Sfameni Gasparro, 'Atti apocrifi') et Ead., 'Motivazioni protologiche', 154 et 169 s.; cf. aussi P. Nagel, 'Die Wiedergewinnung des Paradieses durch Askese', *FuF* 34 (1960) 375-7. Sur la typologie Adam et Eve/André et Maximille, cf. Prieur, 204-7.

[89] Cf. Prieur, 321; sur l'"homme intérieur", voir aussi *infra*, §7.
[90] Cf. Y. Tissot, 'Encratisme et Actes apocryphes', dans Bovon, *Les Actes apocryphes des apôtres*, 109-19 et notamment 111 (désormais Tissot, 'Encratisme').
[91] Cf. Tissot, 'Encratisme', 116.
[92] Cf. Tissot, 'Encratisme', 115. Pour une allusion au schéma des conversions avec motivation encratite, cause de la mort de l'apôtre, cf. également Sfameni Gasparro, 'Atti apocrifi', 301.
[93] Cf. les chapitres 18-19 et 23; voir également le chapitre 11, qui fait allusion à une intervention d'André ayant pour but de dissoudre un mariage: cf. Prieur, 42 s., 45, 49 s., 322 s.; Flamion, 254-8.

grecs, Maximille se convertit et choisit une vie de continence absolue. Cette résolution constitue la cause de la décision de son époux, Egéate, de condamner à mort André. L'épisode de la conversion de Maximille et la prédication de l'apôtre qui l'a provoquée ont été perdus. En revanche, nous connaissons les mots d'exhortation par lesquelles André invite la femme à rester ferme dans ses propos de chasteté[94]. La perte du texte grec relatif à la conversion de Maximille, ainsi que le caractère hypothétique des épisodes encratites reconnus dans l'épitomé latin, avaient poussé Tissot (avant la publication du commentaire de Prieur) à adopter une position de doute face à l'encratisme des *AA*. D'après lui, le caractère fragmentaire du texte n'offre pas d'éléments suffisants pour évaluer l'éventuelle position encratite de l'auteur[95]. Dans ce contexte, on voit ressortir de manière encore plus évidente le rôle fondamental joué par les passages arméniens ici considérés, qui contiennent une condamnation radicale et explicite du mariage et de la procréation, dépourvue des traits édulcorés et moralisateurs supposés par Prieur (voir *supra*, analyse de la structure du passage A). Leur appartenance à l'unique prédication missionnaire des *AA*, donc à une section du texte très importante du point de vue doctrinal, augmente leur valeur.

Les passages primitifs attestés uniquement par la version arménienne démontrent donc que l'original grec avait une tendance encratite plus marquée que celle du texte conservé dans les manuscrits grecs. Derrière l'expression 'tendance encratite' il ne faut pourtant pas sous-entendre une intention polémique de la part de l'auteur des *AA*. Comme l'a bien souligné Prieur, en effet, 'l'auteur... écrit à une époque où la doctrine est encore flottante et l'orthodoxie mal définie, et où l'on peut exprimer des idées comme les siennes sans l'intention de s'écarter de la pensée orthodoxe et de s'opposer à d'autres chrétiens'[96]. Si le texte arménien nous permet donc de dégager l'intention

---

[94] Cf. P 37, 40, 45 ainsi que la prière d'André du chapitre 16.
[95] Cf. Tissot, 'Encratisme', 117 s. et Id., 'Actes de Thomas', 4422, note 49. L'article de Tissot présuppose déjà la connaissance du manuscrit Sinaiticus gr. 526, qui atteste le fragment le plus étendu des *AA*.
[96] Cf. Prieur, 408 s. Sur la régulation de la foi au IIe siècle, cf. E. Junod, 'Observations sur la régulation de la foi dans l'église des IIe et IIIe siècles', *Le Supplément* 133 (1980) 195-213.

idéologique de l'auteur des *AA* grecs, il est important de mettre en évidence que, à une époque postérieure à la composition des *AA*, notamment postérieure aux accusations des hérésiologues contre l'encratisme[97], un copiste grec tardif a vraisemblablement soupçonné d'hérésie les passages en question et a décidé de les épurer, comme l'évêque de Tours l'a fait pour les parties qu'il a résumé dans son épitomé[98]. Par ailleurs, le fait que ces passages n'ont pas subi la même opération dans la version arménienne révèle que ni le traducteur ni les copistes arméniens n'ont ressenti le danger d'une interprétation hétérodoxe.

Une étude de l'encratisme en Arménie reste à faire. Leloir rappelait que l'encratisme typique des cercles syriens avaient pénétré dans les milieux monastiques arméniens[99]. Soulignons au passage que, si le *MartA* arménien nous offre un témoignage intéressant sur la diffusion et la réception de cette doctrine en Arménie, une meilleure connaissance de ce courant religieux et de son impact chez les Arméniens permettrait de mieux situer chronologiquement l'époque d'élaboration de la version arménienne du *MartA*.

7. 'L'homme intérieur'

En guise de conclusion, il me semble intéressant d'analyser un troisième passage de la version arménienne, absent de l'original, qui est parfaitement cohérent du point de vue du contenu avec la pensée des *AA* grecs. Cet extrait aussi fait partie de la prédication missionnaire adressée à la foule par André depuis la croix. Face au gr. ἠρέμα τοιγαροῦν ἄνδρες θαρροῦσιν κτλ., (litt.) 'En vérité les hommes ont paisiblement confiance...', (P 58, 2 s.), le texte arménien (Č' 160, 11-19) a un passage plus étendu (ci-dessous transcrit entre astérisques):

---

[97] Notamment Irénée et Clément d'Alexandrie: cf. F. Bolgiani, 'La tradizione eresiologica sull'encratismo. I. Le notizie di Ireneo', *Atti della Accademia delle Scienze di Torino, II. Classe di scienze morali, storiche e filologiche* 91 (1956-57) 343-419; Id., 'II. La confutazione di Clemente di Alessandria', *ibid.* 96 (1961-62) 537-664.
[98] Cf. Prieur, 267.
[99] Cf. Leloir, 'Rapports', 148.

> ... *ardarew hezs *tesanem zjez orpēs ew kamims. i bac' linel jez yartak'in kerparanac' zi nerk'in mardn*[100] *mer miaban lic'i: Olǰunem zjez šnorhōk'n Astucoy ew sirovn or aṙ na, ew aṙawel jerov miabanut'eambd or aṙ mimeans, heṙanal jez i vnasakarac'n ew dimel i na ew i barin ew i miamtut'iwnn or aṙ na ē ew i miabanut'iwnn or i soyn.* zi ew ayl mardik kaǰaleresc'in ...*

'En vérité je vous vois paisibles, *comme je le veux, rester loin des formes extérieures afin que l'homme intérieur soit en harmonie avec nous. Je vous salue au nom de la grâce de Dieu et de l'amour qui (est) pour Lui et encore plus pour votre accord mutuel[101], (en vous exhortant) à vous éloigner des dangers et à vous élancer vers Lui (*scil.* Dieu) et vers le bien et la loyauté qui est envers Lui et envers la concorde qui (est) en Lui,* afin que d'autres hommes aussi soient confiants...'.

Du point de vue textuel, on remarque un agencement entre les mots grecs ἠρέμα τοιγαροῦν, 'paisiblement en vérité', et l'*incipit* du passage arménien *ardarew hezs*, 'en vérité paisibles'. Si l'adverbe arménien *ardarew*, 'en vérité', équivaut à l'adverbe grec τοιγαροῦν, ayant le même sens, l'adjectif arménien *hezs*, 'paisibles', présuppose, quant à lui, une forme grecque dérivée de ἤρεμος, 'paisible', ou de son synonyme ἠρεμαῖος, au lieu de l'adverbe ἠρέμα. On pourrait donc supposer dans l'original une leçon proche de ἠρεμαίους τοιγαροῦν <ὑμᾶς ὁρῶ...>, 'en vérité <je vous vois> paisibles...'[102]. Les mots grecs ἄνδρες θαρροῦσιν..., 'les hommes ont confiance...', qui suivent gr. ἠρέμα τοιγαροῦν, 'paisiblement en vérité', correspondent à la partie finale du passage arménien (*zi ew ayl mardik k'aǰaleresc'in...*, 'afin que d'autres hommes aussi soient confiants...'); la section arménienne intermédiaire est absente en grec.

L'analyse du texte permet de vérifier l'éventuelle origine primitive de cette péricope arménienne, dont le motif principal est constitué par l'allusion à l''homme intérieur'. Comme l'a remarqué Prieur,

---

[100] Je suis la variante arménienne *nerk'in mardn*, 'l'homme intérieur', attestée par les manuscrits auxiliaires de l'édition de Venise et par les manuscrits 110, 118, 178 de Paris, 1-d de Jérusalem, 2601 et 1325 d'Erevan, à la place de la leçon retenue par Čᶜrak'ean *nerk'ins* ', '(les choses) intérieures'.

[101] Litt. 'qui est l'un pour l'autre'.

[102] L'apparat de Prieur pourrait être corrigé de la manière suivante: 58, 2 *post* τοιγαροῦν *plenius habet arm.*

le thème de l'"homme intérieur" (cf. P 7, 19 ὁ ἐν σοὶ ἄνθρωπος et P 16, 9 τῷ ἔσω ἀνδρί), qui s'oppose au corps apparent, est fondamental dans les *AA* grecs. La connaissance de l'homme intérieur, qui est une conséquence de la révélation, constitue la condition nécessaire pour atteindre le salut. Elle représente le lien qui soude les 'frères' (ἀδελφοί) entre eux, en les distinguant du reste de l'humanité, c'est-à-dire des 'hommes extérieurs' (τοὺς ἐκτὸς ἀνθρώπους) mentionnés dans P 53, 24 (cf. aussi P 57, 2). L'opposition entre l'homme intérieur et l'homme extérieur présuppose en outre une distinction entre les choses intérieures et les choses extérieures; c'est de ces dernières que les hommes, conformément aux nombreuses exhortations d'André, doivent s'éloigner (cf. par exemple P 47; 56; 57). L'invitation à 'être paisibles' est également à la base de la prédication d'André: dans le chapitre 52, 7-8 du texte grec, Stratoclès, un disciple de l'apôtre, rappelle qu'André a enseigné à contenir les excès de colère. Dans P 53, 13-17, par ailleurs, c'est André qui reproche au même Stratoclès son emportement; P 64, 9-10 fait allusion au choix d'"une vie sainte et douce" adopté par Maximille après la mort de l'apôtre. Le thème de l'"accord" ou 'communion mutuelle' rappelle, d'autre part, le grec κοινωνία, 'communion' de P 33, 3 (communion avec Dieu) et de P 57, 19 (communion avec André). L'allusion à 'l'amour qui est pour Lui', pour finir, rappelle le gr. φιλία τῇ πρὸς αὐτόν, 'l'amour pour Lui' de P 58, 4[103].

Du point de vue lexical, on peut remarquer qu'arm. *artak'in*, 'extérieur', est attesté face au gr. ἐκτός, 'extérieur', dans d'autres passages aussi (Č⁽ 152, 15 et 158, 15[104]; 158, 24 et 159, 4). Arm. *hez*, 'doux, paisible', correspond au gr. ἤρεμος, 'paisible', de P 62, 31 et P 64, 10 (= Č⁽ 166, 3 et Č⁽ 167, 3). Arm. *kerparan*, 'forme', est attesté dans Č⁽ 155, 24 face au gr. μορφή, 'forme', (cf. aussi Č⁽ 155, 24-25 *an-kerparann*, 'sans-forme', face au gr. ἄ-μορφον, 'sans-forme'; Č⁽ 156, 1 *kerparanam*, 'donner une forme, figurer', face au gr. μορφόω, 'donner une forme'). Arm. *miaban*, 'concorde, uni', rappelle Č⁽ 166, 20 *miabanakic'* (synonyme de *miaban*), utilisé face au gr. συγγενής, 'de même origine, qui a une affinité avec', (P 63, 10). Le substantif

---

[103] Sur l'"homme intérieur" et les 'choses extérieures', cf. Prieur, 179-84, 201 s., 293, 313 s., 318 s., 332 *et passim*; Luttikhuizen, ce volume, ch. VIII.2; sur la 'communion mutuelle', cf. Prieur, 312.

[104] Dans les deux passages, il s'agit d'une *varia lectio*.

arménien *miabanut'iwn*, 'union, communion', est employé dans Čʿ 167, 26 face à κοινωνία, 'communion', (P 65, 6) et dans Čʿ 157, 28 face à σύνοδος, 'réunion, union', (P 56, 6); il est également attesté dans Čʿ 154, 19-20 et Čʿ 164, 3, dans des extraits dépourvus d'équivalent en grec. Arm. *šnorh(k')*, 'grâce', est utilisé pour traduire le gr. χάρις, ayant le même sens, dans Čʿ 165, 13; 166, 14 et 167, 4. Finalement, arm. *vnasakaran*, 'dangers', rappelle arm. *vnasakarsn*, 'les dangers', de Čʿ 146, 5, traduction de P 47, 4 s. ἐπιβλαβέσιν, 'les fantaisies-pernicieuses'.

Toutes ces considérations permettent de supposer une vraisemblable origine primitive du passage sur l'"homme intérieur"[105]. La nature particulière des passages examinés plus haut pouvait peut-être encore soulever quelques doutes quant à leur origine primitive chez les savants qui ne reconnaissent pas une influence encratite dans les *AA*. L'absence néanmoins, dans le texte grec, d'extraits dépourvus d'éléments qui auraient pu se prêter à révisions ou à épurations orthodoxes prouve que les coupures subies par la tradition directe grecque ne se sont pas limitées aux parties les plus 'gênantes' du point de vue doctrinal. Cette hypothèse est par ailleurs corroborée par deux autres exemples d'abréviations du texte original qu'on peut supposer sur la base de l'arménien. Je me réfère, sans pouvoir les analyser ici, à deux extraits contenus dans le discours du chapitre 61, qui ne sont attestés qu'en arménien et qui ont vraisemblablement une origine primitive[106].

Conclusion

Le *MartA* arménien est un cas exemplaire qui illustre bien l'importance des traductions arméniennes des textes apocryphes[107]. La version arménienne du *MartA* nous livre, en effet, un témoignage pré-

---

[105] Cf. aussi Prieur, 268.
[106] Cf. Calzolari, 149-55.
[107] Sur la littérature apocryphe en langue arménienne, cf. par exemple Calzolari *et al.*; Leloir, 'Ecrits', VII-IX; M. E. Stone, 'Travaux actuels sur la littérature apocryphe arménienne', *Apocrypha* 1 (1990) 303-11; Id., *Selected Studies in Pseudepigrapha & Apocrypha With Special Reference to the Armenian Tradition* (Leiden, 1991); S. J. Voicu, 'Gli Apocrifi armeni', *Augustinianum* 23 (1983) 161-80.

cieux sur l'interprétation donnée – à une époque qu'on suppose peu éloignée de l'époque de rédaction des *AA* – à des passages qui sont désormais pour nous obscurs. En outre, elle nous permet de retrouver la pensée des *AA* dans des endroits où la tradition directe grecque a été victime de coupures, surtout à la suite de révisions doctrinales. La traduction arménienne nous permet ainsi de repérer les traces de manipulations d'inspiration orthodoxe subies par les *AA* grec et de connaître, en même temps, les conditions de leur réception dans les deux milieux chrétiens, grec et arménien.

XIV. Bibliography of *Acts of Andrew*

JAN N. BREMMER AND PIETER J. LALLEMAN

Texts

MacDonald, D.R., *The Acts of Andrew and the Acts of Andrew and Matthias in the City of the Cannibals* (Atlanta, 1990).
Prieur, J.-M., *Acta Andreae*, 2 vols (Turnhout, 1989).
T.S. Richter, 'P. Ien. inv. 649: Ein Splitter vom koptischen Text der Acta Andreae', *Arch. f. Papyrusforschung* 44 (1998) 275-84.

Translations

Bovon, F., and P. Geoltrain (eds), *Écrits apocryphes chrétiens* I (Paris, 1997) 875-972 (J.-M. Prieur).
Elliott, J.K., *The Apocryphal New Testament* (Oxford, 1993) 231-302.
Erbetta, M., *Gli Apocrifi del Nuovo Testamento, II: Atti e Leggende* (Torino, 1966) 395-449g.
James, M.R., *Apocryphal New Testament* (Oxford, 1924) 337-63.
Klijn, A.F.J. (ed), *Apokriefen van het Nieuwe Testament* II (Kampen, 1985) 161-82.
Moraldi, L., *Apocrifi del Nuovo Testamento* II (Torino, 1971) 1351-1429.
Prieur, J.-M, *Actes d'André* (Turnhout, 1995).
Schneemelcher, *NTA* II, 101-51.

Apocryphal Acts in general

Bovon, F., *et al.*, *Les Actes Apocryphes des Apôtres* (Geneva, 1981).
—, 'Miracles, magie et guérison dans les Actes apocryphes des apôtres', *J. Early Chr. Stud.* 3 (1995) 245-59.
—, (ed), *The Apocryphal Acts of the Apostles* (Cambridge MA, 1999).

Bremmer, J.N., 'The Novel and the Apocryphal Acts: Place, Time and Readership', in H. Hofmann and M. Zimmerman (eds), *Groningen Colloquia on the Novel* IX (Groningen. 1998) 157-80.
Elliott, J.K., 'The Apocryphal Acts', *Expository Times* 105 (1993-94) 71-7.
Kampen, L. van, *Apostelverhalen. Doel en compositie van de oudste apokriefe Handelingen der apostelen* (Diss. Utrecht. 1990).
Lipsius, R.A., *Die apokryphen Apostelgeschichten und Apostellegenden. Ein Beitrag zur altchristlichen Literaturgeschichte* II.1 (Braunschweig, 1887).
Plümacher, E., 'Apokryphe Apostelakten', in *Paulys Realencyclopädie der classischen Altertumswissenschaft*, Supplementband XV (1978) 11-70.
Rebell, W., *Neutestamentliche Apokryphen und Apostolische Väter* (München, 1992) 137-80.
Rordorf, W., 'Terra Incognita. Recent Research on Christian Apocryphal Literature, especially on some Acts of Apostles', in his *Lex orandi – Lex credendi* (Freiburg, 1993) 432-48.
Rostalski, F., 'Die Gräzität der apokryphen Apostelgeschichten', in *Festschrift zur Jahrhundertfeier der Universität Breslau am 2. August 1911* (Breslau, 1911) 59-69.
Söder, R., *Die apokryphen Apostelgeschichten und die romanhafte Literatur der Antike* (Stuttgart, 1932).
Warren, D.H., 'The Greek Language of the Apocryphal Acts of the Apostles: A Study in Style', in Bovon, *Apocryphal Acts*, 101-24.
Zachariades-Holmberg, E., 'Philological Aspects of the Apocryphal Acts of the Apostles', in Bovon, *Apocryphal Acts*, 125-42.

Acts of Andrew

Barns, J., 'A Coptic Apocryphal Fragment in the Bodleyan Library', *JTS* 11 (1960) 70-6.
Baumler, E.B., *Andrew in the City of the Cannibals: a comparative study of the Latin, Greek, and Old English texts* (Diss. Kansas 1985).
Blatt, F., *Die lateinischen Bearbeitungen der Acta Andreae et Matthiae apud Anthropophagos* (Giessen, 1930).

Calzolari Bouvier, V., 'La versione armena del *Martirio di Andrea*: alcune osservazioni in relazione all' originale greco', *Studi e ricerche sull' oriente cristiano* 16 (1993) 3-34.

—, 'Particolarità sintattiche e lessicali della versione armena del *Martirio di Andrea*, messa a confronto con Teone armeno', *Le Muséon* 106 (1993) 267-87.

—, 'La versione armena del *Martirio di Andrea* e il suo rapporto con la tradizione manoscritta dell' originale greco', *Le Muséon* 111 (1998) 141-56.

Cirillo, L., 'L'uomo interiore negli Atti Apocrifi di Andrea e il 'Nous' nella visione di Mani secondo Baraies (*CMC* 17, 7ss', in L. Cirillo and A. van Tongerloo (eds), *Manichean Studies* III (Turnhout, 1997) 11-21.

Deeleman, C.F.M., 'Acta Andreae', *Geloof en vrijheid* 46 (1912) 541-77.

Détorakis, Th., 'An Unpublished Martyrdom of St. Andrew the Apostle' (in New Greek), in *Acts of the Second International Congress of Peloponnesian Studies* I (Athens, 1981-82) 325-52.

Dvornik, F., *The Idea of Apostolicity in Byzantium and the Legend of the Apostle Andrew* (Cambridge MA, 1958).

Flamion, J., *Les Actes d'André et les textes apparentés* (Louvain, 1911).

Hilhorst, A., 'The Apocryphal Acts as martyrdom texts: the case of the Acts of Andrew', in Bremmer, *Acts of John*, 1-14.

Hornschuh, M., 'Acts of Andrew', in E. Hennecke (ed), *New Testament Apocrypha* II, ed. W. Schneemelcher (London, 1965) 390-425.

Kampen, L. van, '*Acta Andreae* and Gregory's *De miraculis Andreae*', *VigChr* 45 (1991) 18-26.

Karasszon, I., 'Old Testament Quotations in the Apocryphal Acts', in Bremmer, *Acts of John*, 57-71.

Leloir, L., 'La version arménienne de la Passion d'André', *Handēs Amsōreay* 90 (1976) 471-4.

—, 'Les Actes apocryphes d'André', in A. van Tongerloo and S. Giversen (eds), *Manichaica Selecta* (Louvain, 1991) 191-201.

MacDonald, D.R., 'Odysseus's Oar and Andrew's Cross: The Transformation of a Homeric Theme in the Acts of Andrew', in D.J. Lull (ed), *SBL 1981 Seminar Papers* (Atlanta, 1981) 309-12.

—, 'The *Acts of Andrew and Matthias* and the *Acts of Andrew*', *Semeia* 38 (1986) 9-26, with responses by J.-M. Prieur (27-33) and MacDonald (35-9).

—, 'Intertextuality in Simon's "Redemption" of Helen the Whore: Homer, Heresiologists, and the *Acts of Andrew*', in D.J. Lull (ed), *SBL 1990 Seminar Papers* (Atlanta, 1990) 336-43.

—, *Christianizing Homer: The* Odyssey, *Plato, and the* Acts of Andrew (New York and Oxford, 1994).

Milazzo, A.M., 'Gli "Atti di Andrea" ed il romanzo antico', in *La narrativa cristiana antica* (Rome, 1995) 53-75.

Nasrallah, L.S., '"She Became What the Words Signified": The Greek *Acts of Andrew*'s Construction of the Reader-Disciple', in Bovon, *Apocryphal Acts*, 233-58.

Pao, D.W., 'The Genre of the *Acts of Andrew*', *Apocrypha* 6 (1995) 179-202.

—, 'Physical and Spiritual restoration: The Role of Healing Miracles in the *Acts of Andrew*', in Bovon, *Apocryphal Acts*, 259-80.

Peterson, P.M., *Andrew, Brother of Simon Peter. His History and His Legends* (Leiden, 1958).

Prieur, J.-M., 'Les Actes apocryphes de l'apôtre André: Présentation des diverses traditions apocryphes et état de la question', *ANRW* II.25.6 (1988) 4384-4414.

Quispel, G., 'An Unknown Fragment of the Acts of Andrew (Pap. Copt. Utrecht 1)', *VigChr* 10 (1956) 129-48.

Santos Otero, A. de, in Schneemelcher, *NTA* II, 443-51.

Trigalet, M., 'La crucifixion de S. André *inverso capite* dans un fragment de légendier du prieuré de Chiny (Belgique)', *Analecta Bollandiana* 113 (1995) 317-20.

Wagener, K.C., '"Repentant Eve, Perfected Adam": Conversion in *The Acts of Andrew*', in *SBL 1991 Seminar Papers 30* (Atlanta, 1991) 348-56.

Zelzer, K., 'Zur Frage des Autors der Miracula B. Andreae Apostoli und zur Sprache des Gregor von Tours', *Grazer Beiträge* 6.2 (1977) 7-41.

Index of names, subjects and passages[1]

Abel 51
Abraham 7, 43, 44, 71, 72
Achaia 2, 16
Achilles Tatius, *Leucippe and Clitophon* 18; 1.1-2: 111
Acta Sanctorum, Sept. vol. VII, 204ff.: 25
Acts of Andrew 1: 16, 20, 117; 2: 21, 27-8, 117, 143; 3: 8, 28-9, 117, 143; 4: 8, 16, 32, 77, 105, 117; 5: 28, 30-1, 76, 105, 115, 117; 6: 7, 89, 117; 7: 76, 82, 100, 167; 8: 7, 21, 82, 89, 92, 115; 9: 82, 89, 92, 118, 120; 10: 7, 82, 101, 120, 142; 11: 82, 100-1, 106, 142; 12: 82, 92, 100-1; 13: 21, 48, 119-20, 142-3; 14: 54, 116, 119; 15: 16; 16: 48, 91, 143, 167; 17: 7, 48, 119; 18: 7, 21, 48; 19: 8, 33; 20: 115; 22: 22; 23: 54, 115-6; 25: 8; 26: 8, 116; 27: 54; 28: 8; 29: 92, 121, 143; 32: 5, 142; 33: 8; 36: 21, 34, 119-20; 37: 5, 7, 48, 50-1, 84, 89, 96, 99, 121, 167; 38: 5, 66, 84, 91, 96-7, 99, 105; 39: 5, 7, 53, 84, 92, 96, 99, 158; 40: 7, 48, 53, 84, 91, 96, 106, 146; 41: 84, 96; 42: 7, 85-6, 90, 92, 100; 43: 21, 85-6, 89-90, 100, 115, 146; 44: 85-6, 90, 92, 109, 119; 45: 33, 85-6, 167; 46: 5, 21, 48, 96, 142; 47: 5, 86, 89, 91, 94, 105, 121, 159, 166-7; 48: 86, 89, 92, 121, 143; 49: 86, 143, 155, 159, 161-2, 167; 50: 5, 86, 91-2, 160-1; 51: 33, 55, 86-7; 52: 86-7, 101, 158; 53: 86-7, 120, 157; 54: 86-7, 157; 55: 86-7; 56: 87-8, 90, 99, 120, 155; 57: 87-8, 91, 99, 120; 58: 87-8, 91, 99, 120; 59: 87-8, 89, 91; 60: 34, 87-8; 61: 87-8, 91, 94, 121; 62: 55, 87-8, 102, 157; 63: 87-8, 99, 106; 64: 87-8, 141, 155, 158; 65: 88, 92, 94, 99, 141, 145, 158; *Martyrium Prius* 3-4: 32; 6: 31; 14: 145; Coptic 9: 20, 28; 10: 24-5; 14: 30, 145; Latin 3: 15, 143; 4: 22, 34, 37; 5: 16, 26-7, 30-1, 38; 6: 148; 7: 27-8, 31, 144; 9: 20; 11: 18, 25, 39-40, 148; 12: 17, 142; 13: 31, 144; 14: 144; 15: 142; 16: 144; 17: 29; 18: 31, 32, 34; 19: 142, 144; 20: 144, 146; 21: 144; 22: 16, 27, 28, 144; 23: 16, 17, 23, 26, 27, 28, 41, 42, 105, 144, 148; 24: 21, 31, 105; 25: 16, 44-5;

---

[1] The editor would like to thank Ilse Roos for her kind assistance in making the index.

26: 144; 27: 26, 28-30, 105; 28: 23, 42-43, 92; 29: 16-7, 28-9; 30: 21, 45, 144; 34: 16, 27-8, 30; 35: 45; and *Acts of John* 129, 140-8; Andrew in 6; Armenian translation 149-85; author of 16; date of 19-20; devil in 160-1; eroticism 35-46, God in 145; inner man 100-3; Middle Platonism 95; miracles 6; *Passion of Andrew* 112-26; place of composition 15-16, 132-3; Poimandres 104-9; rhetorical purpose 98; rite of initiation 89; spiritualism 147; women 24

Acts of Andrew and Matthias 1: 8, 10-1, 13; 3: 11; 4: 6, 9-10, 13; 5-16: 5; 5: 9, 11, 13; 6: 8, 11; 7: 11; 8: 9, 11; 10: 9; 11-5: 4, 7, 9, 11; 14-5: 5; 16: 9, 13; 17: 8-9, 13; 18: 5, 13; 20: 5, 7, 167; 21: 6, 8; 22: 5; 24: 25; 25: 11; 26: 11; 27: 6, 11; 28: 6, 9; 29: 6, 7; 30: 6, 9, 11; 31: 11; 32: 5, 11; 33: 6, 11, 13; and *Acts of Thomas* 1, 128; and Homer 13

Acts of John 62: 87: 142; 19: 144; 20: 144; 24: 142; 40: 143; 43: 143; 45: 146; 47: 142; 49: 143; 56: 144, 148; 57: 148; 58: 144; 59: 144; 64: 143; 73: 142; 76: 142; 81: 142; 82: 142, 144, 147; 83: 142, 144, 167; 84: 167; 87: 142; 88: 147; 89: 5, 105, 147; 90: 144, 146-7; 91: 147; 92: 147; 93: 147; 97: 147; 98: 147; 99: 134, 145; 101: 146; 106: 143; 109: 134; 112: 167; 115: 142-3; 122: 105; and *Acts of Andrew* 140-8; date and place of 128-30

Acts of Justin 6: 8;

Acts of Paul 4: 142; 7: 142; 11: 142; 12: 50; 3Corinthians 150

Acts of Paul and Thecla 21: 141; 25: 142; Armenian 151

Acts of Peter 4: 141; 5:142; 8: 50; 11: 30; 14: 57; 20: 147; 21: 141, 147; 28: 33; 33-5: 33;

Acts of Peter and Andrew 10

Acts of Philip 3.12: 142; 38: 167

Acts of Thomas 10-11, 141; 10: 94; 11: 142; 26: 142; 27: 142; 32: 105; 39: 94, 167; 47-8: 94; 48: 147; 49: 142; 54: 142; 73: 30, 142; 74: 29-30, 142; 77: 30; 87: 142; 120: 142; 131: 142; 144-8: 141; 151: 142; 152: 142; 153: 142, 147; 154-5: 142; and *Acts of Andrew and Matthias* 128

Adam 5, 50-1, 52, 76, 79, 84, 97, 99-100

Aegeates 5, 7, 17, 21, 33, 34, 47-55, 58, 65-6, 70, 74-5, 77, 82, 87-8, 91, 96, 98, 102, 106, 113, 116-7, 119, 121, 124

agapê 114

Agrippa 74

Ahab 72-4

Albinus, *Didaskalikos*, 32: 94

Alcman 16

Alcmanes 16, 21, 27-31, 82

Alcaeus 16

Alexander Romance 14

Alexandria 120-30
allotrios 105, 168
Amasea 15, 22
Amphilochus of Iconium, *Fragmenta* X, 1-3: 178
anaidês 49
anarchos 161-70
Angels 9
Antiphanes 16, 28-9
apathês 47
Aphrodisias 17
Apocalypse of Baruch (Greek) 13.2: 167
Apocalypse of Moses 2.4: 167; 7.2: 167; 19.3: 177; 25: 167; 28: 167
Apocryphal Acts of the Apostles, common elements 141-3
Apocryphon of John 51
Apollonius Rhodius 2.537ff:13, 598ff: 13
Apotactici 177
Apuleius *Met.* 3.8: 27, 4.26:19
Aretaeus 3.6: 28
Aristophanes 63; *Acharnians* 1024: 61; *Birds* 69: 61; *Ecclesiazusae* 592: 61; *Frogs* 1-20: 62; *Knights* 638: 61; 658: 61, *Lysistrata* 443-8: 61; *Plutus* 302-8: 61, 309-15: 61; *Wasps* 801-8: 61, 1177: 61
Archontes 107
Artaxerxes 72
Ascension of Isaiah 49; 11: 168
Aseneth 71
Augustine, *Contra Felicem* II, 6: 159; *De gestis cum Emerito* 9: 22

Bandits 19
Bakhtin, M., 63
Bath 26, 38-9, 41, 105
Beach 34
Belkira 49
Bêma 34, 74
Bible: *Gen* 1.1-3: 78; 1.11,24: 78; 2.22: 50; 2.7: 7; 3: 7; 5.3: 52; 6.1-4: 7; 6-8: 7; 9.11: 7; 16.1-16: 71; 29.21-30; 41.50: 71; *Ex* 29.14: 59; 31.18: 7; 32.6: 67; *Lev* 11-15: 56; 16.28: 59; *Num* 19.5ff: 59; *Deut* 23.13-5: 56; *1Sam* 1.12-4: 67; 2.12-7: 67; 9.22-4: 67; *2Sam* 24.3ff: 60; *1Kings* 14.10: 59; 17.18: 29; 22: 73; *2Kings* 6.25: 59; 6.28-9: 59; 7.1: 60; 9.37: 59; 18.37: 60; 27; *Job* 20.7: 59; *Ps* 23: 165; 28.3: 165; 83.10: 59; *Is* 9.6: 33.17: 165; 77; 11.4f: 77; 14.12-15: 169; 16.5: 77; 25.10: 59; *Jer* 8.2: 59; 9.22: 59; 16.4: 59; 23.5f: 77; 25.33: 59; 33.15: 77; *Ez.* 4.12,15: 60; 6.11: 59; 9.1f: *Zeph* 1.17: 59; *Mal* 2.3: 60, 61; *Mt* 1.20: 77; 2.12-13: 77; 5.1: 8; 8: 156; 8.1: 8; 8.20: 7;

8.23-7: 7; 8.28: 27; 8.29: 29; 9: 158; 10.7-10: 7; 10.16: 8; 11: 158; 11.5: 7; 12: 156; 12.24: 8; 12.45: 27; 13: 156, 158; 13.25: 167: 167; 13.38: 160; 13.39: 167; 14.14-21: 7; 14.5: 78; 15: 158; 15.17-8: 56; 19: 77; 19.27: 7; 22: 156; 24: 156; 24.35: 8; 25: 156; 27.19: 74; 27.46: 3, 8, 9; 30: 156; 42: 156; 43: 158; 50: 156; 51: 156; *Mk* 1.24: 29; 1.25: 30; 1.26: 31; 1.43: 30; 2.12: 30; 5.13: 31; 5.2,3,5: 27; 5.7: 29; 5.8: 30; 7.19: 57; 9: 156; 9.11-13: 74; 9.20: 28, 31; 9.25: 30; 16.9: 27; *Luke* 8.2: 27; 8.27: 27; 8.28: 29; 10.19: 167, 169; 11.26: 27; 13: 156; 21.18: 8; 22.31: 168; 23.47: 77; 23.8-12: 8; 18: 156; 28: 156; *John* 2.1-10: 7; 3.1-20: 89; 6.68-9: 93; 8: 158; 8.44: 7; 8.51: 93; 10.18: 168; 12.31: 168; 16.11: 16918.4-8: 8; 20.30-1: 92; 21.24-5: 92; *Acts* 7: 75, 156; 7.2: 165; 12.21-3: 65; 16.18: 30; 16.25: 8; 20: 158; 26.14: 9 27.34: 8; 54: 156; *Rom* 16: 168; 16.16: 8; 17-20: 168; *1Cor* 2.6: 107; 2.8: 165; 15.22,45: 76; 15.24: 107; *2Cor* 2.11: 168; 3: 157; 4.16: 101; 11,3-15: 168; 14-16: 168; 18: 157; *Eph* 1.21: 107; 2.2: 107; 3.16:101; *1Tim* 2.4: 8; *James* 2.1: 165; *1Petr* 3.22: 107; 3.4: 101; *1John* 2.26: 169; 3.10: 160; 5: 158; 5.2: 169; *2Rev.* 12: 78, 79; 12.16: 79; 12.9: 51
Bithynia 16
Blandina 33
bonitas 17
brothel 23, 41, 42
bSanh 107b: 25

Cain 7, 51-2
Caliopa 16, 37, 44
Calisto 41
Callista 17, 26
Callistus 21
Celsus 132
Chamber pots 57, 65
Chaos 107-8
Chariton, *Callirhoe and Chaereas* 1.1: 111
Christ, appearance of 142
Chrysostom, John, *Homiliae in Col.* 5.3: 166
Clement of Alexandria, *Stromateis* 3.66.1-2: 50; III, VI, 45.1: 177; III, VI, 49.1: 176; III, IX, 66.1: 177; III, IX. 63, 1, 25,1-4: 177, XIII, 93.3: 176
coniungere 44
contingere 23
Corpus Hermeticum IV, 3: 167
Council of Epaon 19; of Auxerre 19
Cratinus 16, 28, 30-1
Crucifixion 22

Cruelty 18, 22
culleus 22
Cultic practices 89
Cyprian 25; *Conf.* 12: 25; *Ep.* 69.15: 30

David 7
Demaenete 37
Demon, black 27; as dogs 27; number of 27; striking by 27-8; and water 38
Devil 44, 47-55, 106
Diana 44
dianoia 92

Edification 89
Efidama 45
Egypt 25
Eleusis 106
Elijah 72-4
Encratism 18, 40, 46, 76, 124, 171-81, 177-8
Encratites 177
endogamy 18
epieikeia 17
epieikês 17
Epiphanius, *Pan.* 47.1.5: 177; 61.1.5: 178
Epistle of Barnabas 128, 138-9
Epistula Apostolorum 128
Epistula Titi 140
Eros 111, 114-5; in Greek novel 124; Plotinus and 123
eroticism 66
Esther 72
Eukleia 21-2, 33, 46-7, 84
Euangelium 23
Eucharist 39
Eusebius, *Historia Ecclesiastica* 3.25: 149; 4.29.3: 176; 5.1.41-2: 33; 6.3.9-12: 130; 6.8.1-3: 130
Evagrius Ponticus, 125; *Tractatus practicus*, 78: 94
Eve 5, 7, 50-2, 76, 84, 97, 99-100
Excrement 58
Exegesis on the Soul 52
exercere 23
Excerpta ex Theodoto 42.1: 145; 26.2: 145; 35.1: 145
Exorcism 24-32
Exousiai 107
Exuos 17, 25

INDEX

Fielding 63
First Book of Enoch 14
first of the city 15
Flora 62
Foucault, M. 64, 67

Geisterbannung 31
Gesta Romanorum: 42
Gnosticism 18, 93-4, 102
Gospel of Thomas 93-4; saying 11: 100
Gospel of the Egyptians 50
Gospel of Philip 51, 53; 78-79: 100
Gratianus 105
Gratinus 16, 36, 38
Gregory, *Liber de miraculis*, date of, 19
Gregory of Nyssa 125

Hagar 71-2
hairesis 137
Haman 72
Heliodorus, *Aethiopica*, 9: 37
Herod 8, 74, 77
Herodias 74, 77
Hippolytos 37
Hippolytus, Refutatio 1.19 166; 6.31.5-6: 145; 9.12.24-5: 21
Historia Apollonii regis Tyri 16; 33-5: 42
Historia Lausiaca 8: 23
Hrotsvitha, *Abraham* 43-4
hylikos 48
Hymenaeus *et al., Epistula ad Paulum Samosatenum* 2: 166

Ignatius, 145; *Epistula ad Trallianos* 8.1: 49, *Epistula ad Philadelphios* 6.2: 49
incest 19, 22, 40
Inscriptions *IGR III*.115: 15; *I. Iznik* 196: 16; 1062: 16; 1201: 16; 1208: 16; *I. Prusias* 7.2.22: 33; *RECAM* ii. 324: 16; *SEG* 35.1330: 17, 35.1363: 17, 37.544: 33, 43.441: 16, 43.850: 17; *TAM II*.3.739: 17; *TAM III*. 118.3: 33, 180.3: 33, 596.2: 33, 697.1: 33
inludo 23
inner man 181-4
Innocent 126
Interpretation of Gnosis 102
Iphidamia 84

Irenaeus 26, 129; *Adversus haereses* 1.3.5: 145, 1.10.2: 130, 1.13.3: 26, 1 28.1: 176
Isaac 7

Jacob 7, 71-2
Jehu 73
Jerome, *Praef. In Comm. Ad Tit.* 75; *Prol. com. in ep. ad Titum* 685: 176; *Vita Hilarionis* 12.10: 28
Jesus 2-3, 6-9, 77, 89; divinity 9
Jews 9
Jezebel 72-4
John 146-7
John the baptist 74, 77-8
Joseph 71-2
Josephus, *Ant.* 8.47: 29
Justin 129-30; *Ap.* I 29.2-3: 130
Juvenal 6.422f: 26

Knemon 37
koinos logos 87, 90, 99
koitôn 118

Leah 71
Leopard 33
Lesbios 16, 22, 26
Letter of Lyons 33
Letter of Peter to Philip 102
Letter of the Presbyters and Deacons of Achaea 5: 177-8
Life of Adam 17: 167
Life of Shenute 10
Livia 39.8-18: 39
logos 92, 106; *logoi* 93
Longus, *Daphnis and Chloe*, prologue: 111
Lucian, *Demonax* 67; *Philopseudeis* 16: 28-30; 31: 30; 34-6: 25
Lucius of Patras, *Metamorphoseis* 19
Lycia 18

1Macc 9.22: 146
2 Macc 7.4: 22
4 Macc 10.19: 22; 10.20: 22
Magic 5, 24-32
Magician 24-5
Manicheans 122

Maria 43-4
Marriage 176; age at 19
Martial 3.51: 39; 7.35: 26; 11.2.4: 21; 11.104.5: 21; 11.75: 26; 12.43.10: 21; 72: 39
Martyrdom of Pionius 11.5: 8; 18.12: 8
Matthias 2, 6, 8
Maximilla 5, 7, 15, 17, 21, 29, 37, 40, 44, 47-55, 58, 66, 70-1, 73, 75-8, 82-5, 89, 91-2, 96-100, 106, 113-21, 124, 177, 180
Meliton of Sardes, *Homilia in Passionem Christi* 120: 167
metrios 17
military service 20
miniature codices 23
Minucius, *Octavius*, 8.4: 39
Miracles 6
Miracle stories 142
Mordecai 72
Moses 7

Narrative of Zosimus 76
Nepos, *Praef.* 4: 39
Nicaea 27
Nicodemus 89
Nicolaus 42-3
nous 108, 121, 167
Novel, and Apocryphal Acts 110-26

Odes of Salomon 38: 168
Odysseus 70; and *Acts of Andrew and Matthias* 13
Odyssey 70
oikonomos 16
Old Comedy 62-3, 66
Origen 125-6; *Contra Celsum* 1.28, 38, 46: 25; 5.48: 167; 6.28: 167; *De principiis* 125, IV.2.4: 53; *Dialogus cum Heraclide* 2: 166; *Homiliae in Jer.* 5.17: 167
Ovid *AA* 2.619-20: 21, *Am* 1.5.7-8: 21

Papyri: *P.Diog.* 6.3: 33; *PGM* I.1-3: 26, IV.1227: 30, 1242-4: 30, 3007ff: 30, 3037-41: 29; V.158: 30; VII.282: 28; XII.79: 25; XIII.242-4: 29; 25; XXXVI.76: 28; *P.Kell.* 91, 92, 94: 23; *P.Kell.Copt.* 1.: 23; *P.Kron.* 3.1: 33; *P.Oxy.* 3.486.1: 33; 9.1201.16: 33; 12.1475.10: 33; 14.1642: 33; 1727.1: 33
parhedros 26
Parricide 22

Passio Perpetuae 33
Patras 26
Paul 8
Penelope 70
Peri Pascha 51.9: 145
Peter 8
Phaedra 37
Philippi 18, 39
Philo, *De Agricultura* 9: 101; 108: 101; *De Plantatione* 42: 101
Philostratus, *Life of Apollonius* 3.38: 30; 4.20: 28, 30
Pilate 74, 77-8; wife 77-8
Plato, *Laws* 166; *Phaedo* 119, 120; *Politeia* IX.589A,B: 101; *Republic*, 440: 48; *Theaetetus*, 118; *Tim.* 89A: 94; Pseudo-Plato, *Tim. Locr*.102 E: 94
Platonism 114-26
Plautus 62-3, 66
Pliny, *NH* 33.153: 39
Plotinus 121; *Against the Gnostics* 1.2.3: 123; 1.2.5: 123; 1.2.6: 123; 2.9: 123; *Enneads* 1.4.14: 122; 3.5.1: 123-4; 4.8.1: 123; 4.8.2: 123; 4.8.4: 123; 4.8.5: 123; 5.1-2: 167;
Plutarch, *M*.849B: 22
Polybius 5.54.10, 8.21.3: 22
Polymorphy 147
Poimandres 4, 107; 5: 108; 20: 108; 23: 108; 28: 109; 29: 109; 56: 109
Pontus 16
Porphyrius, *De abstinentia* 2.40.1: 168
Potiphar 71
pragmateutês 16
praotês 17
Prayer 141
Procula Claudia 77
prosênês 17
Ptolemy, *Tetrabl.* 3.14: 28

Quintilian 5.9.14: 39;

Rabelais, *Gargantua* I.13: 63; III.22: 64
Rachel 71-2
Relationships 21
Revelation of Adam 100

Sammael 25, 52
Sammoth 25

Sappho 16
Sarah 71-2
Satan 7
Saturnalia 62, 66, 68
Scatology 56-69
Second Apocalypse of James 55; 15-20: 54
Secret Gospel of Mark 3.4-5: 89
Seed, image of 93
sella 58
sella pertusa 65
Semmath 25
Seneca, *Controversiae*, 1.2.1: 41
Sentences of Sextus 130-1
Serpent 107
Seth 52
Simon Magus 49, 61, 65-6
Sirach 43.27: 146
Socrates 117-20
Sostratus 22, 37
sphragis 101, 142
Spirit 108
storgê 114, 116, 119
Supplication 27
Stratocles 20-2, 27-28, 33-4, 47, 70, 82-3, 85, 87, 89-90, 92, 100, 113-9, 124, 147
syggenês 104, 146

Tacitus, *Annales* 15.27: 21
Targum Pseudo-Jonathan 4.1: 52; 5.3: 52
Tatian 132, 176; *Address to the Greeks* 70, 166
Teachings of Silvanus, NHC VII, 4: 168
Tehom 106
Telemachos 70
Tertullian, *Ad uxorem* 2.8: 21; *De corona* 1: 20
Testament of Dan 6.3: 167
Testament of Joseph 8.5: 8
Testamentum Solomonis 5.2ff: 29; 8.1: 27; 10.1-4: 27, 13.2: 29; 17.2: 27
Theodoretus of Cyrrhus, *Commentarii in Pss. 108.6*: 168; *Historia Ecclesiastica* 5: 168, 11: 168
Theophilos, *Autolyc.* 2.8: 29
thymoeidês 48
Tiamat 106
Toilet 21

Trofima 23, 37, 40-3

Varianus 33
Venantius Fortunatus 39
venatores 33

Walking 21
We-form 141
Whipping 33
Wisdom of Solomon 6-9: 93
Words of Life 81-95

Xenophon, *Ephesian Tale* 1.1-2: 111

BS
2880
.A7
A66
2000

PRINTED ON PERMANENT PAPER • IMPRIME SUR PAPIER PERMANENT • GEDRUKT OP DUURZAAM PAPIER - ISO 9706
ORIENTALISTE, KLEIN DALENSTRAAT 42, B-3020 HERENT